AF615063

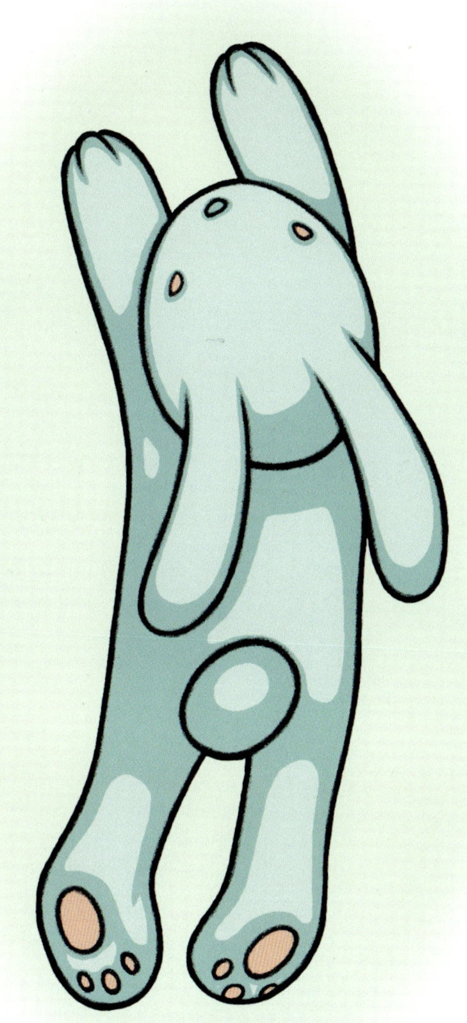

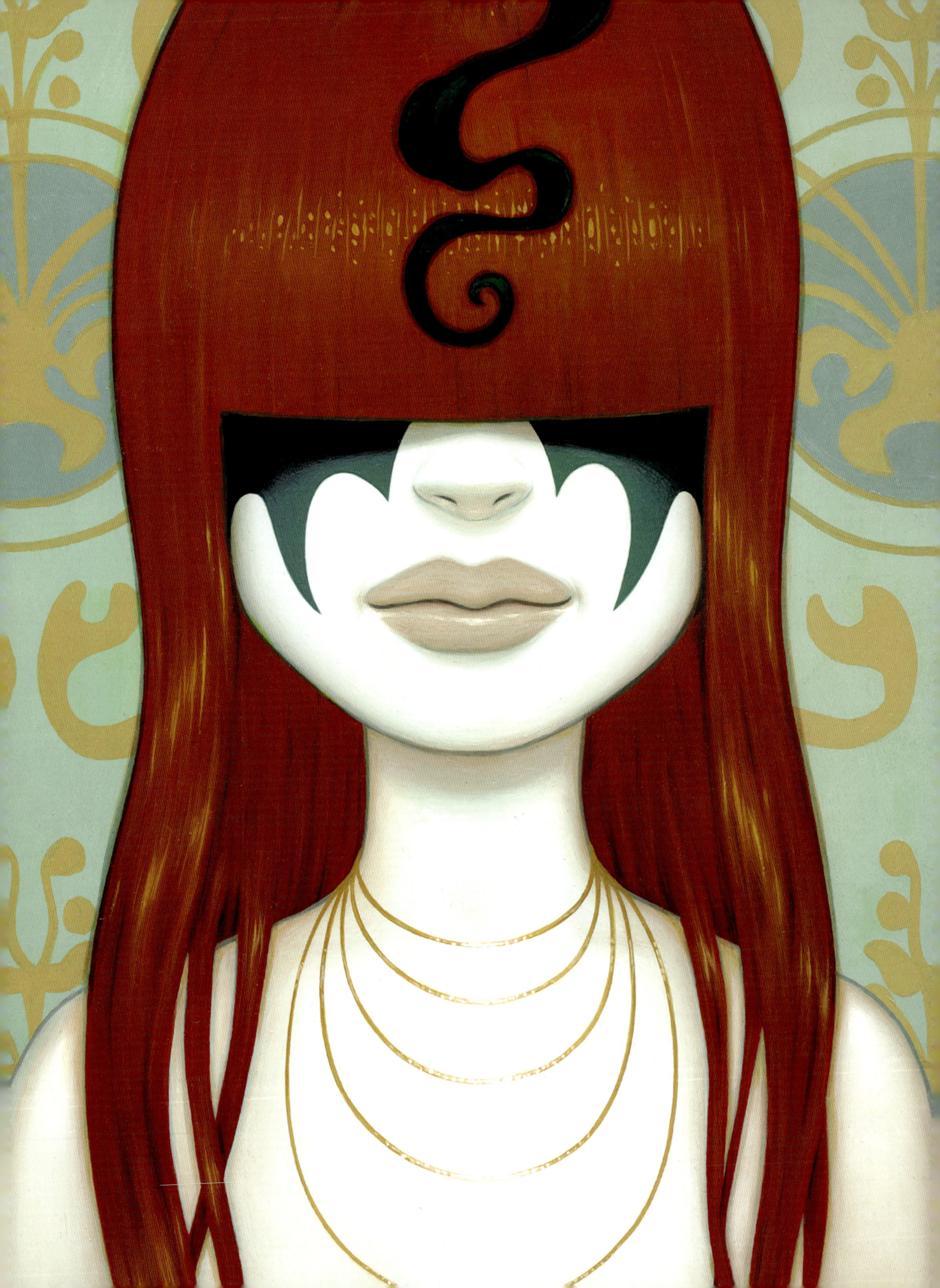

Lost Constellations

The Art of Tara McPherson

Volume II

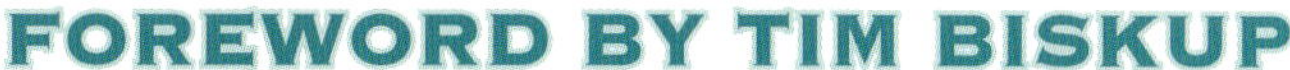

FOREWORD BY TIM BISKUP

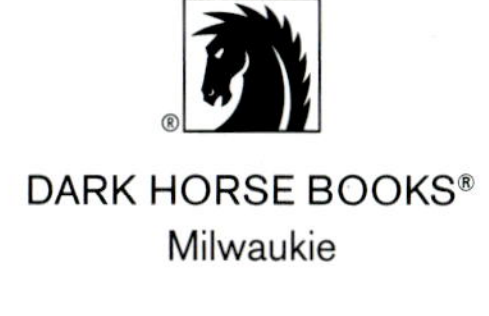

DARK HORSE BOOKS®
Milwaukie

THIS BOOK IS DEDICATED TO YOU.

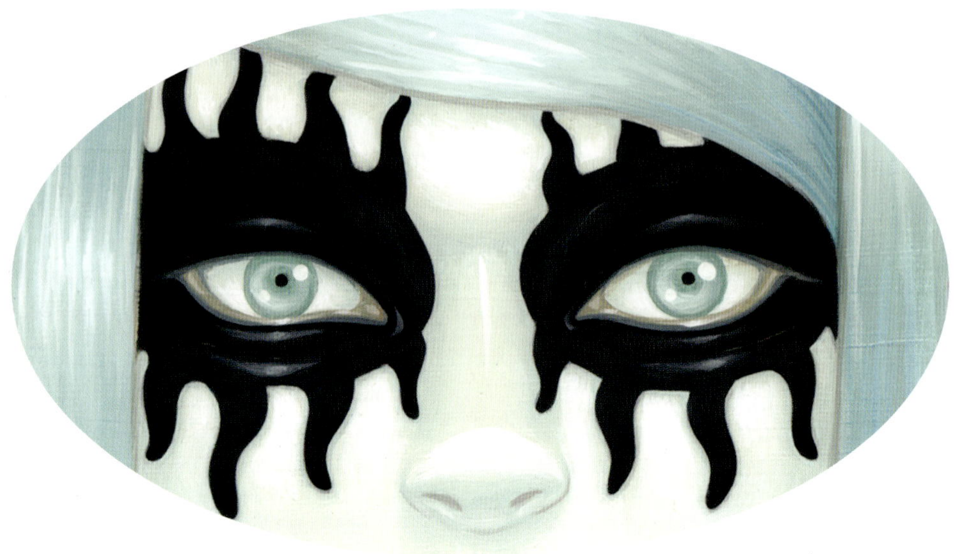

I would like to give special thanks to Tyna Reneé and family; Dad; Grant; Kathy and Marc; Grandma; Jonathan LeVine and everyone at the Gallery; Andy Stern and Diesel Fuel Prints; Anthony Pontius; Esao Andrews; Frank Kozik; Tim Biskup; Lori Earley; Adam Wallacavage; Jonathan Viner; Eric White; Gary Baseman; Liz McGrath; James Jean; Jeff Soto; Shawn Barber; Henry Lewis; Foerdl; JK5; Ralf Krüger; Junko Mizuno; Jonathan Cathey; Thomas Han; Saved Tattoo; Sara Antoinette Martin; Jay Ryan; Geoff Peveto; KB Projects; Svetlana Bahchevanova; Travis Chance; Durbis; Jessie Frances; Kristin; Billie; Holly; Jenny; Rondi; Kelley; Kim; Jessicka; Tomi Monstre; Steven Daily; Shelly Bond; Steven Guarnaccia; Brooklyn Adorned; Red Sparowes; Mastodon; Isis; Torche; Melvins; High on Fire; New York Times; Erik Foss; Jamie O'Shea; William Haugh and *Juxtapoz*; Paul Budnitz and everyone at Kidrobot; Poster Pop; *Royal Flush*; GigPosters; American Poster Institute; Mike Mignola; Chris Warner, David Scroggy, Rebecca D'Madeiros, Jeremy Atkins, Scott Allie, Dirk Wood, Lia Ribacchi, Mike Richardson, and everyone else at Dark Horse; and especially to the fans who have continued to support and explore this strange world that exists in my head.

Thank you.

LOST CONSTELLATIONS: THE ART OF TARA McPHERSON VOLUME II

Publication design by Tara McPherson and Krystal Hennes

Dark Horse Books
10956 S.E. Main Street
Milwaukie OR 97222

darkhorse.com

taramcpherson.com

First edition: April 2009
ISBN 978-1-59582-222-2

1 3 5 7 9 10 8 6 4 2

Printed in China

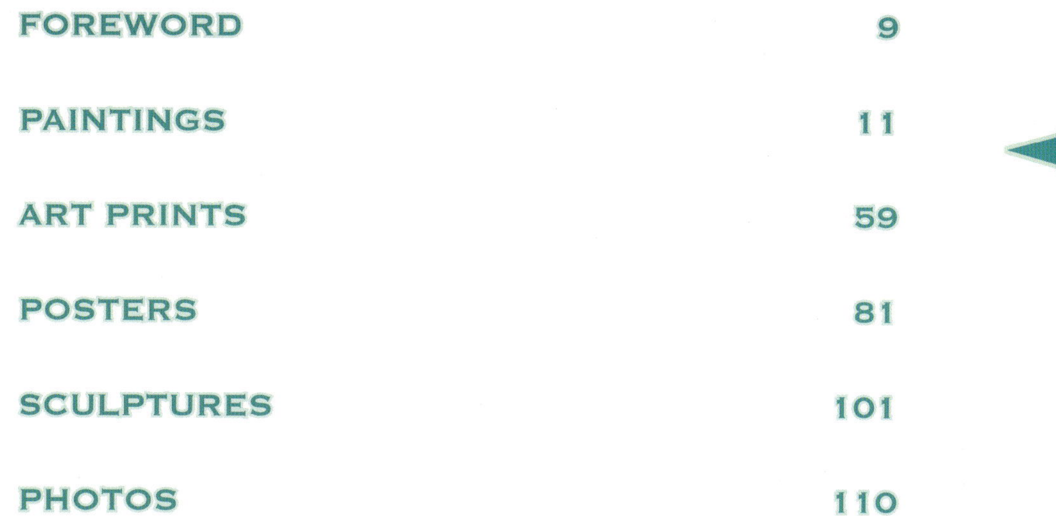

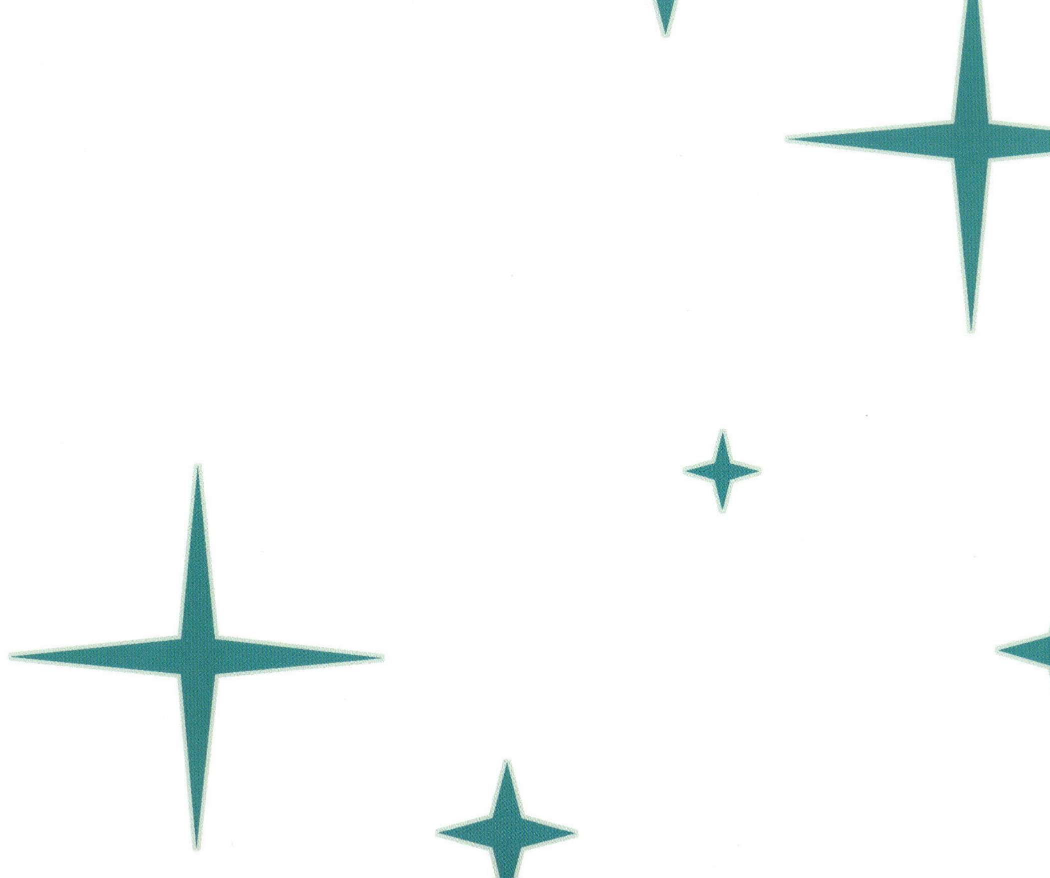

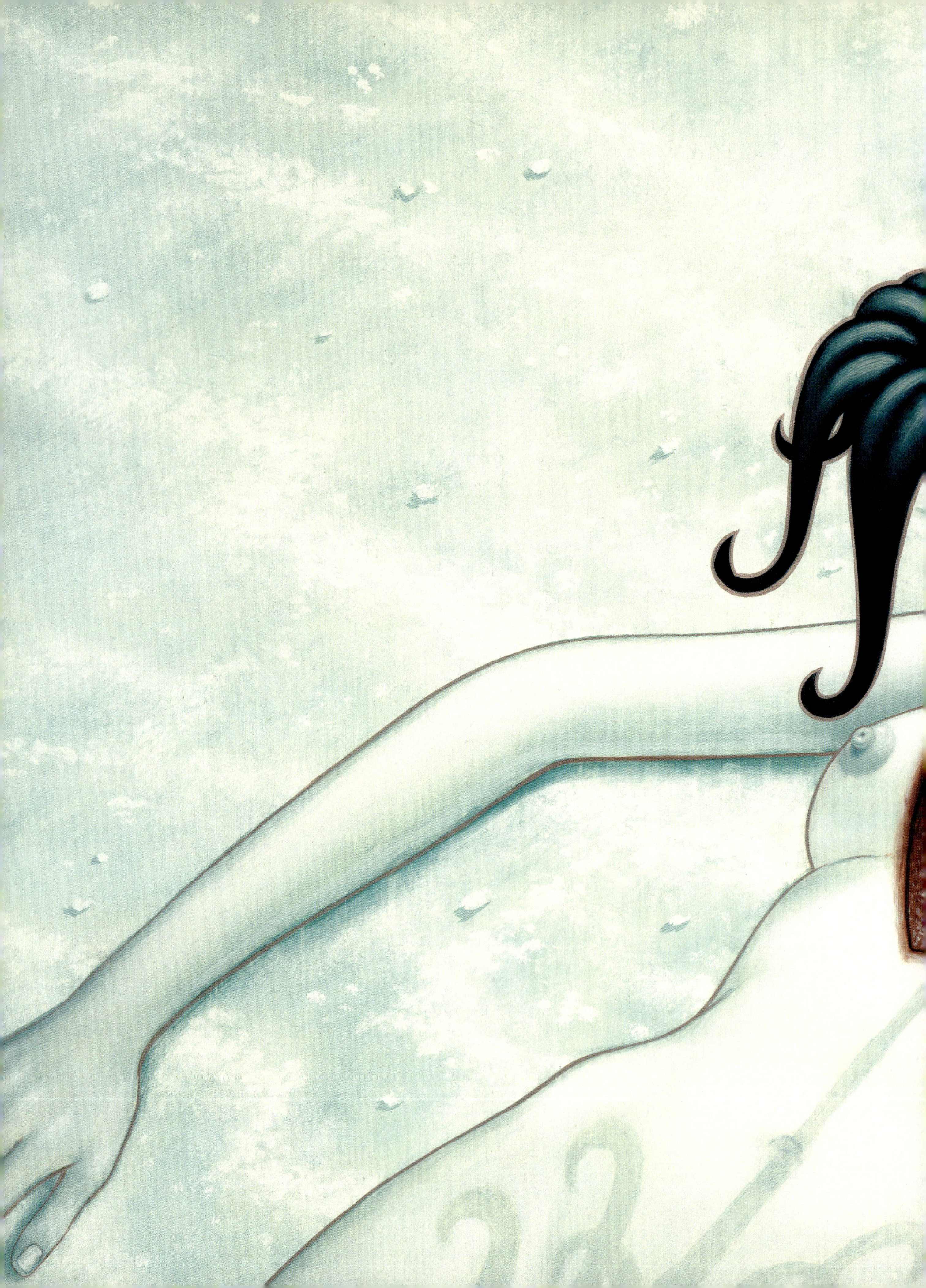

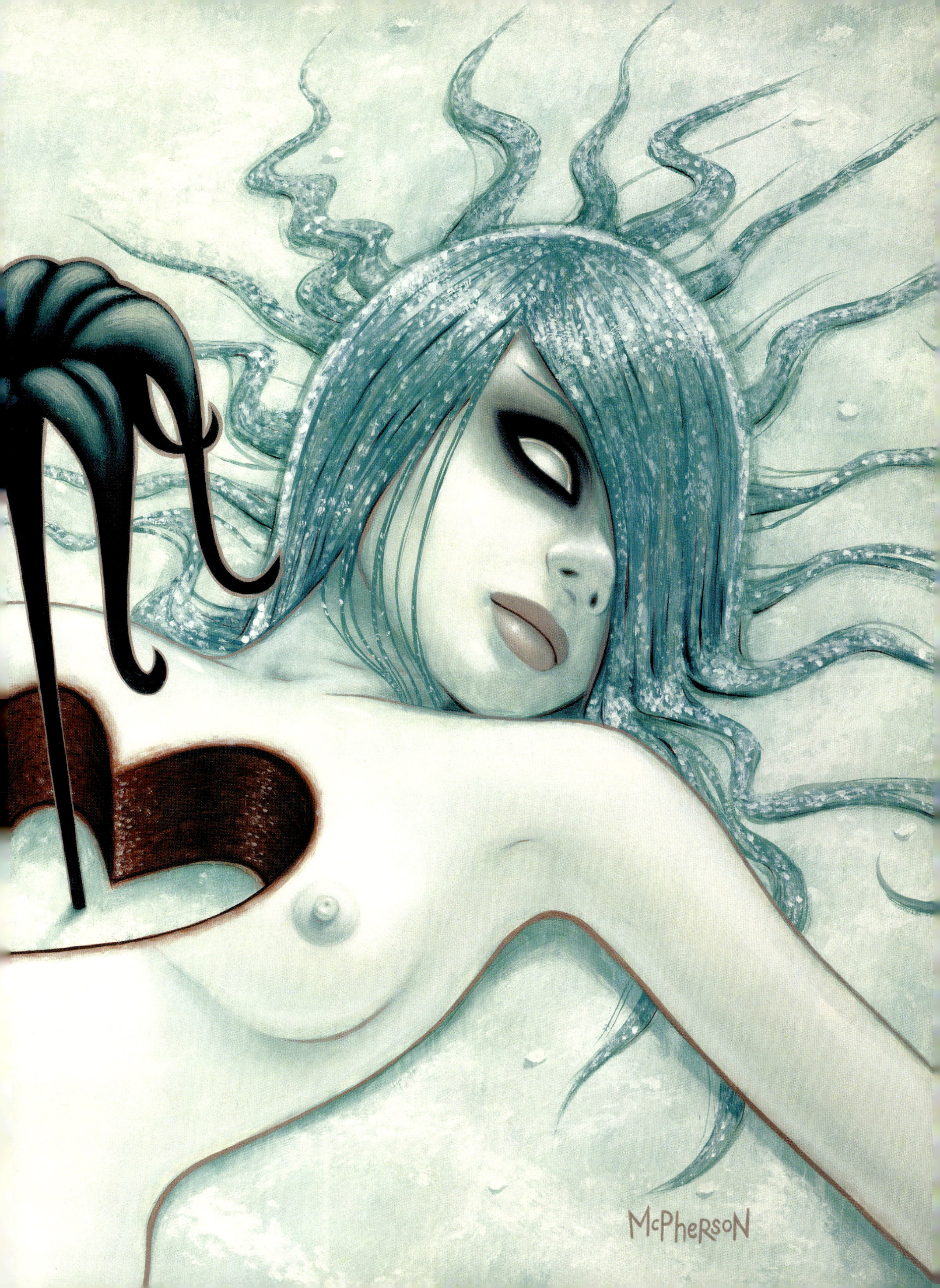
McPherson

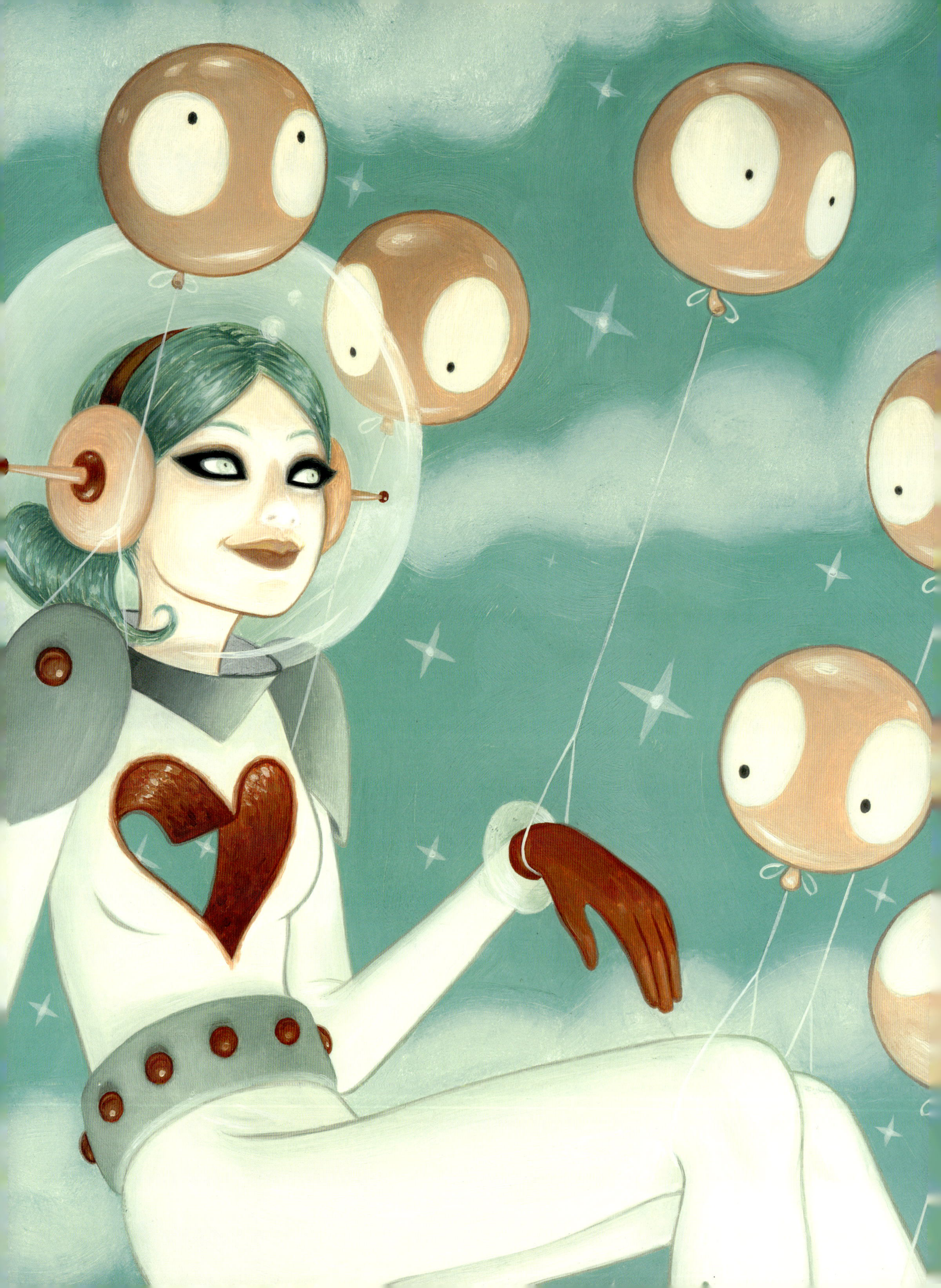

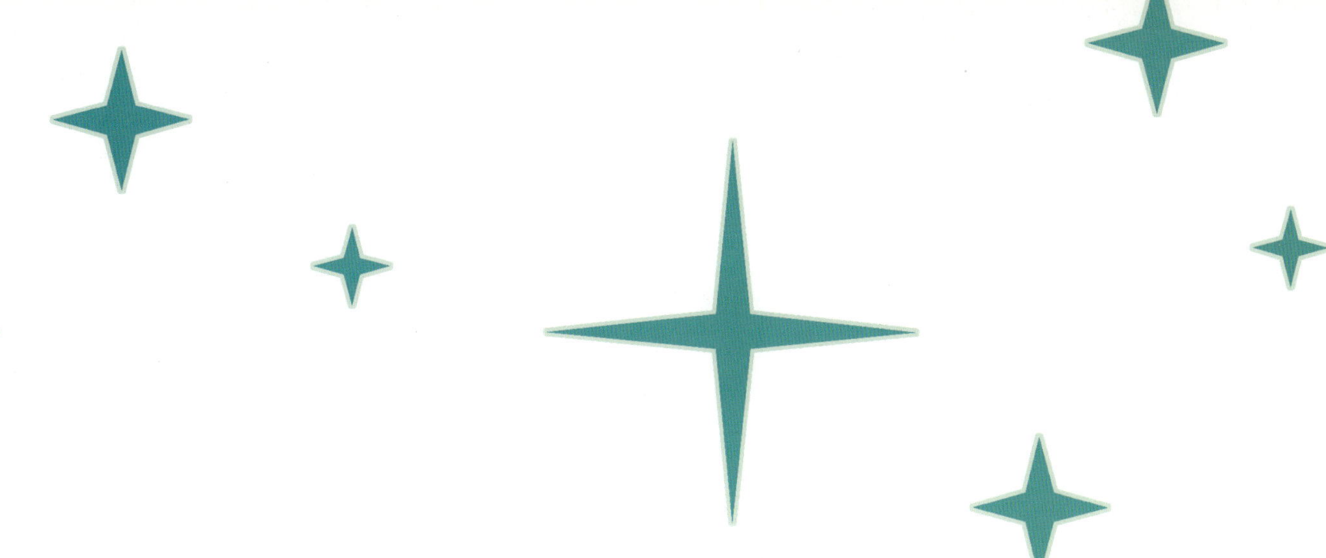

FOREWORD

Stars, planets, bubbles, and girls with their hearts torn out . . . What's not to love? The subjects of Tara's art are often floating weightlessly in space. Their distance from Earth doesn't really make them seem unreal, though. It just puts them in a place where they can relax and present themselves. Perhaps they are there because in our idea of space we lose our sense of time and gravity and everything else that takes us away from what is right in front of us. We can't help but focus, and Tara wants us to pay attention. You can't help but pay attention to her, actually. If you've seen her walk into a room full of people, you know what I'm talking about. Heads turn. She's a bombshell and that is undeniable, but once you get past the platinum locks, the perfect makeup, and the adorable, subtly kitsch outfit she's wearing, you'll notice the tattoos peeking out of her sleeves. They are not just there for decoration. They are an autobiography of her life, and she wants them to be seen. That's the mind-fuck that she brings to her paintings. They are pristine and delicate illustrations that are made just for you to look at. Nothing could be more palatable. But there is a little hint of malevolence sifted into the composition, at times as subtle as a wink and often as direct as a literal hole through the chest in the shape of a heart. You can't mistake the intentionality of the message, but you cannot truly know what it is about. The power of suggestion will keep you in place, head turned, facing the door where she just entered. Maybe you can untangle a few of the knots and reveal a bit of truth, but it is not so important that we know what's going on, is it? We are floating in space, after all.

—Tim Biskup
Pasadena
December 2008

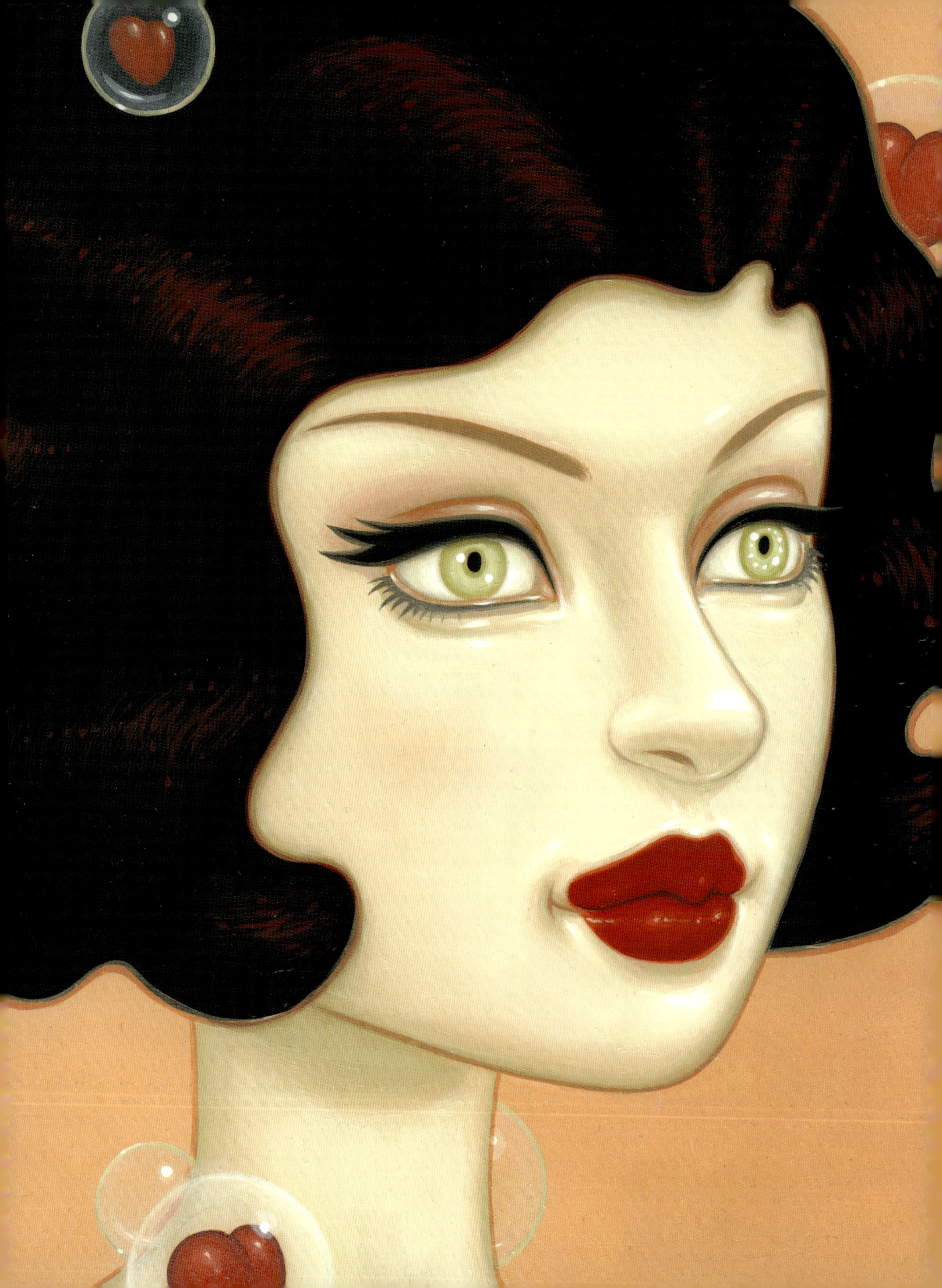

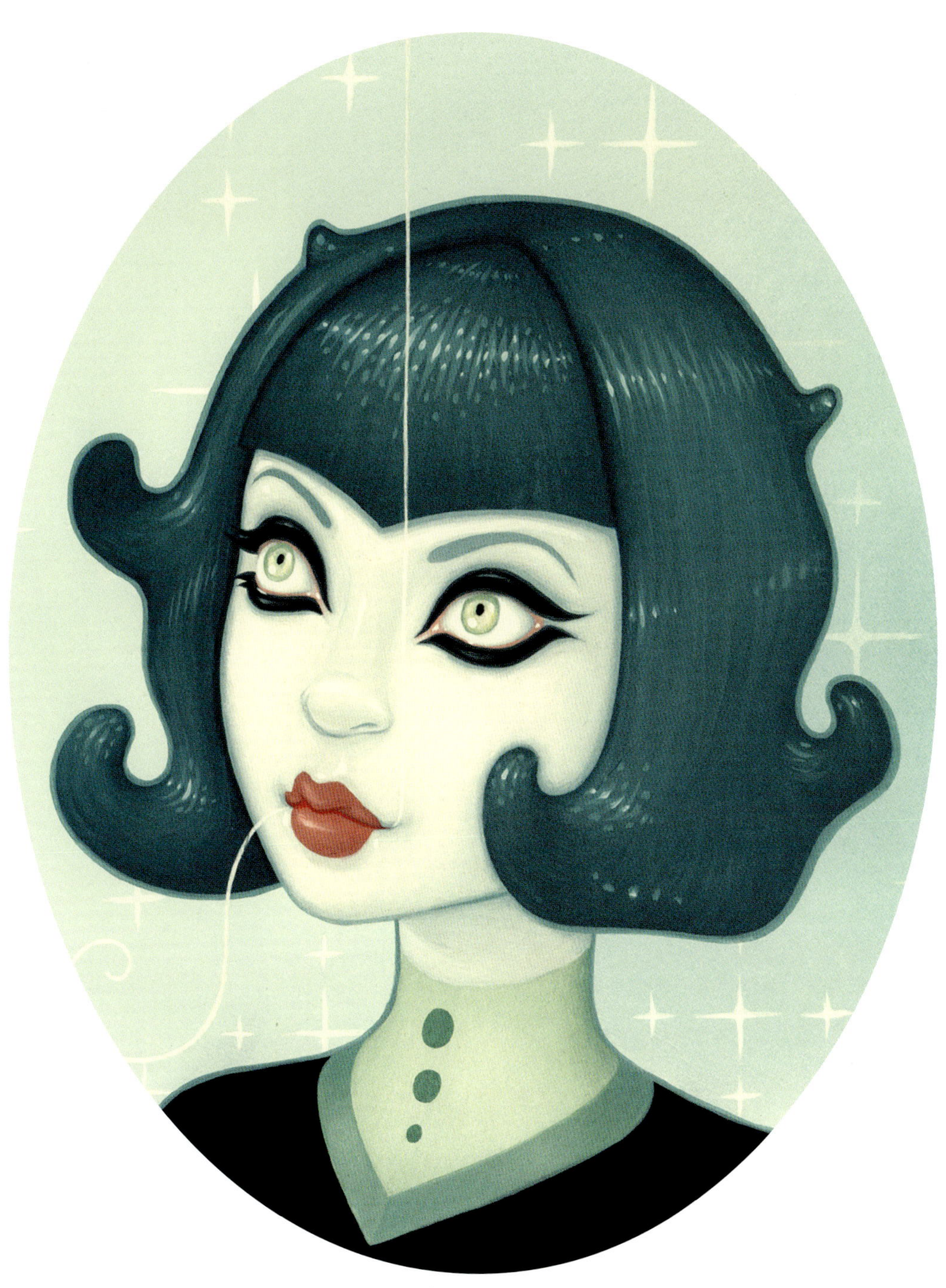

PAINTINGS

Lost Constellations

oil and acrylic on birch
30" x 40"
2007

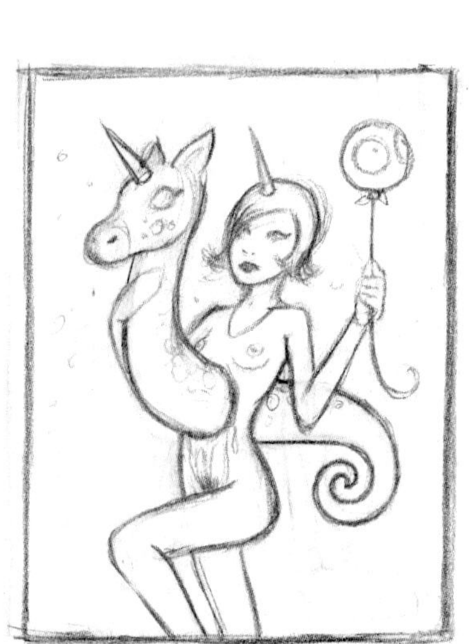

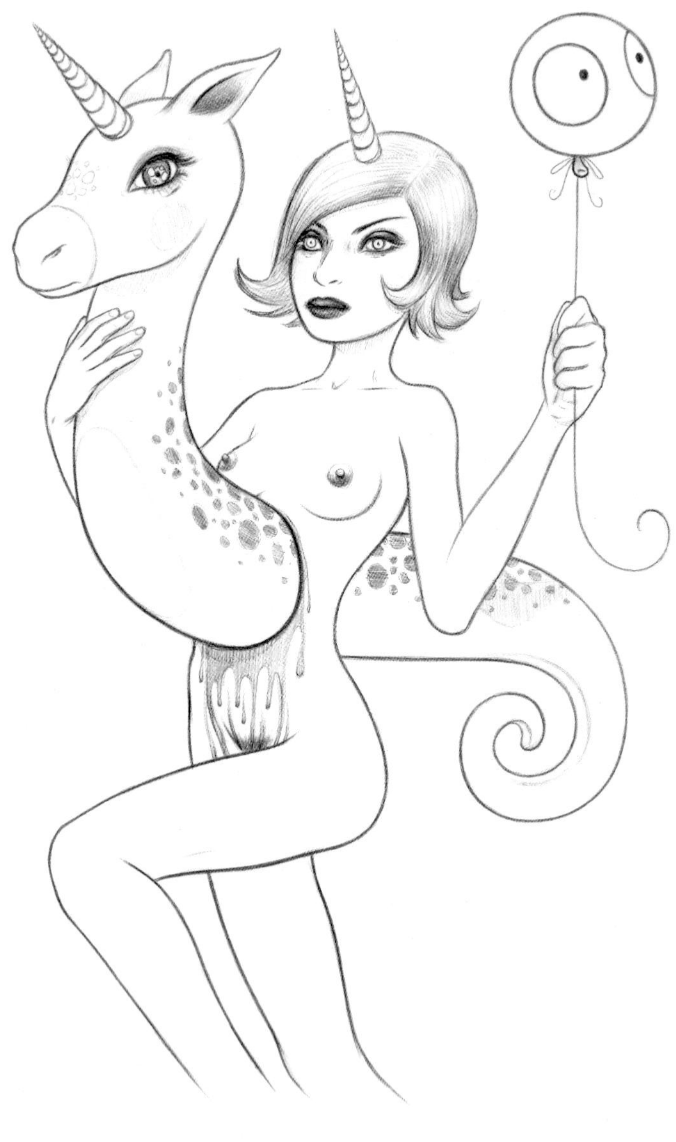

rough
graphite on paper
2" x 3"

drawing
graphite on bristol
14" x 17"

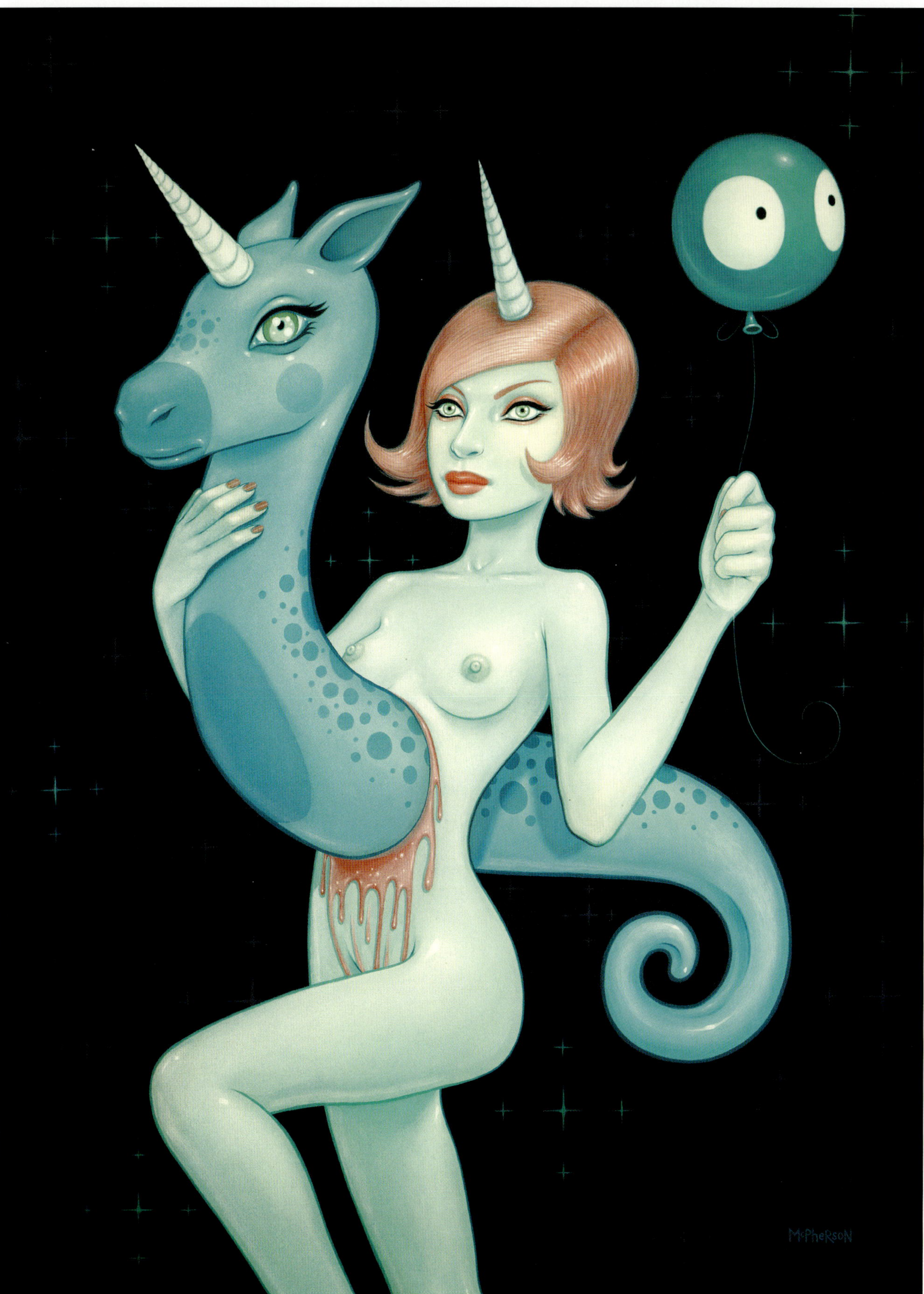
McPHERSON

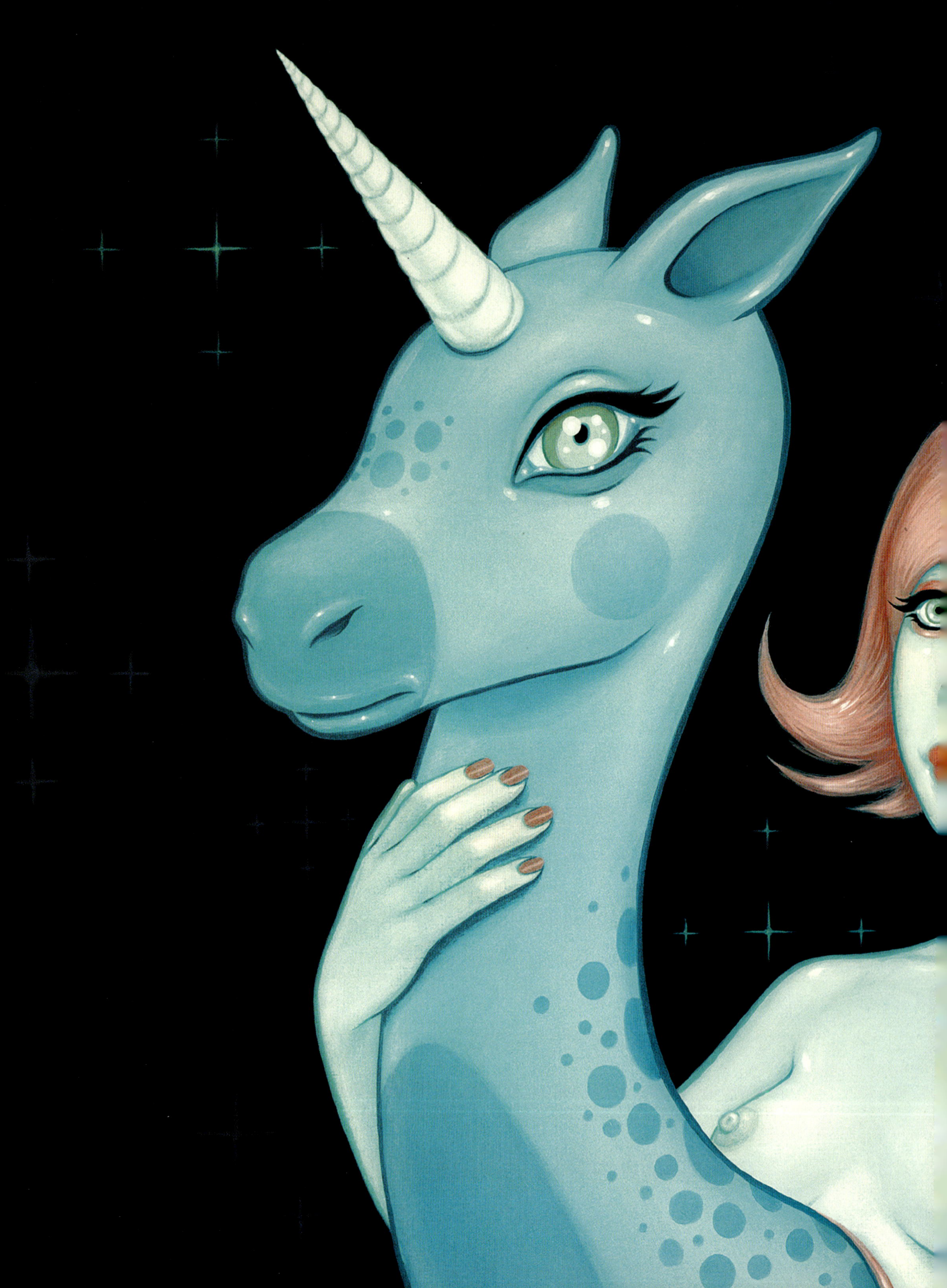

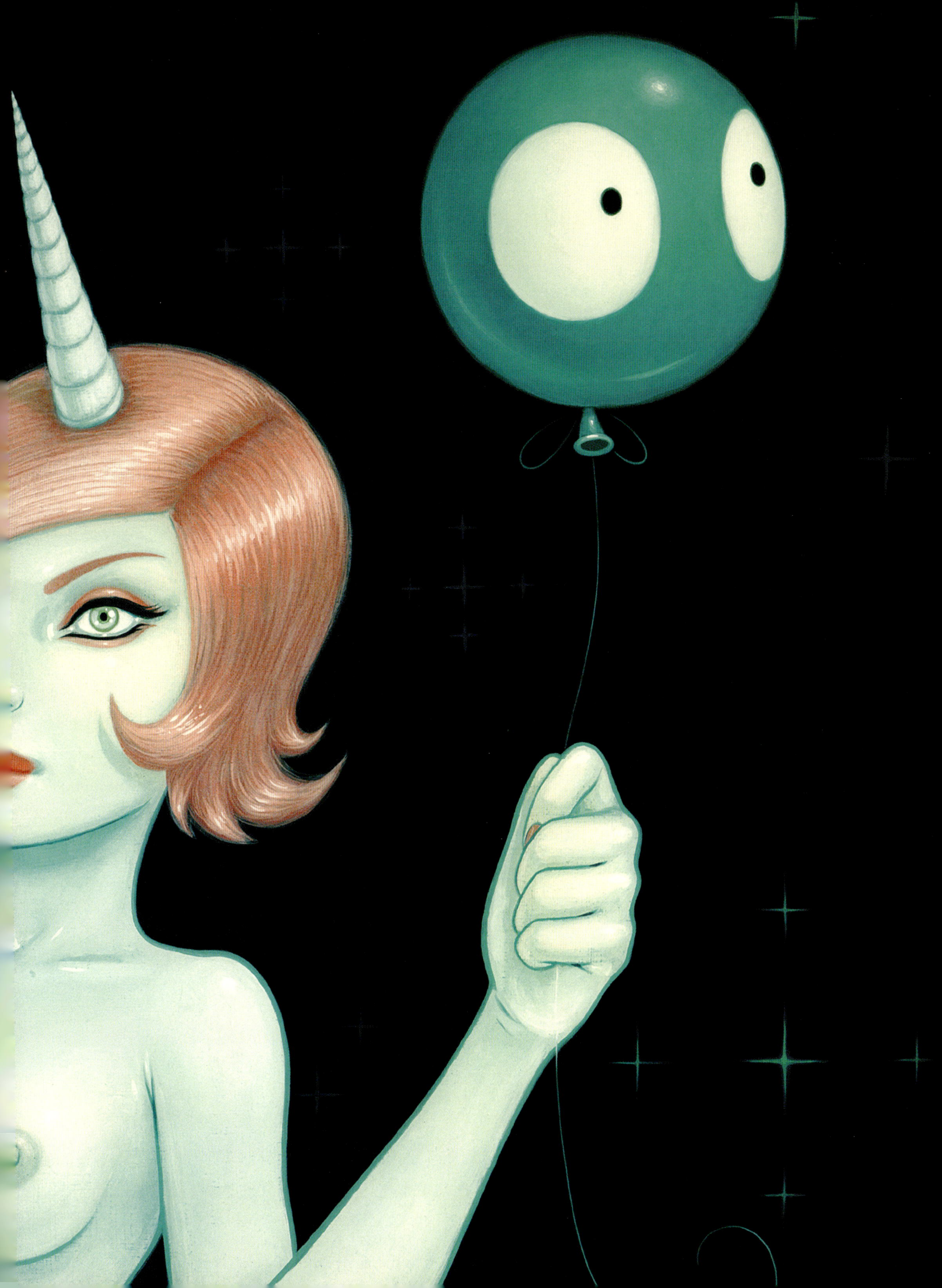

Evolution of Language

oil on birch
20" x 30"
2008

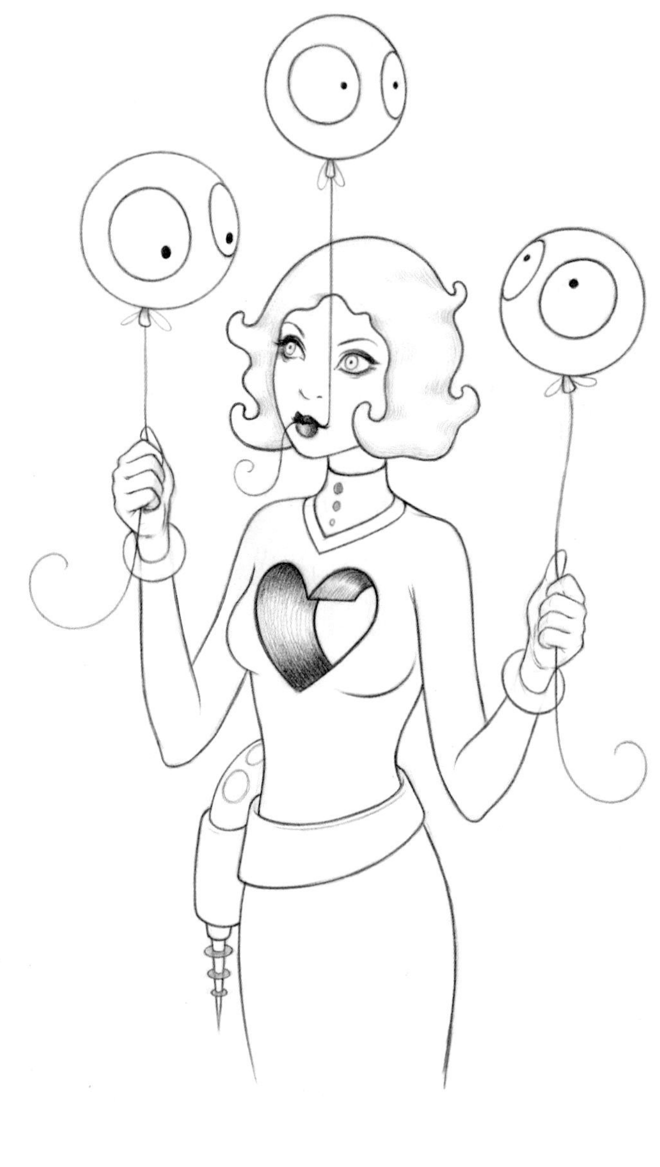

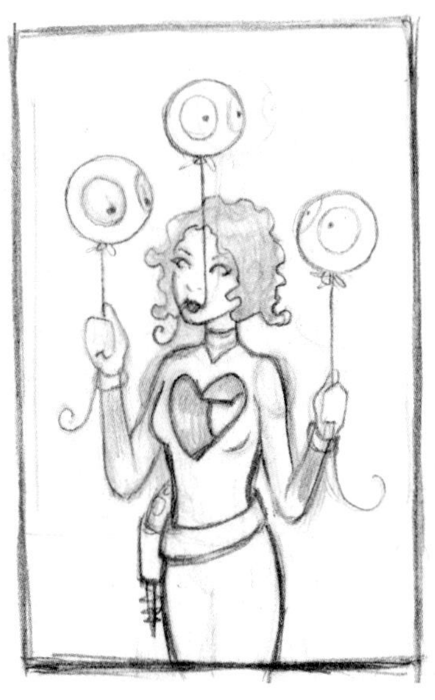

rough
graphite on paper
2" x 3"

drawing
graphite on bristol
14" x 17"

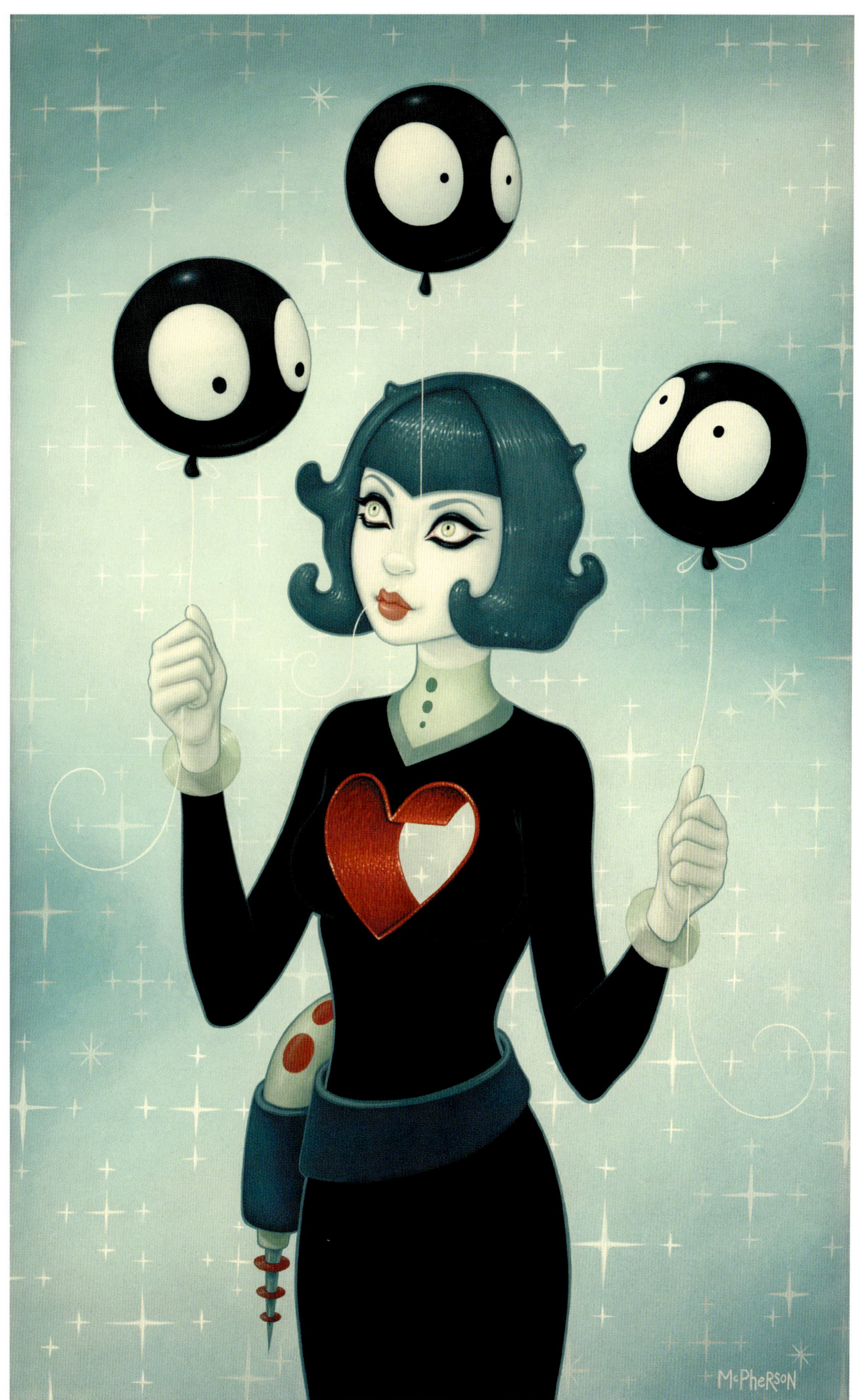
McPherson

The Weight of Water, Part One

oil on birch
30" x 40"
2008

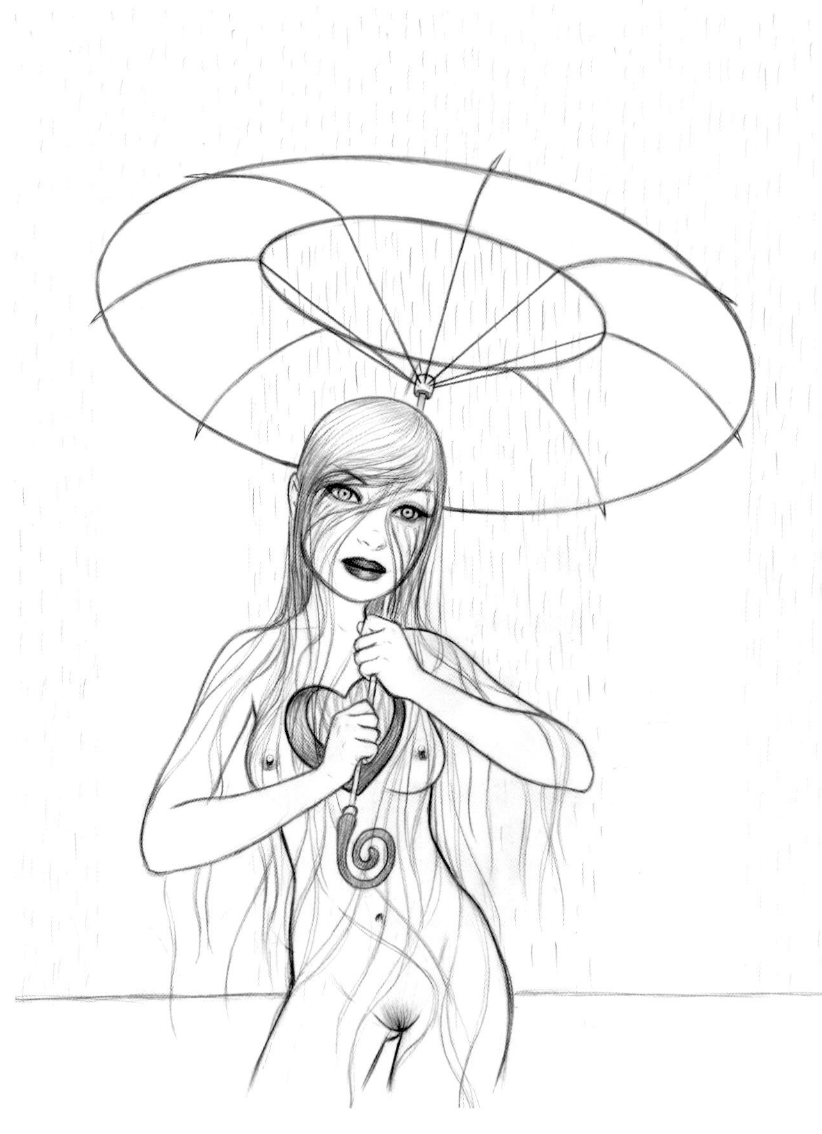

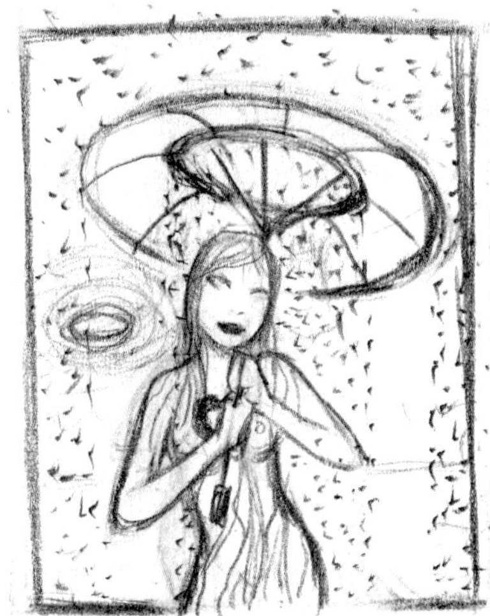

rough
graphite on paper
2" x 3"

drawing
graphite on bristol
14" x 17"

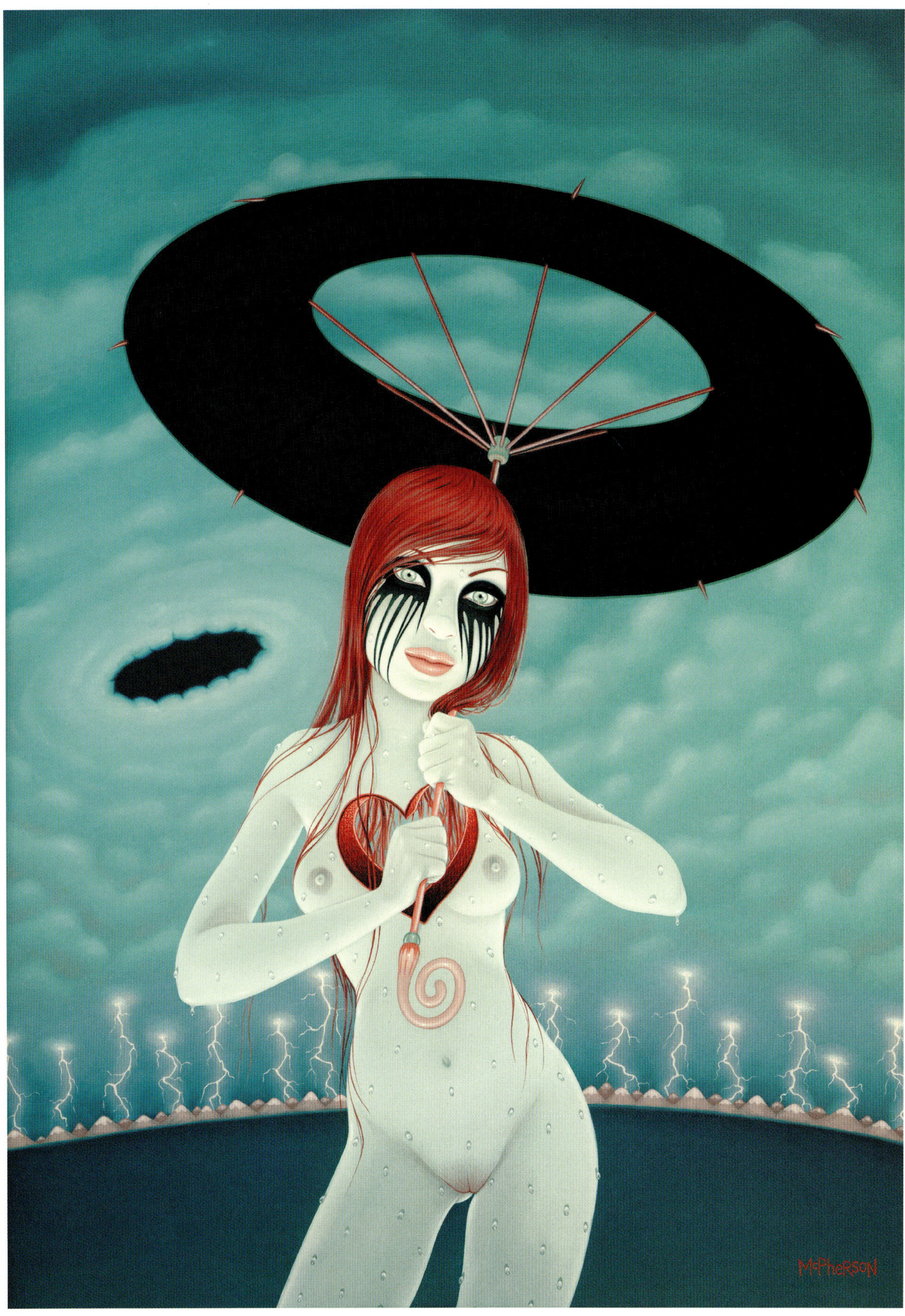
McPHERSON

THE WEIGHT OF WATER, PART TWO

oil on birch
30" x 40"
2008

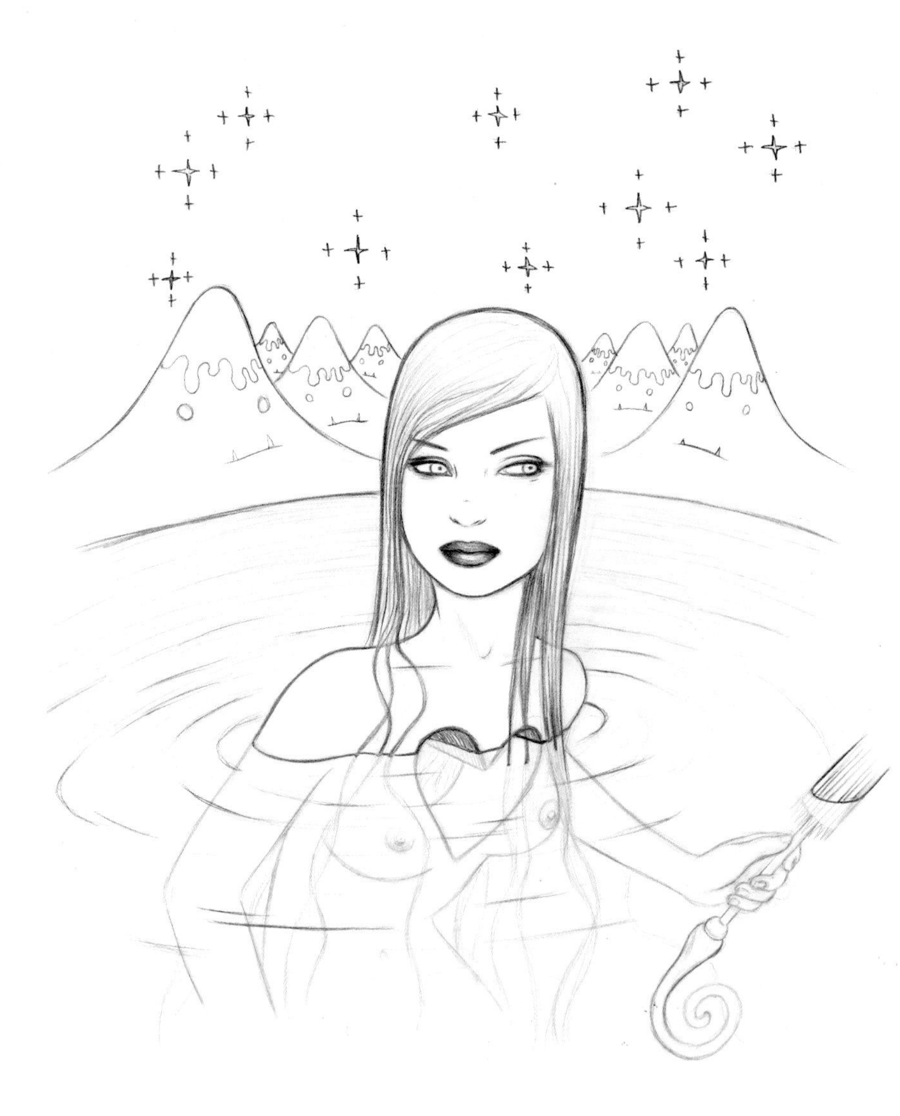

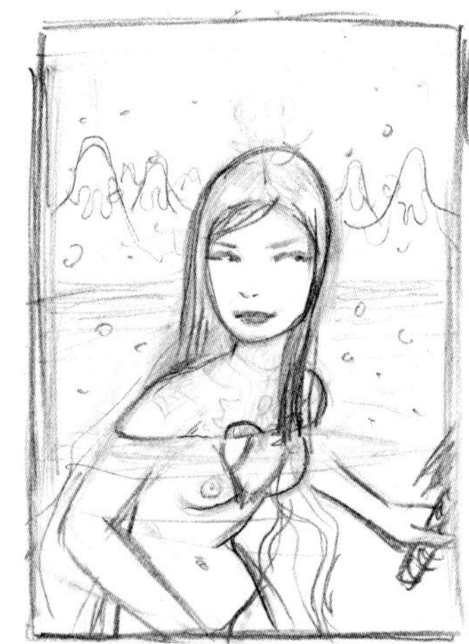

rough
graphite on paper
2" x 3"

drawing
graphite on bristol
14" x 17"

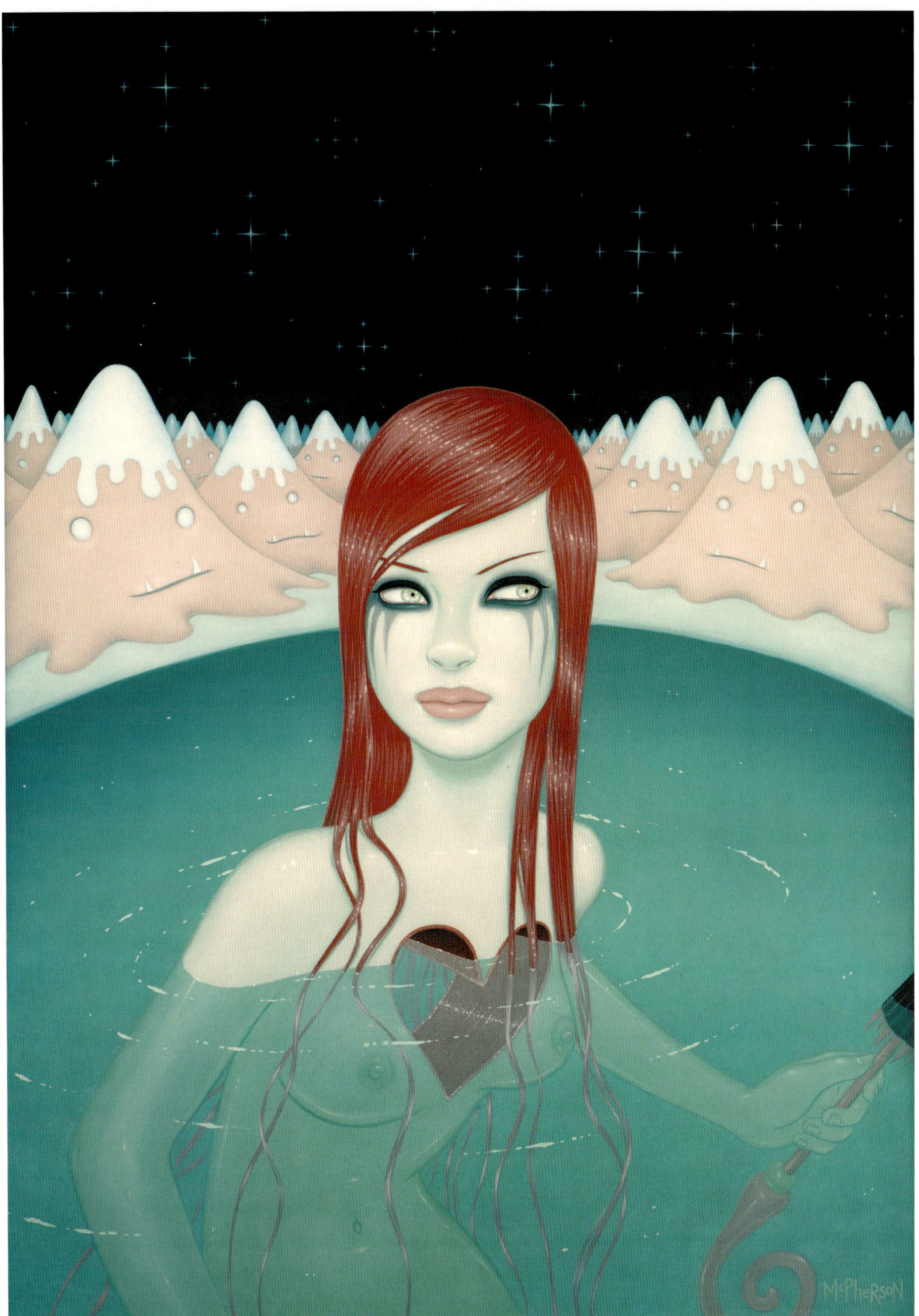
McPherson

The Weight of Water, Part Three

oil on birch
30" x 40"
2008

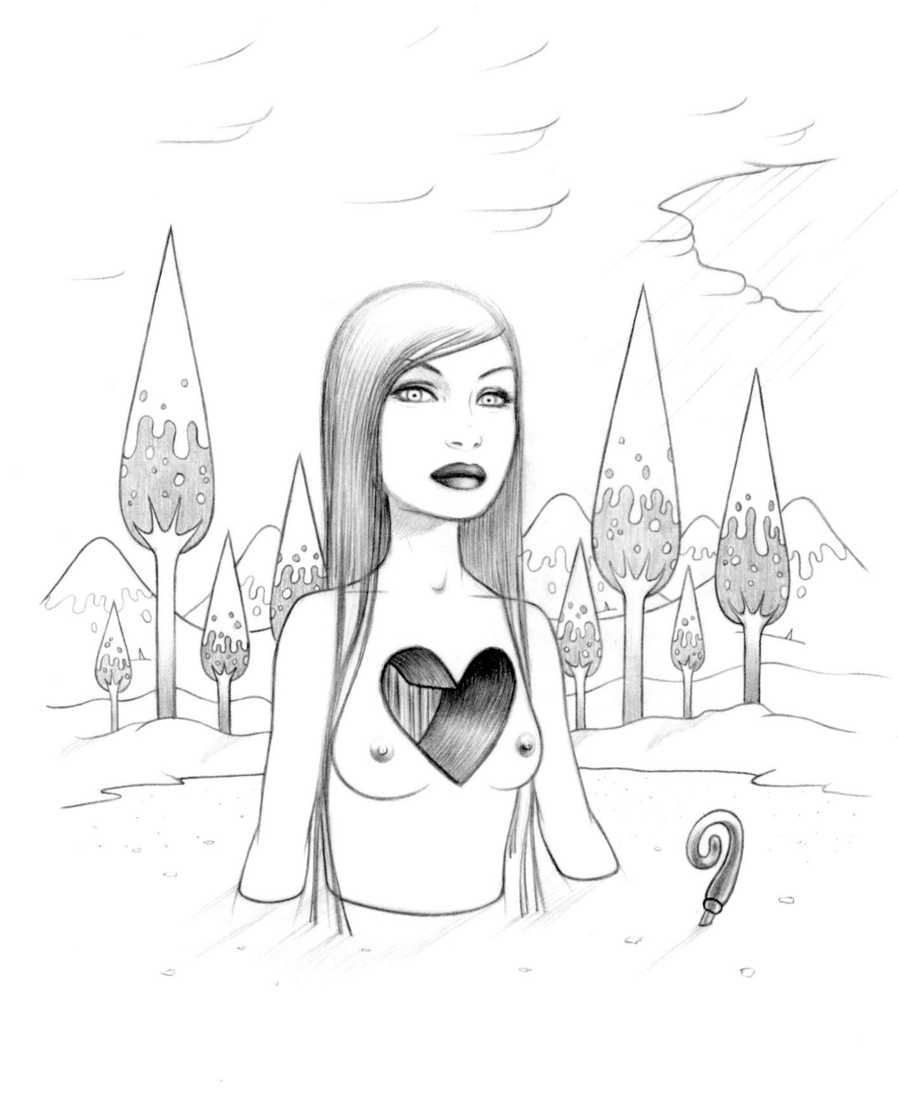

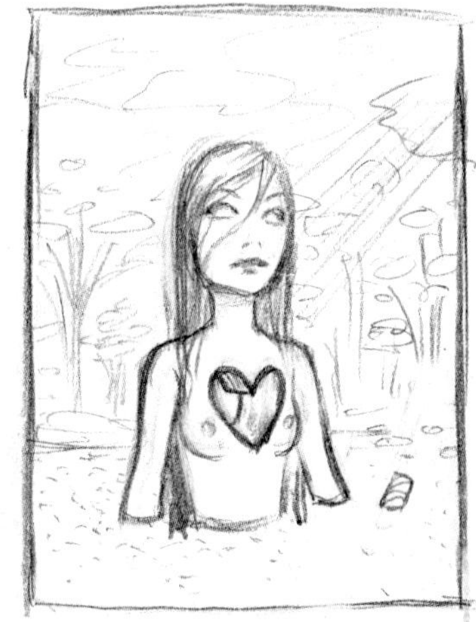

rough
graphite on paper
2" x 3"

drawing
graphite on bristol
14" x 17"

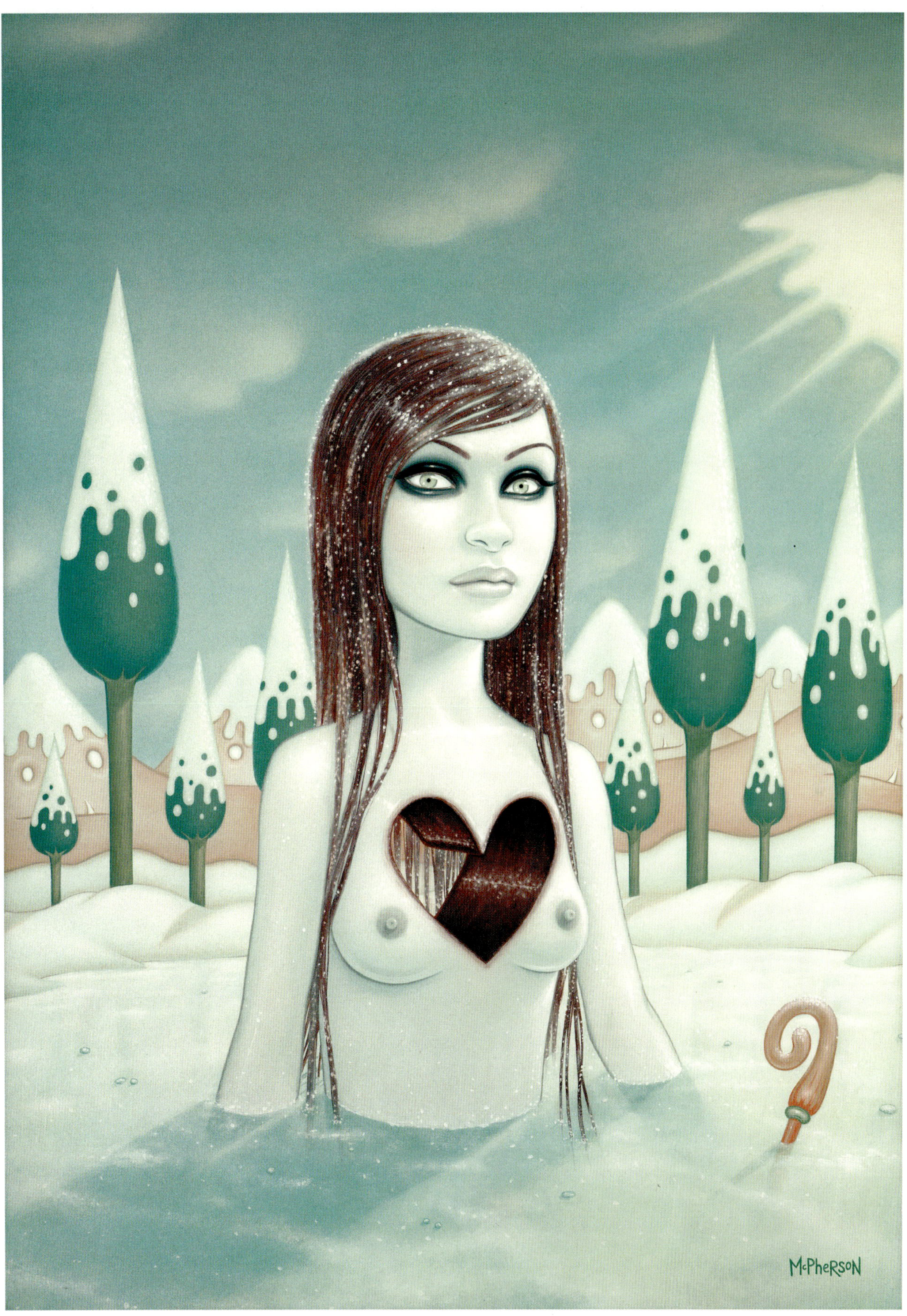
McPherson

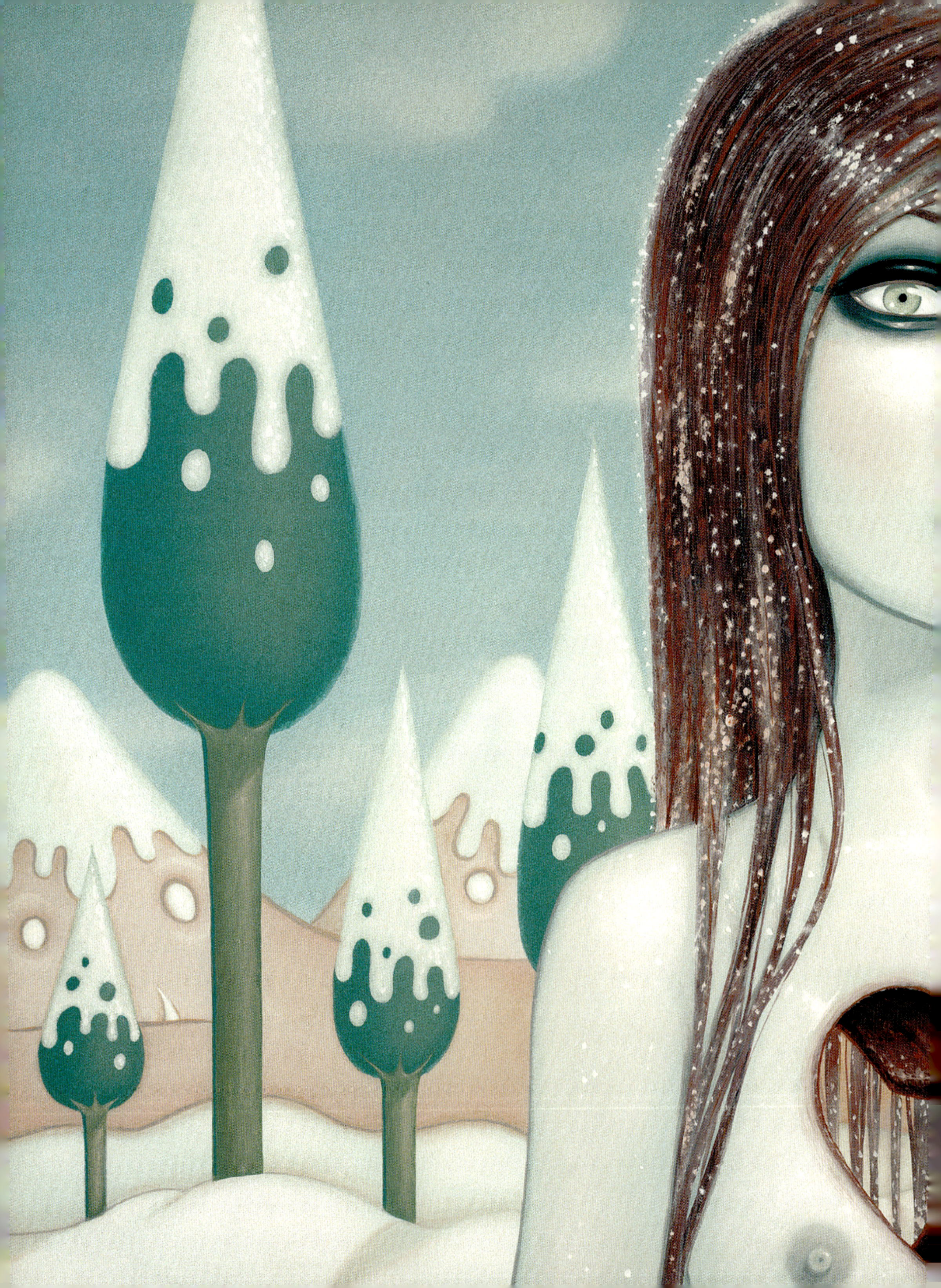

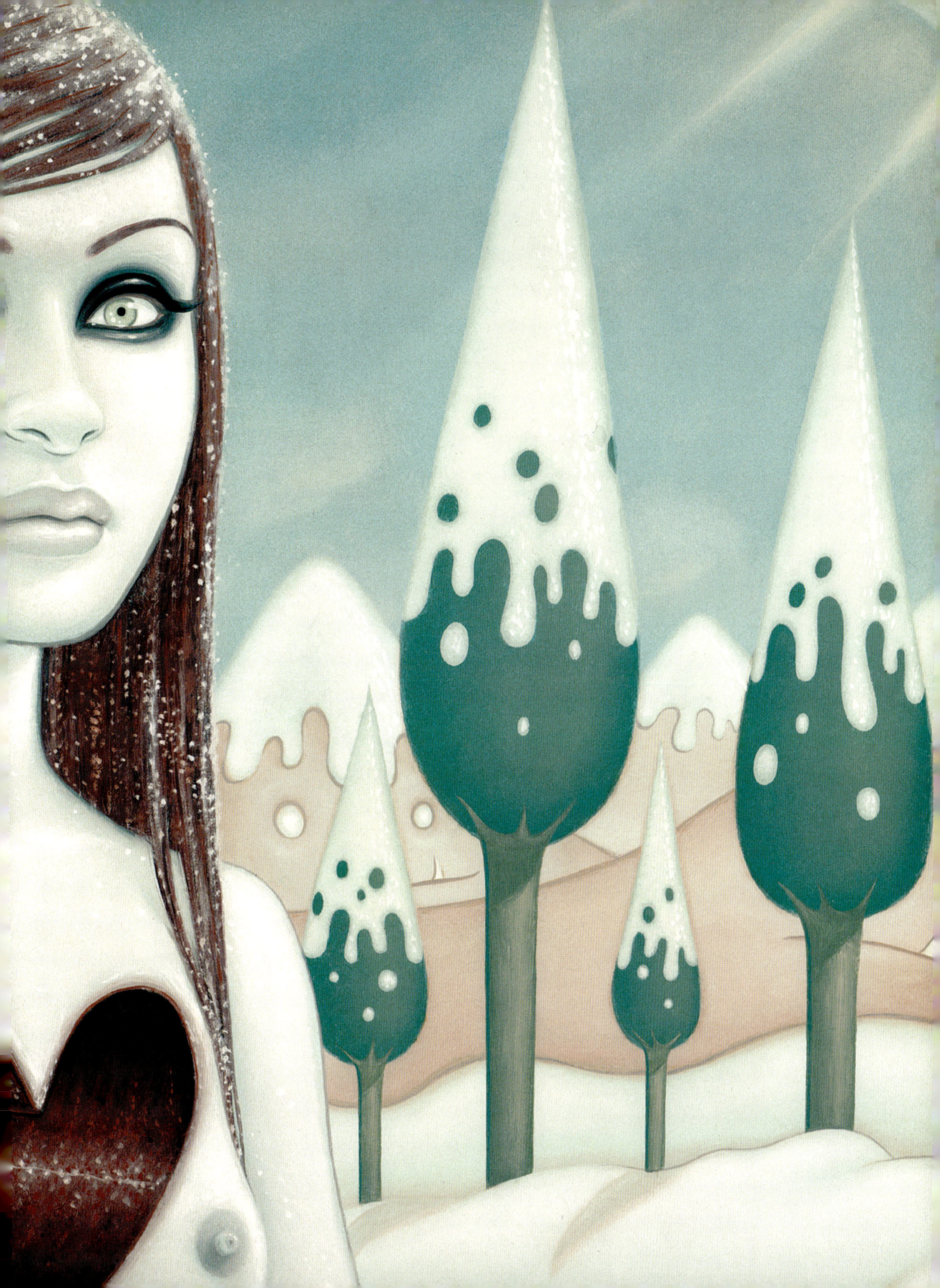

Somewhere Under the Rainbow, Pink

oil and acrylic on birch
12" x 24"
2008

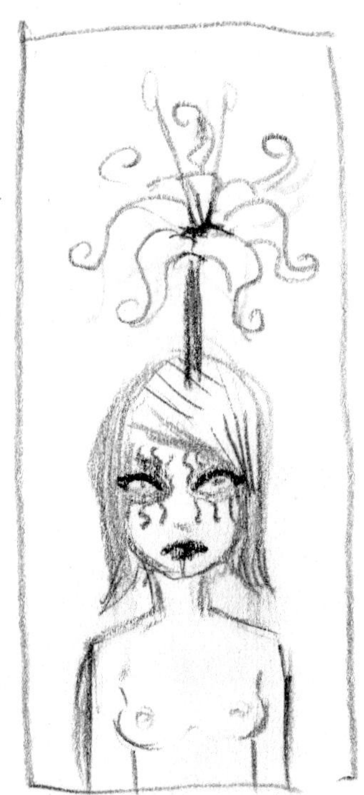

rough
graphite on paper
1" x 3"

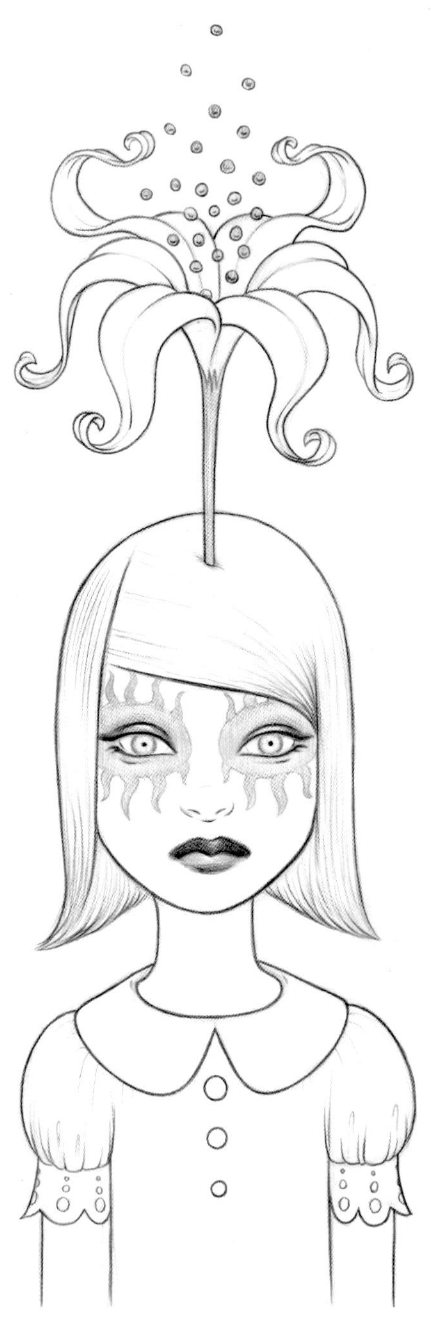

drawing
graphite on bristol
14" x 17"

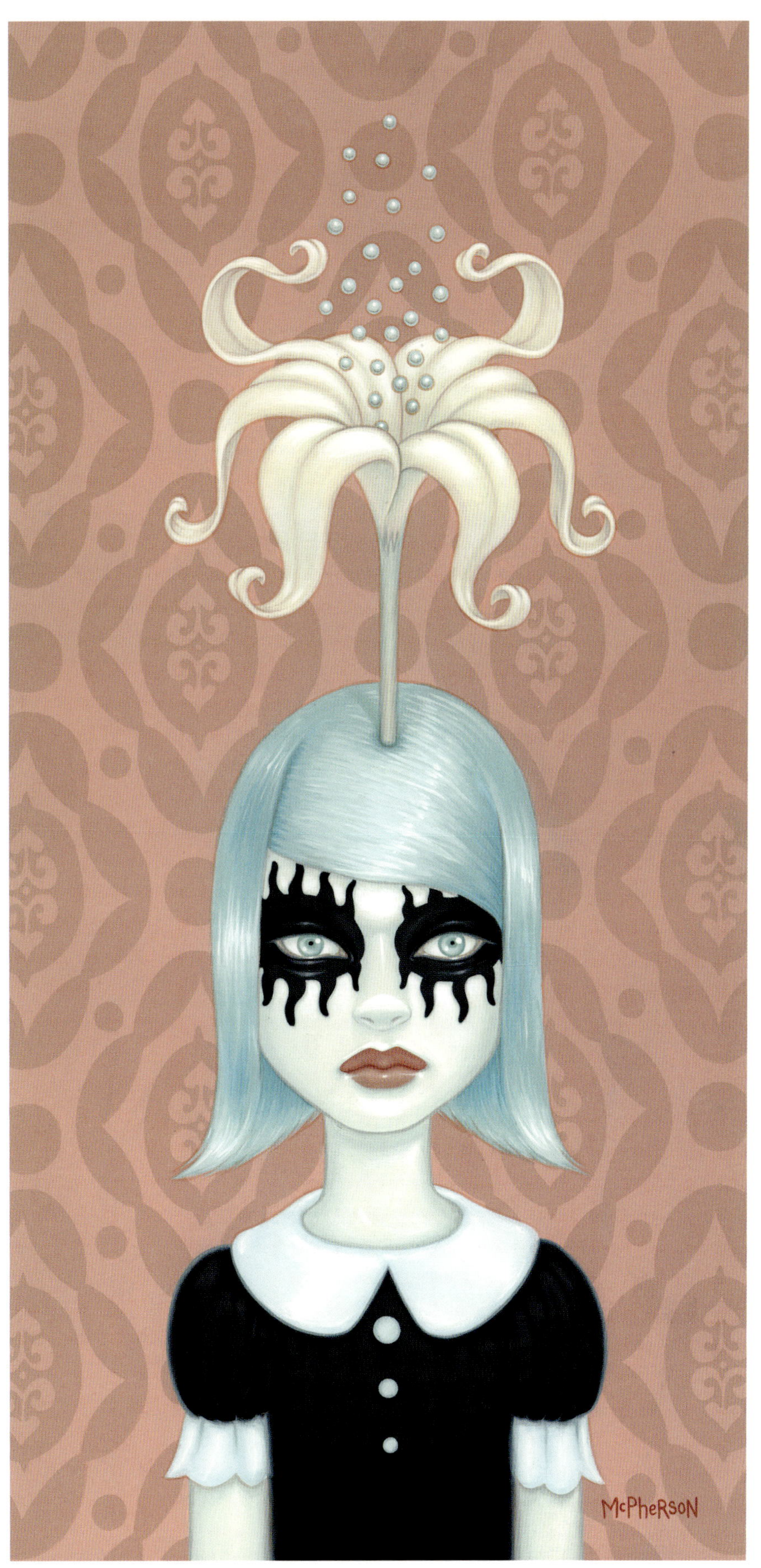
McPherson

Somewhere Under the Rainbow, Peach

oil and acrylic on birch
12" x 24"
2008

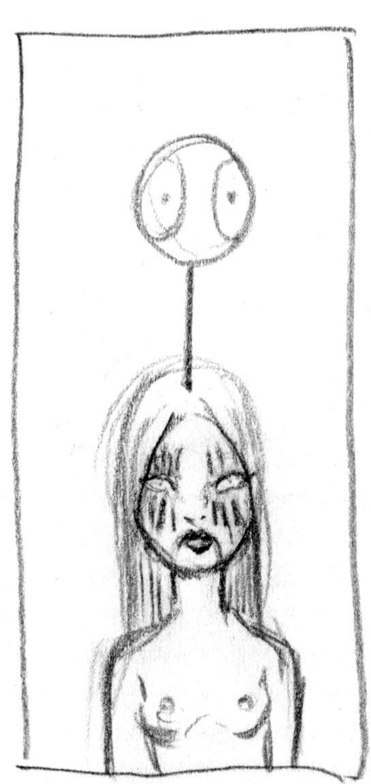

rough
graphite on paper
1" x 3"

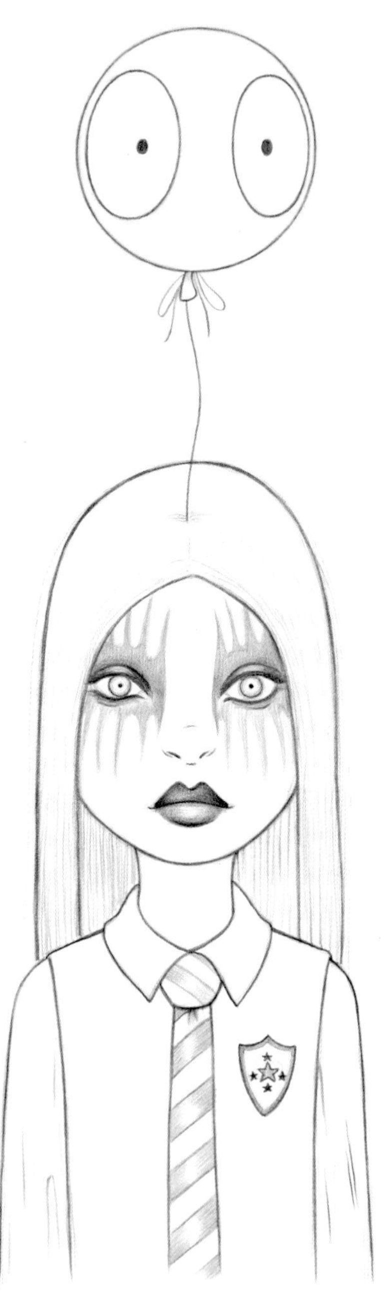

drawing
graphite on bristol
14" x 17"

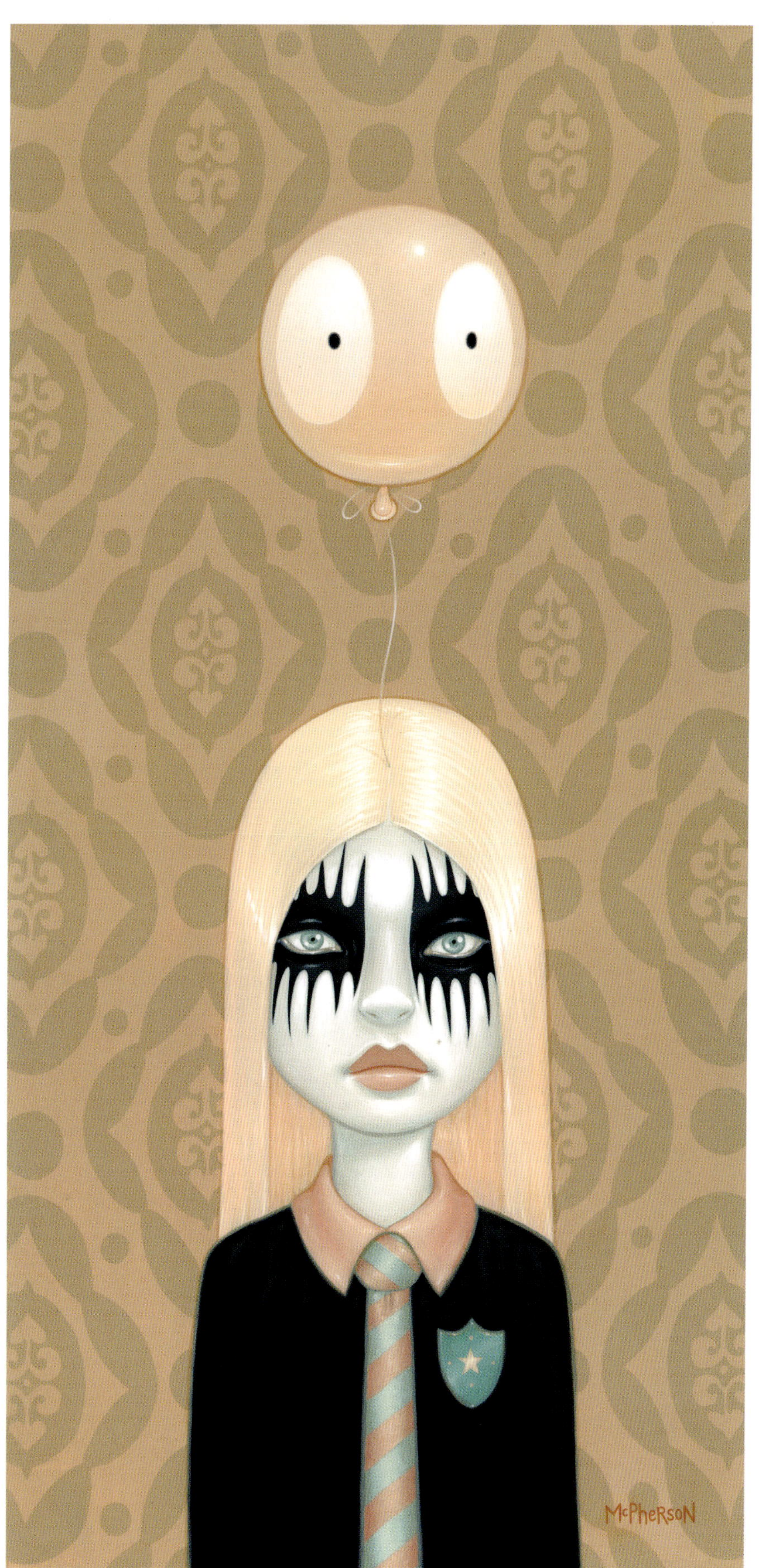
McPherson

Somewhere Under the Rainbow, Green

oil and acrylic on birch
12" x 24"
2008

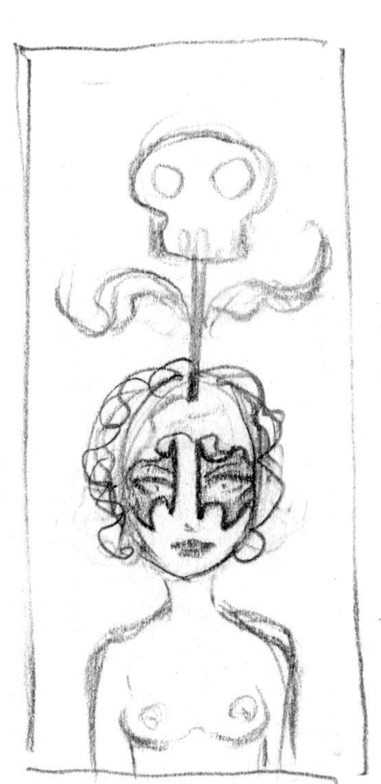

rough
graphite on paper
1" x 3"

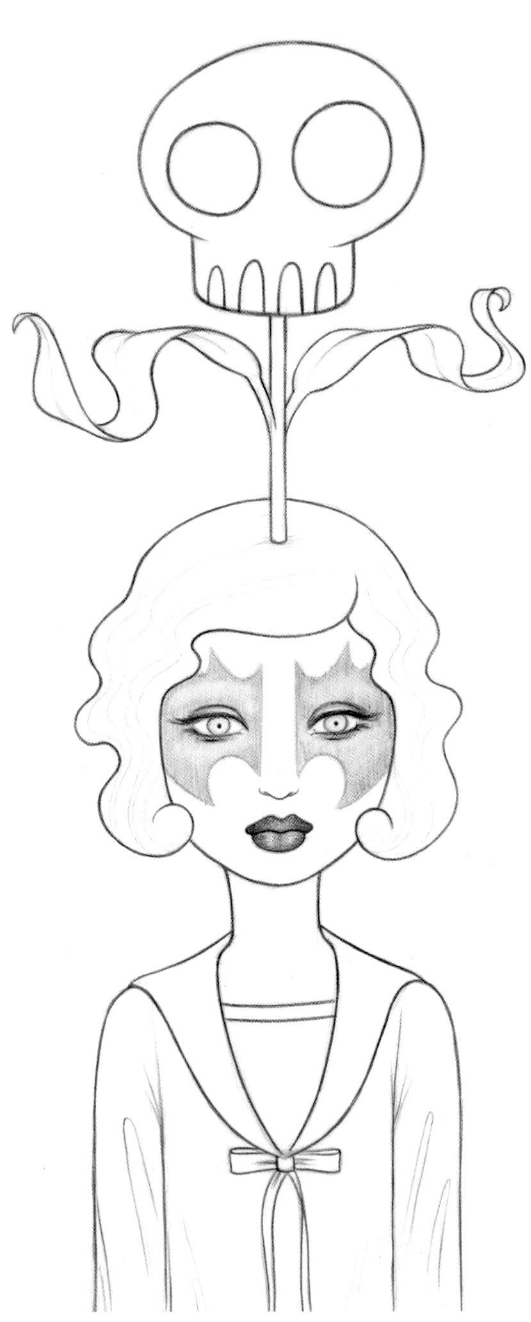

drawing
graphite on bristol
14" x 17"

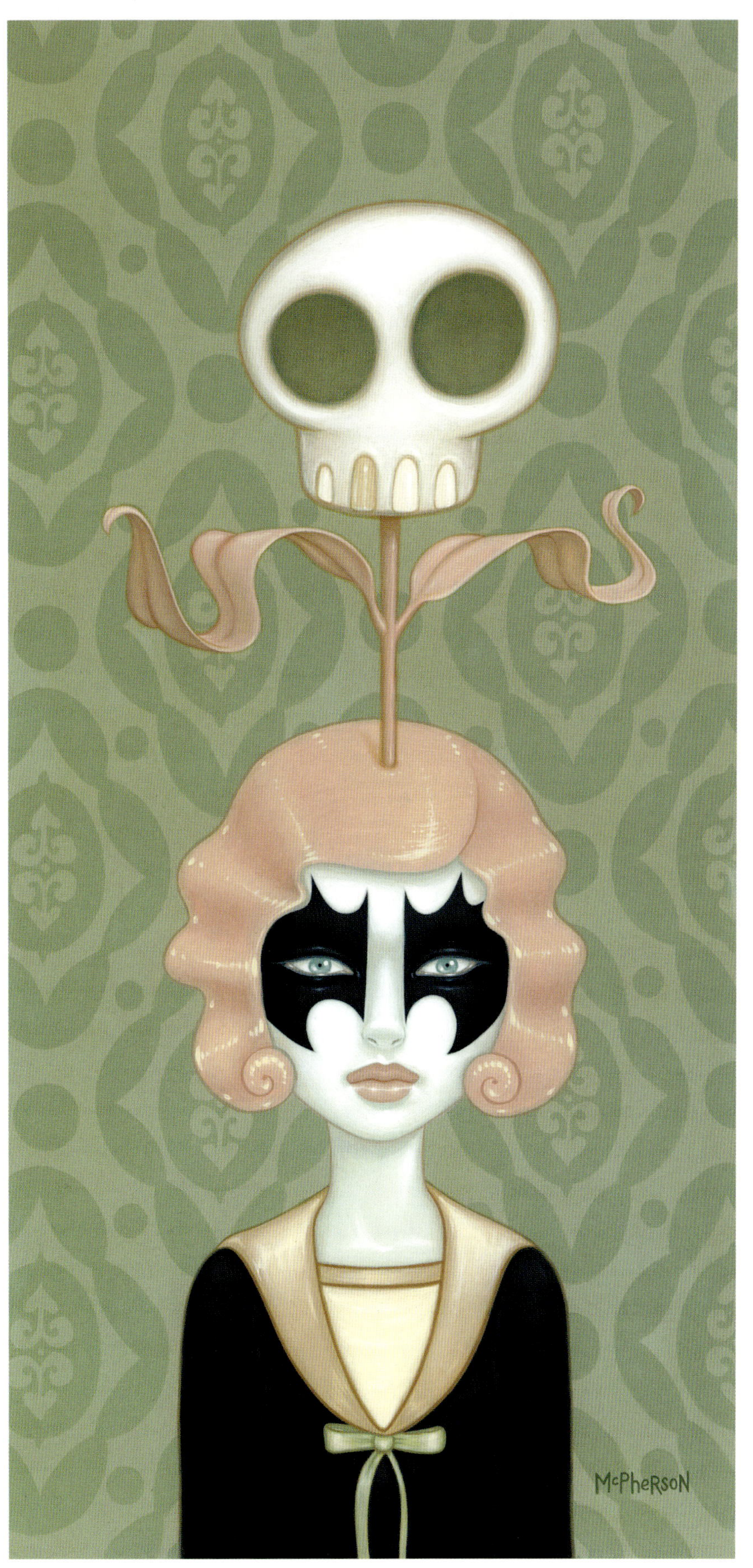
McPherSoN

Somewhere Under the Rainbow, Turquoise

oil and acrylic on birch
12" x 24"
2008

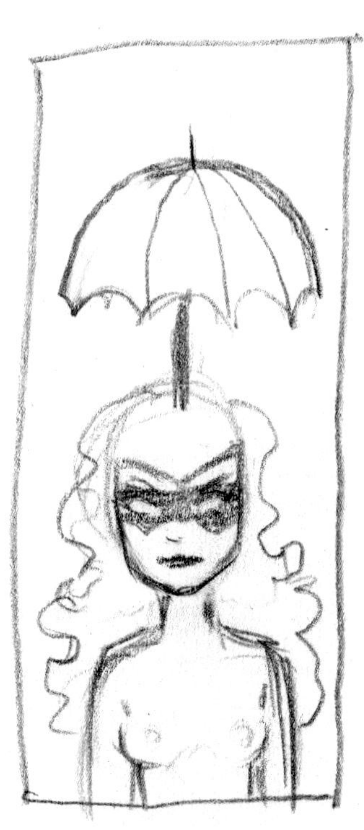

rough
graphite on paper
1" x 3"

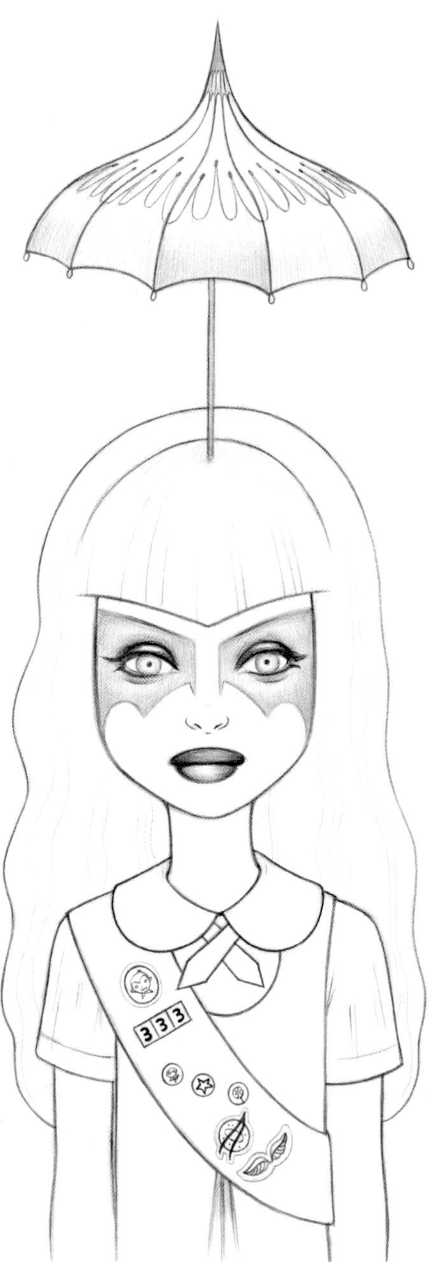

drawing
graphite on bristol
14" x 17"

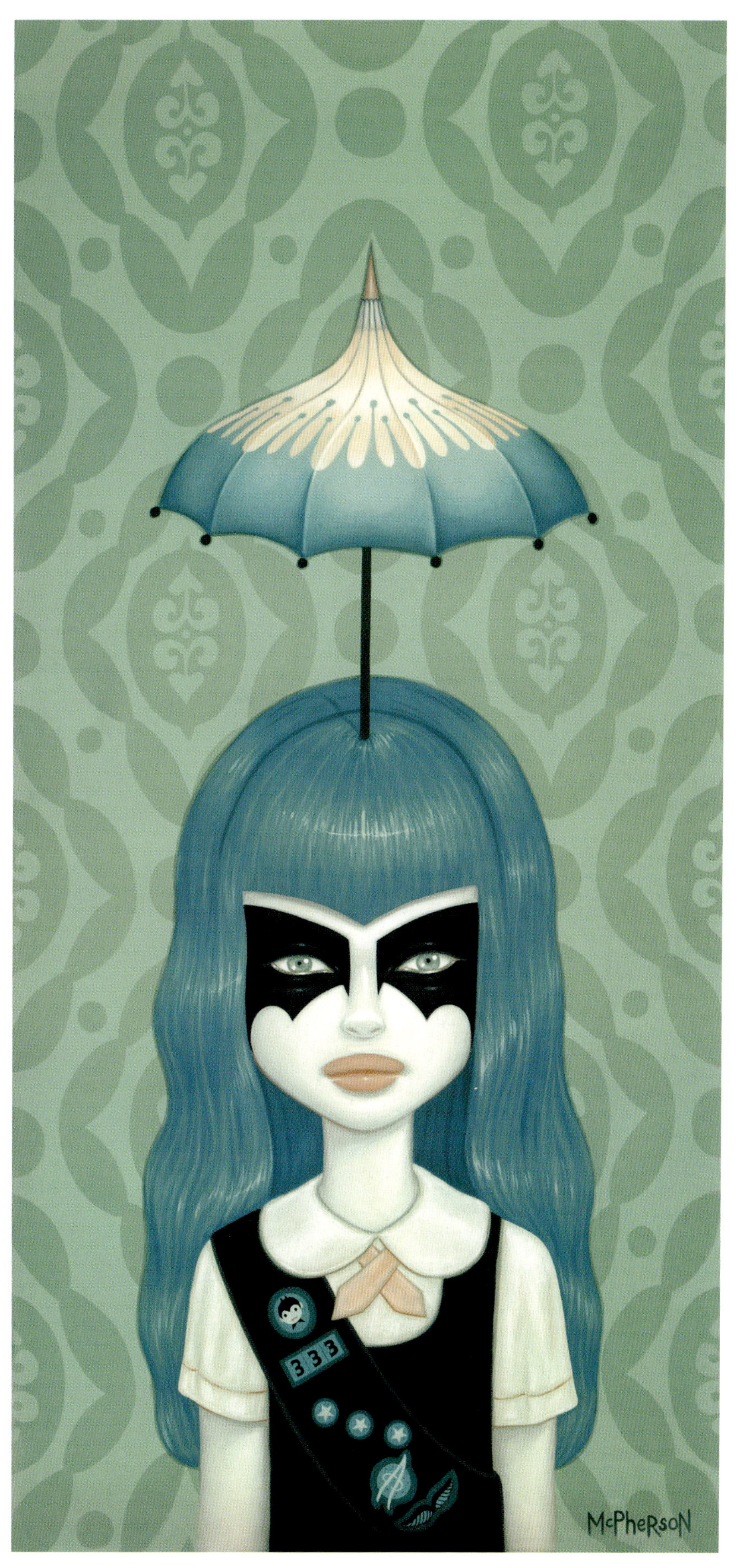
333
McPHERSON

Somewhere Under the Rainbow, Blue

oil and acrylic on birch
12" x 24"
2008

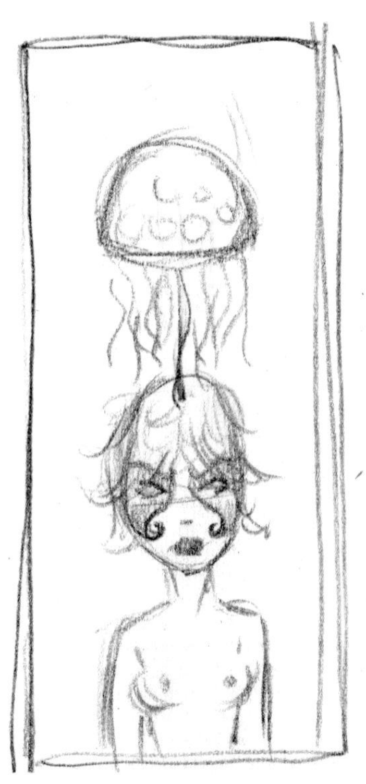

rough
graphite on paper
1" x 3"

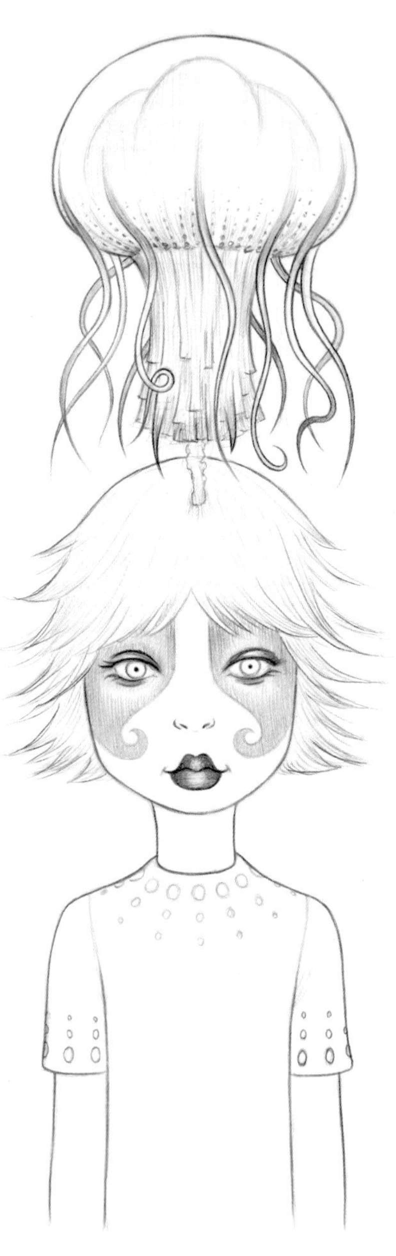

drawing
graphite on bristol
14" x 17"

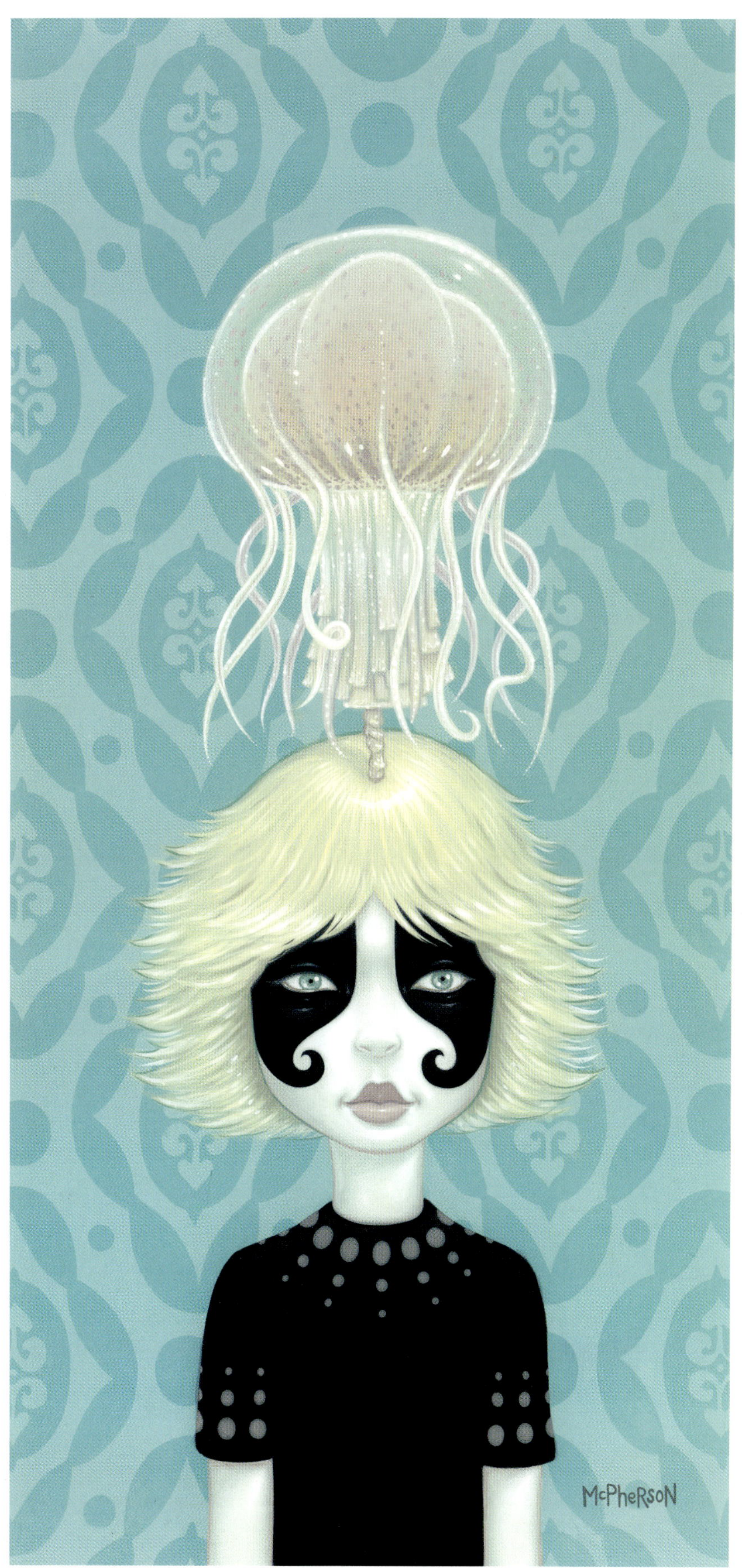
McPherson

How They Fly Away So Easily

oil and acrylic on birch
24" x 30"
2007

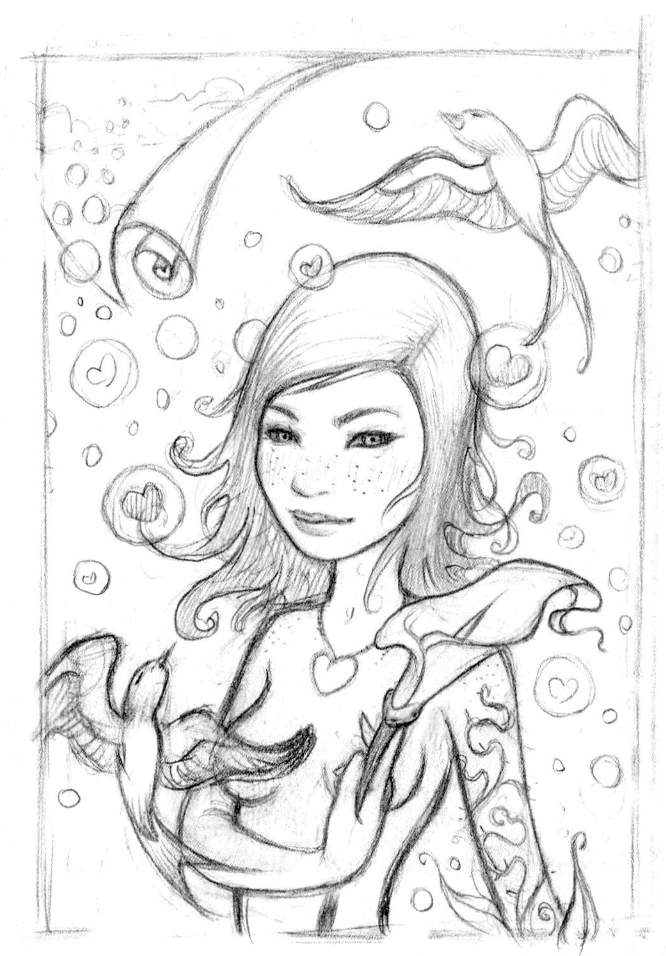

drawing
graphite on bristol
4" x 5"

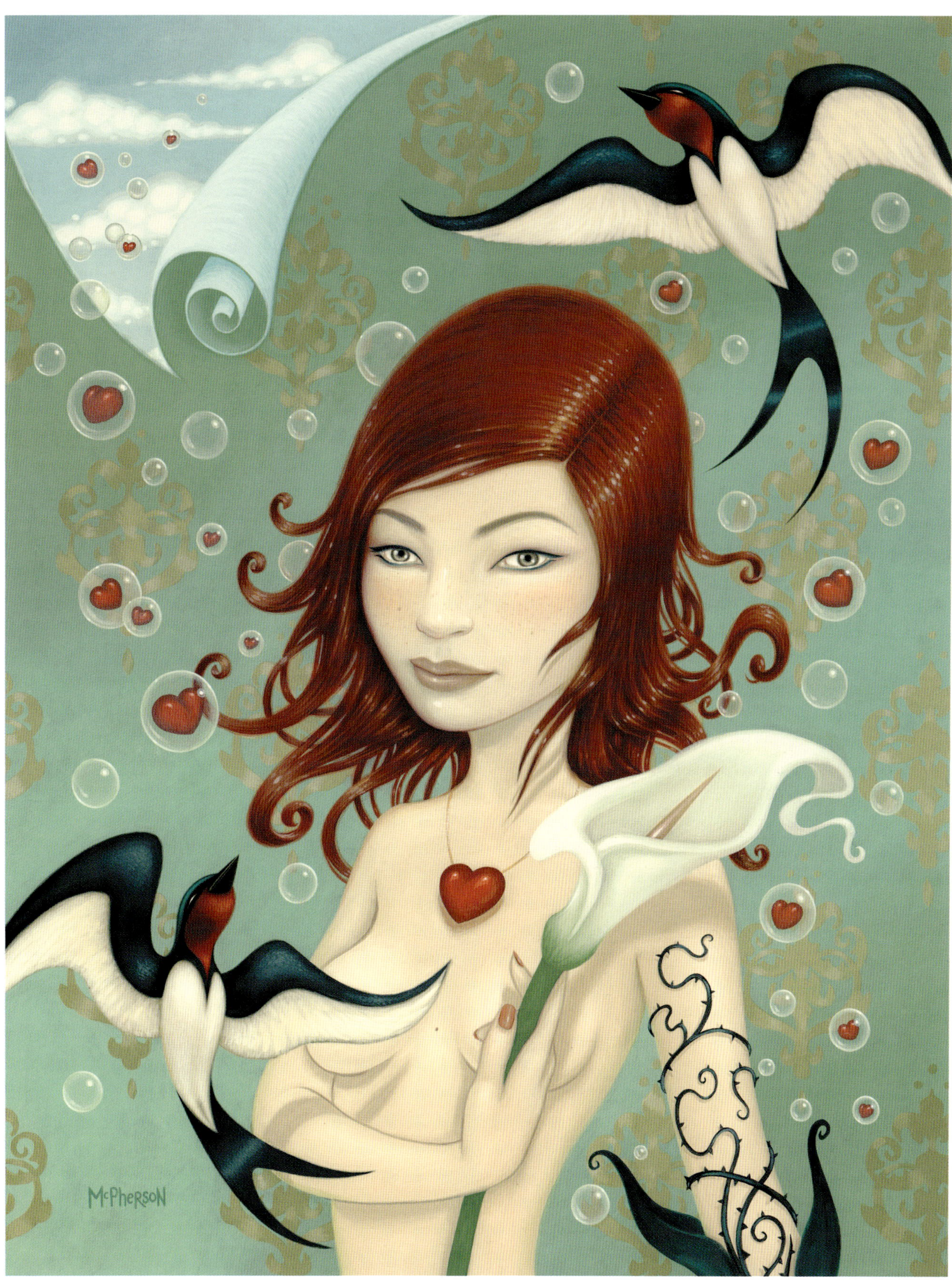
McPHERSON

Untitled

oil on birch
24" x 30"
2008

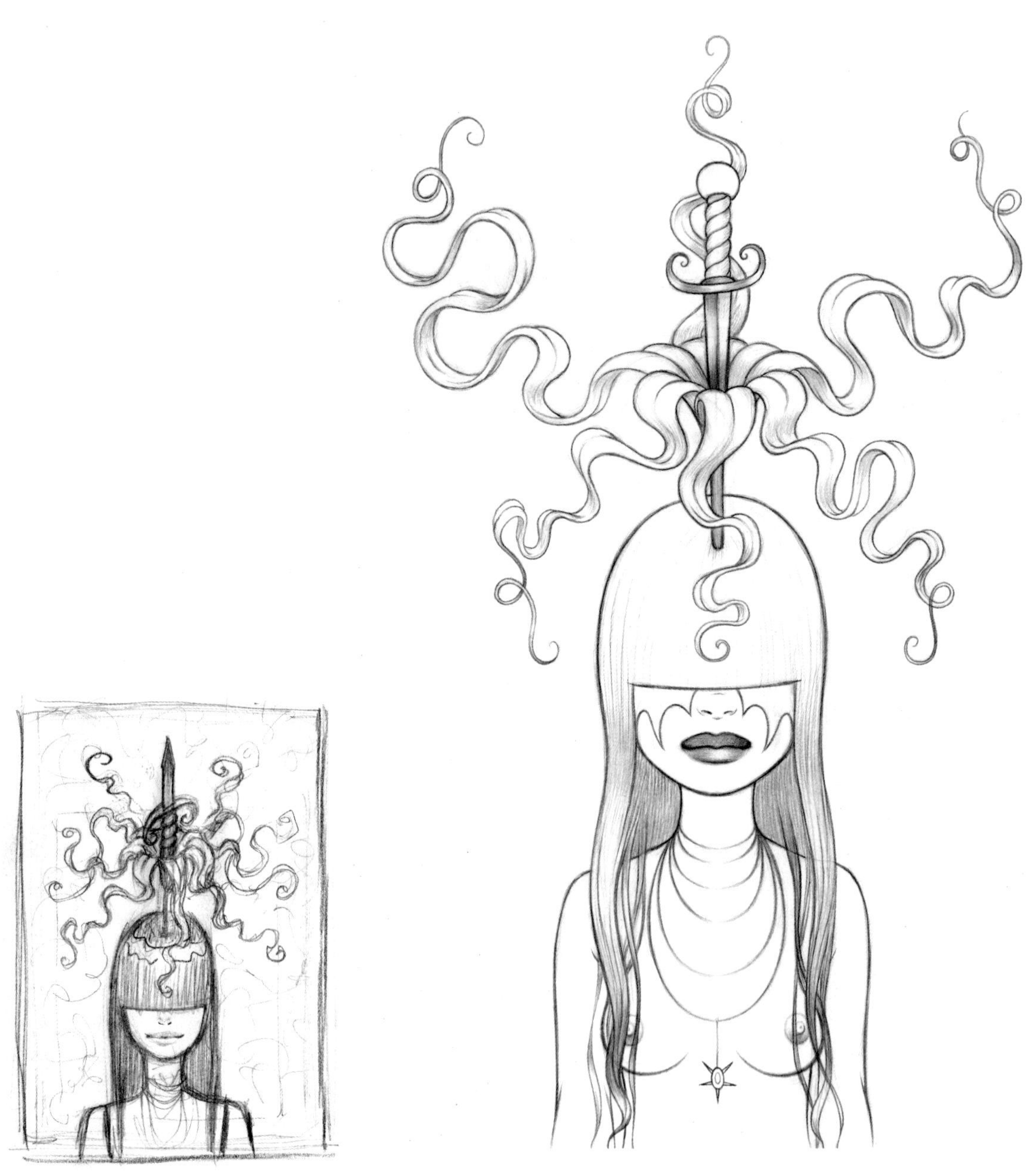

rough
graphite on paper
3" x 4"

drawing
graphite on bristol
14" x 17"

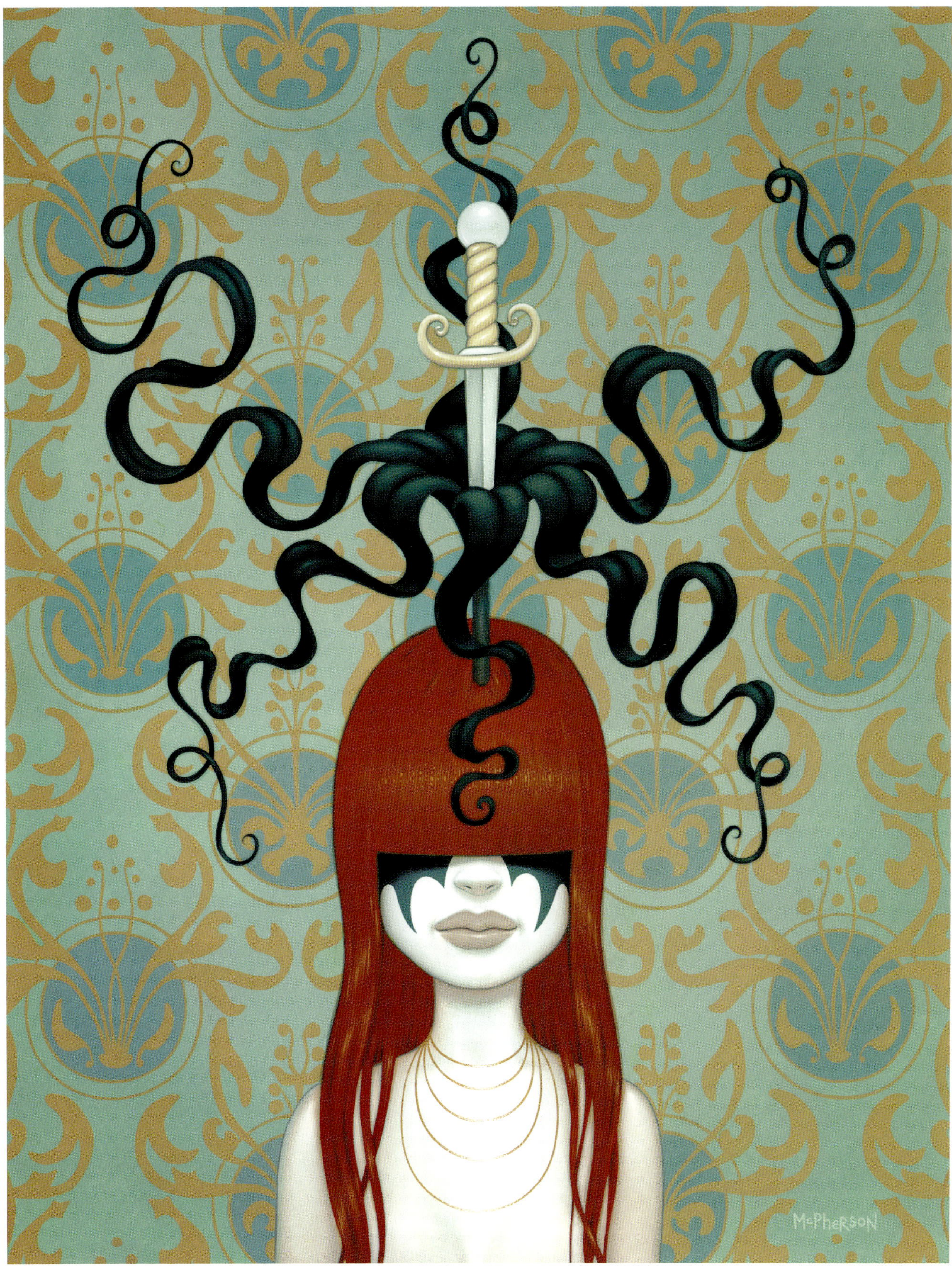
McPHERSON

The Fractioned Second

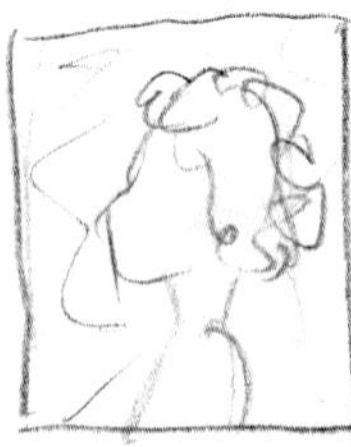

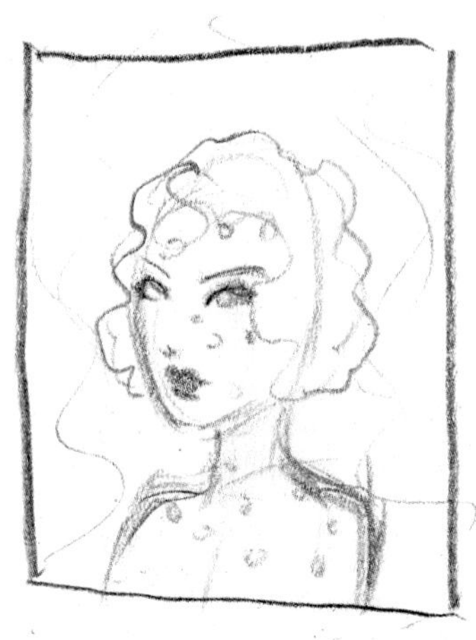

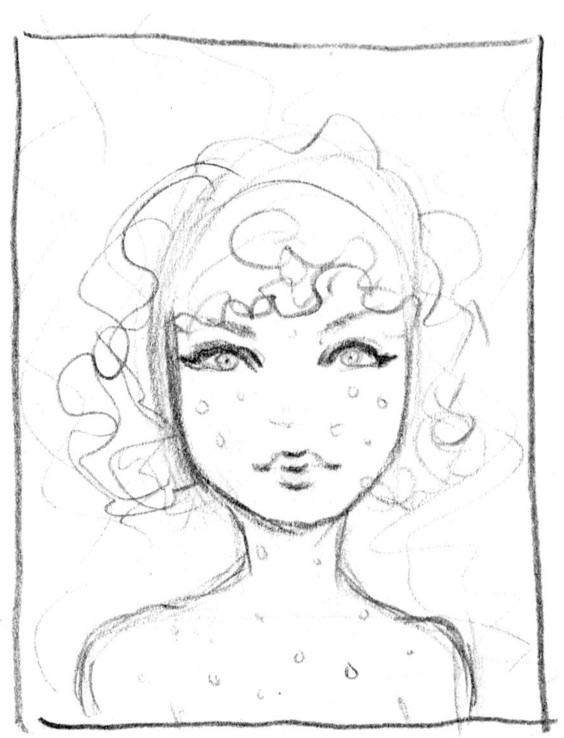

roughs
graphite on paper
1" x 1", 2" x 2", 2" x 3", 2" x 2", 1" x 1"

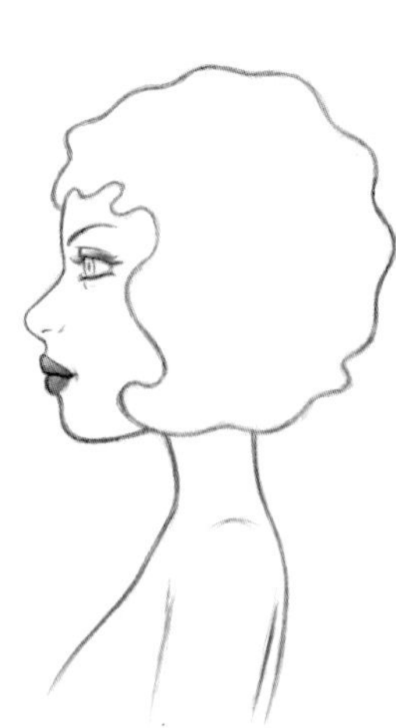

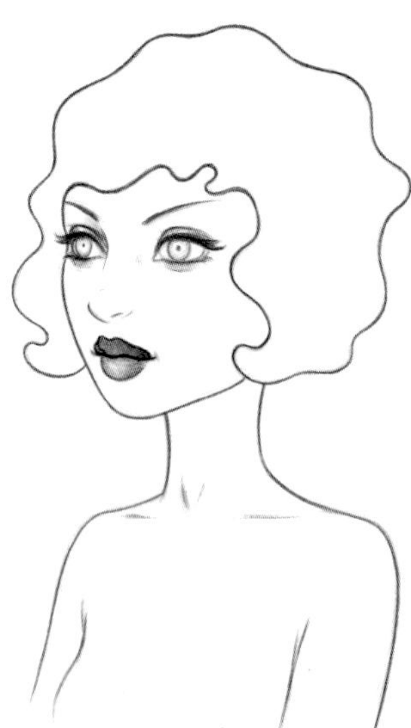

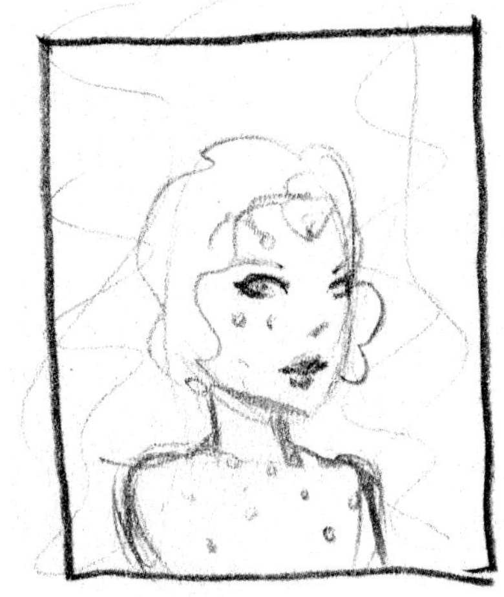

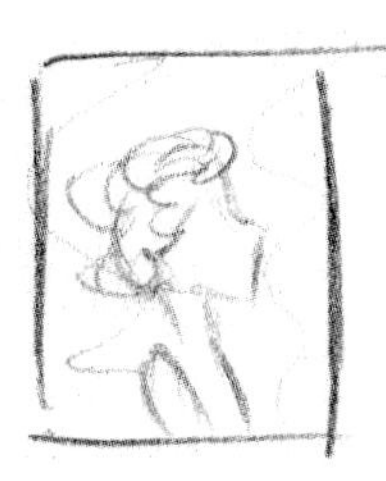

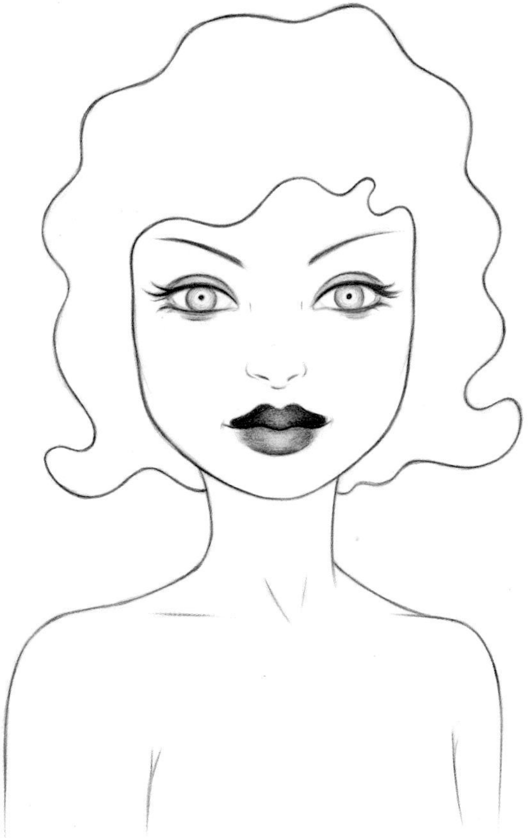

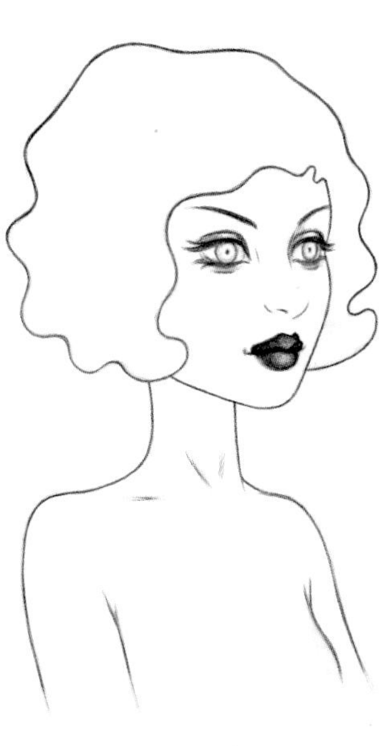

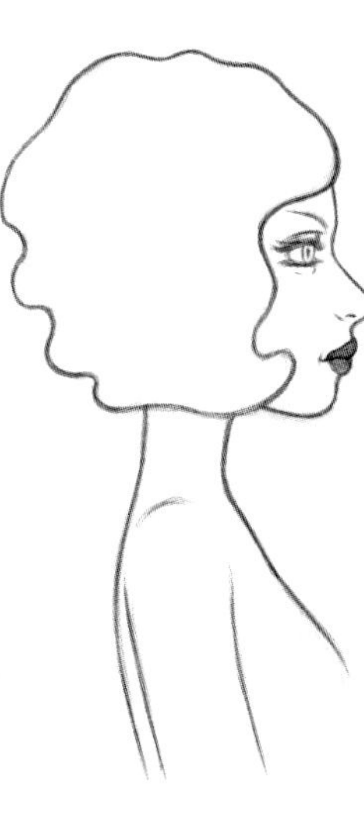

drawings
graphite on bristol
5" x 7", 6.5" x 9", 10" x 14", 6.5" x 9", 5" x 7"

The Fractioned Second

oil on birch
11" x 14", 16" x 20", 24" x 30", 16" x 20", 11" x 14"
2008

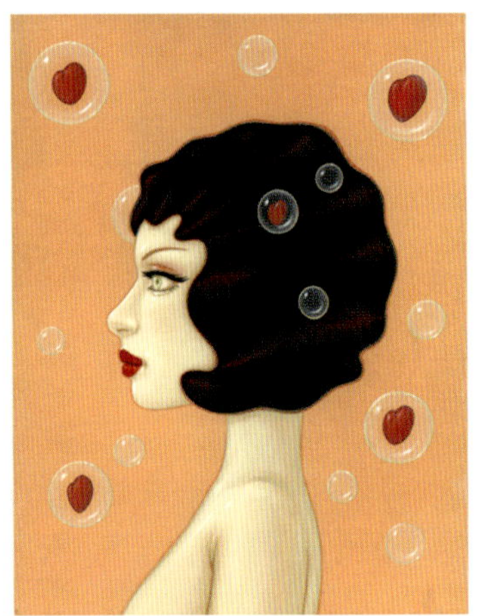

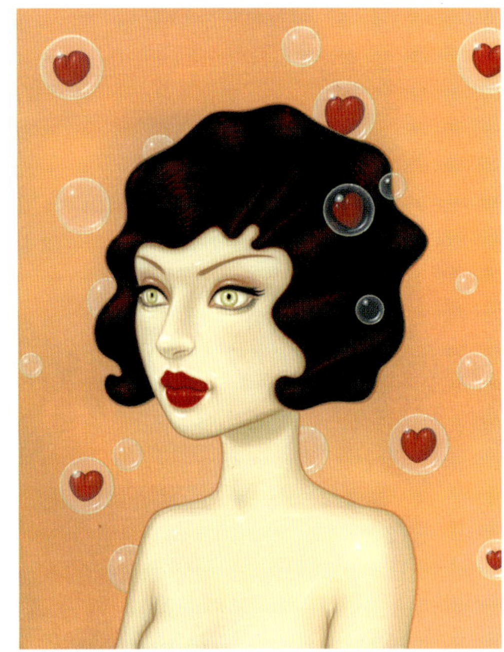

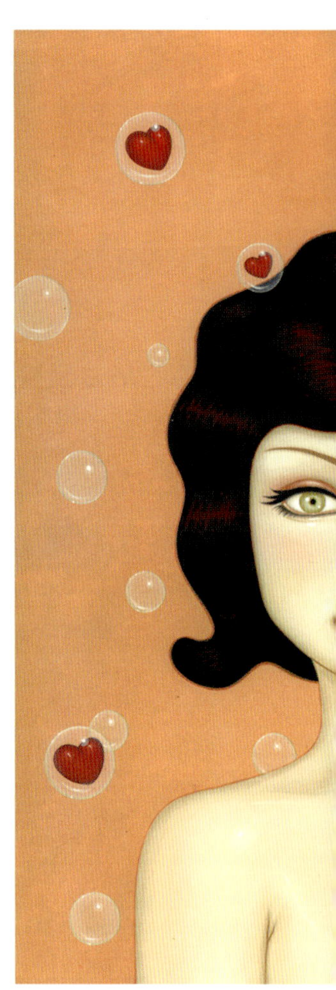

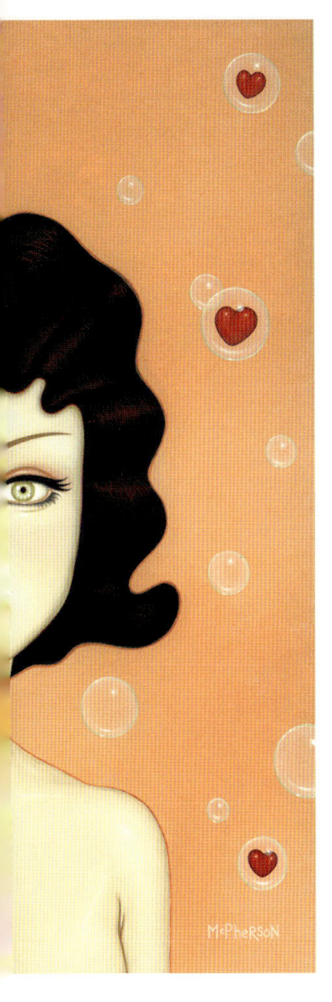
McPHeRSoN

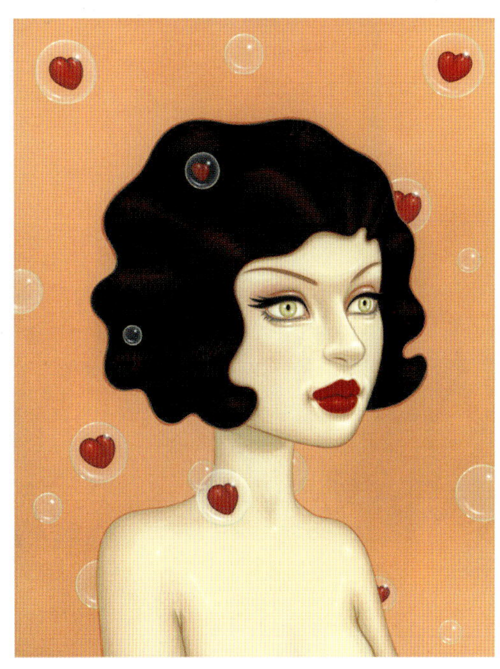

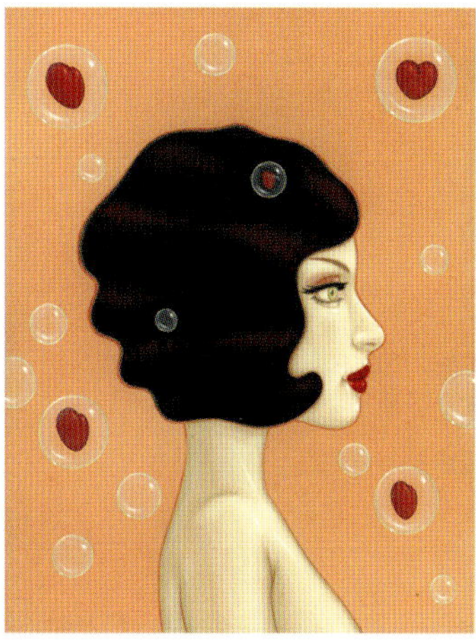

Laughing Through the Chaos of It All

oil on birch
20" x 24"
2008

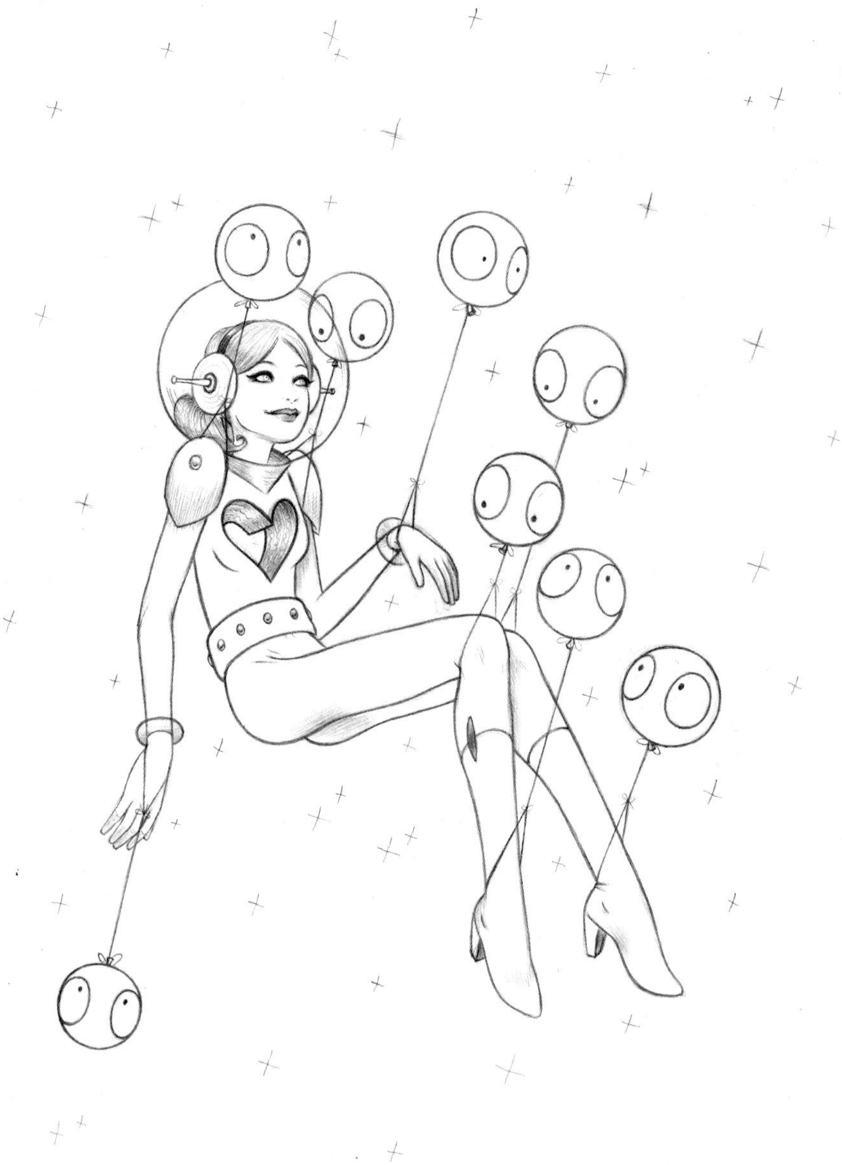

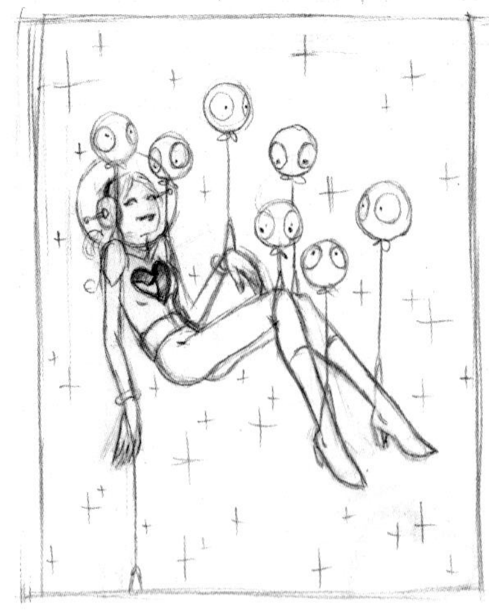

rough
graphite on paper
3" x 4"

drawing
graphite on bristol
11.5" x 16"

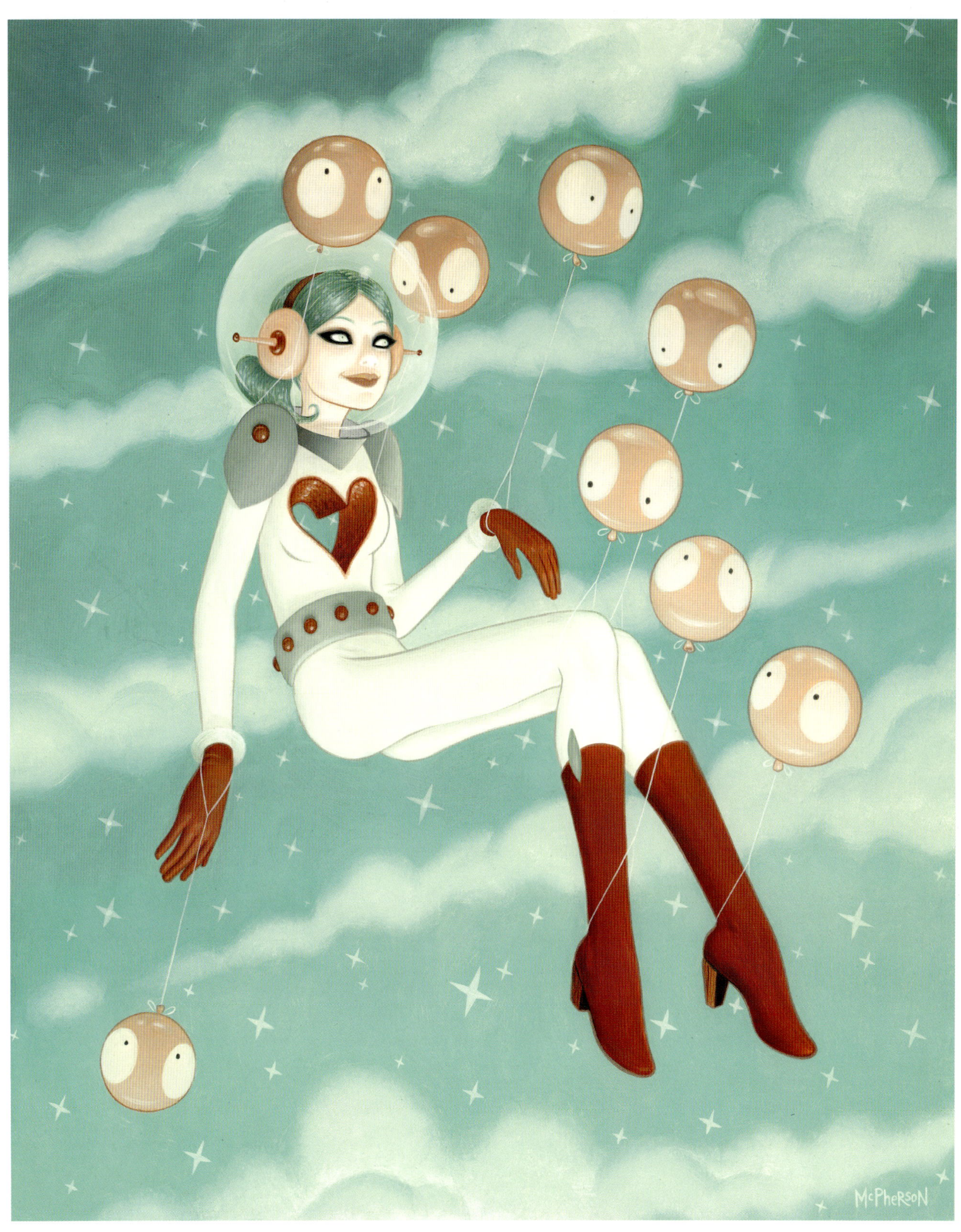
McPHERSON

A Halloween Portrait

acrylic on illustration board
10.5" x 9"
2007

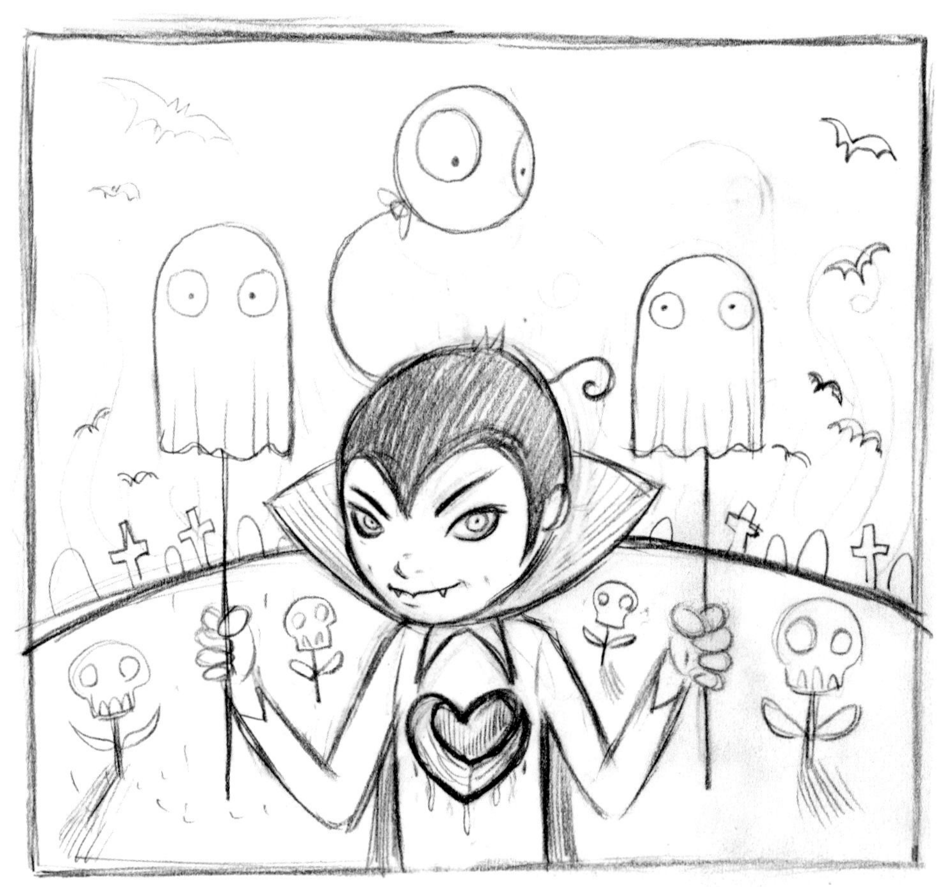

drawing
graphite on paper
5.5" x 5"

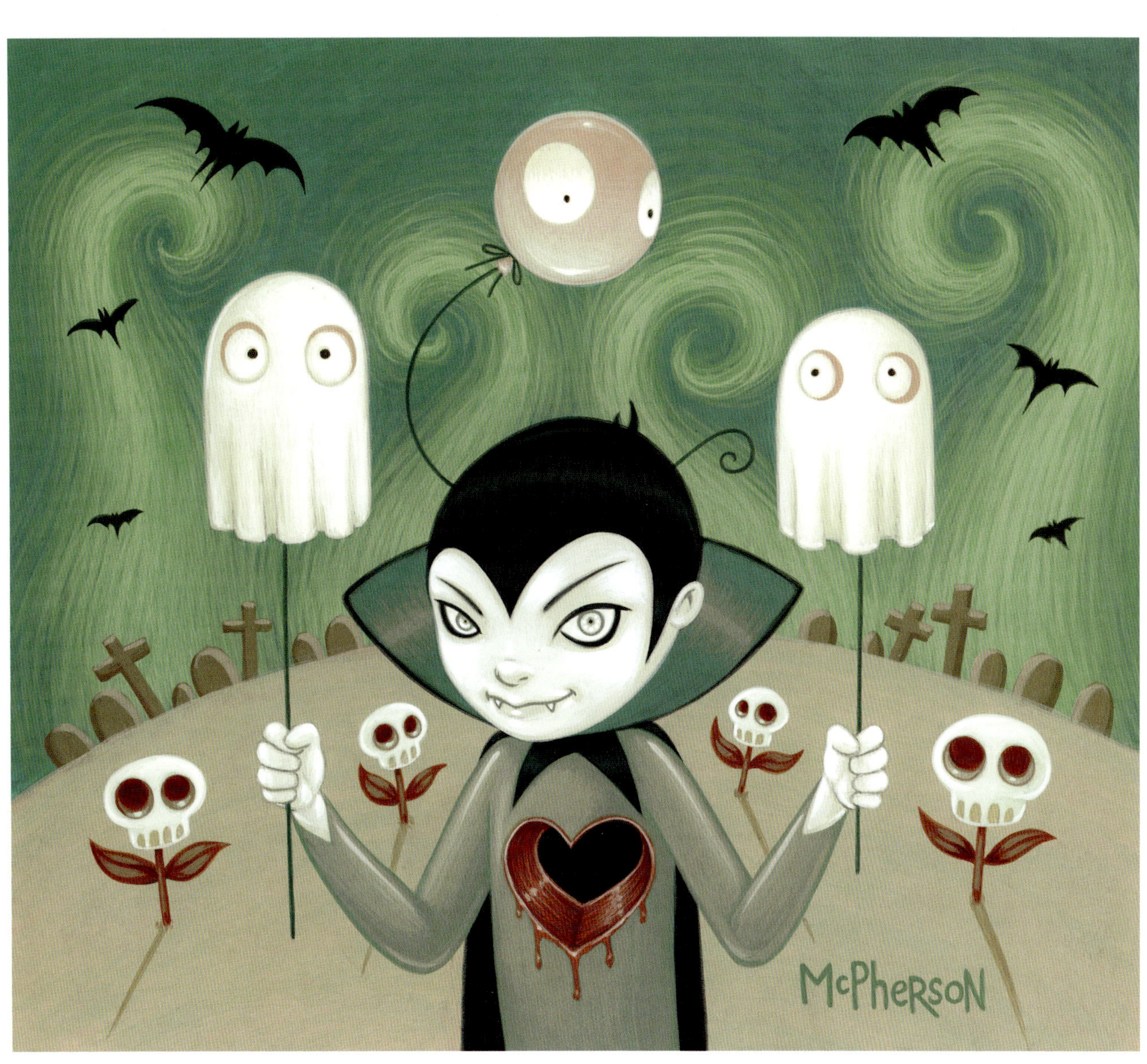
McPherson

Shortly Thereafter

acrylic on birch
5" x 7"
2008

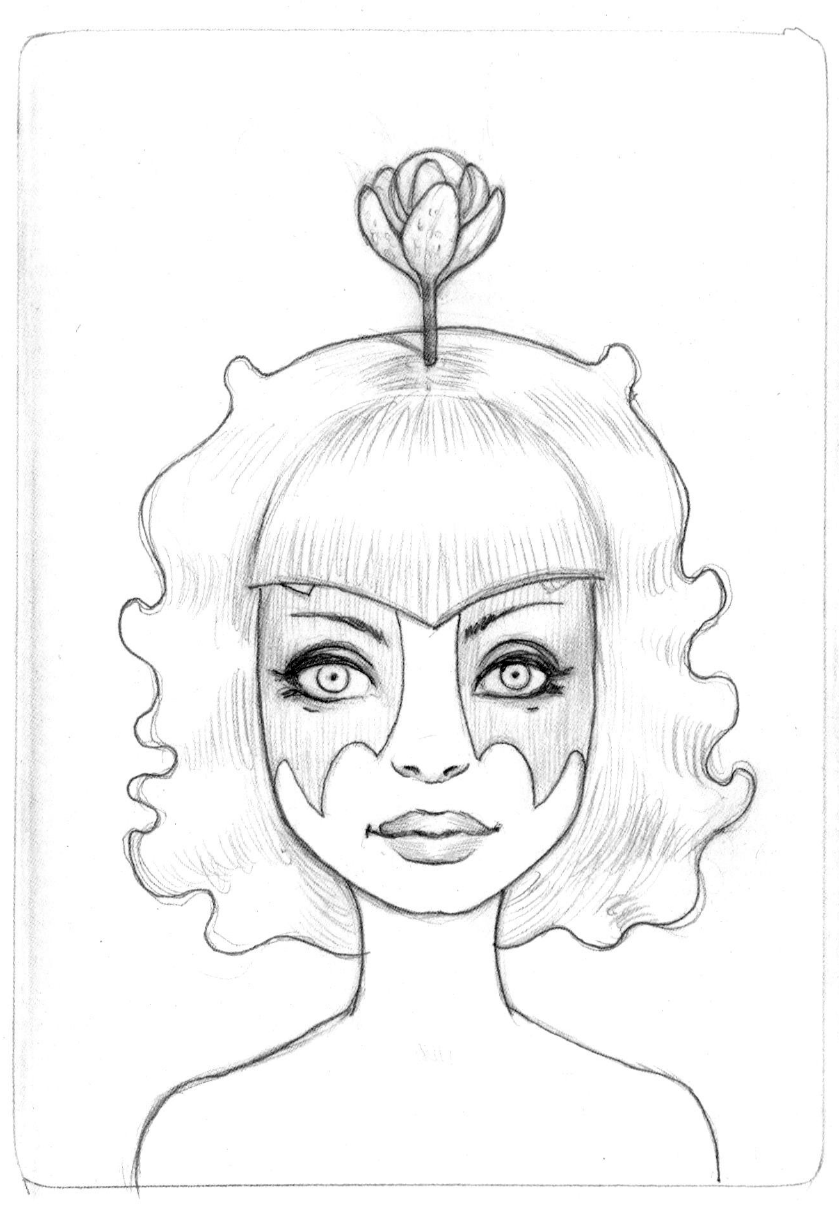

drawing
graphite on paper
5" x 7"

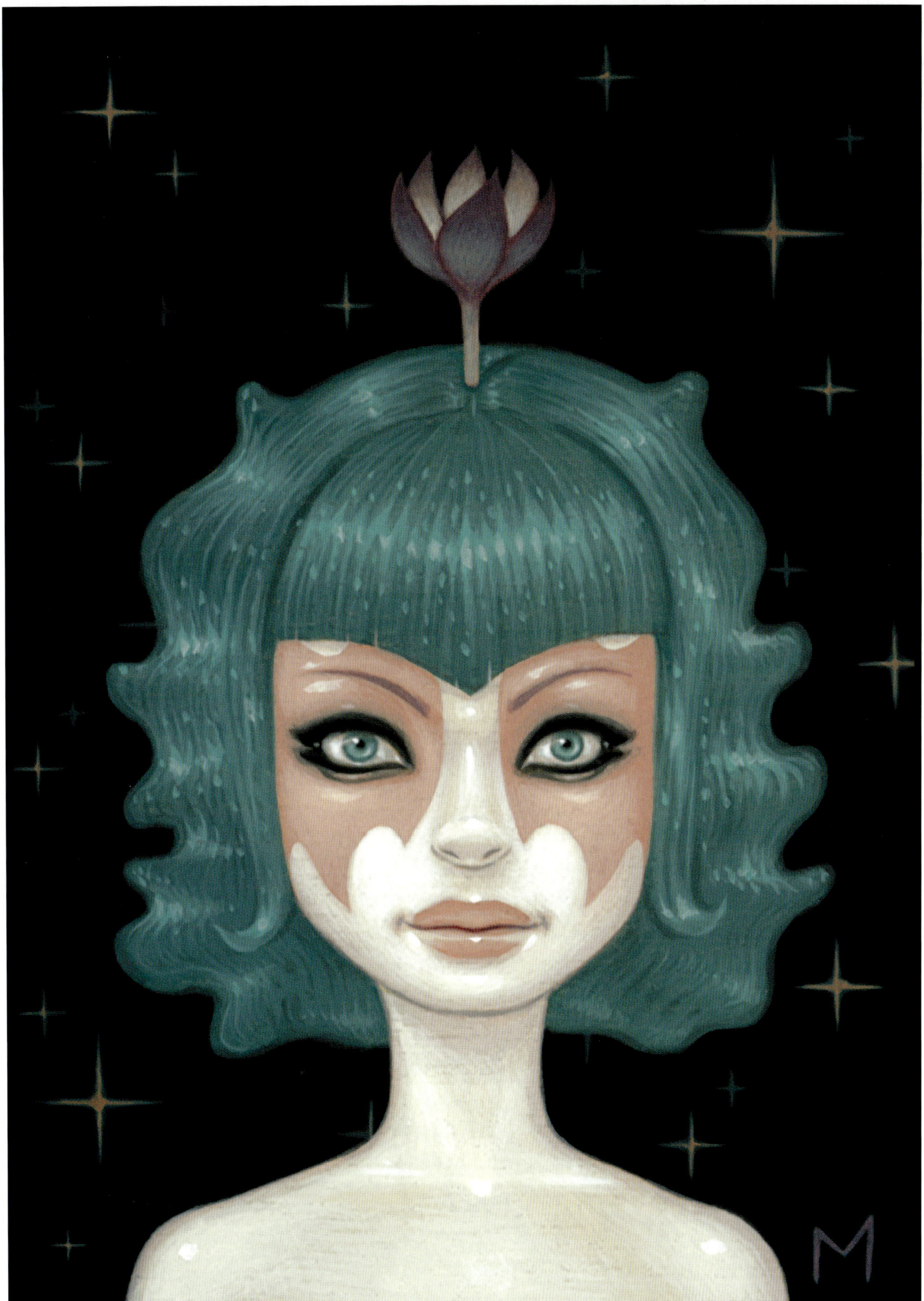

My Love for You Flows Out Like a Waterfall and Goes Nowhere

acrylic on birch
20" x 30"
2008

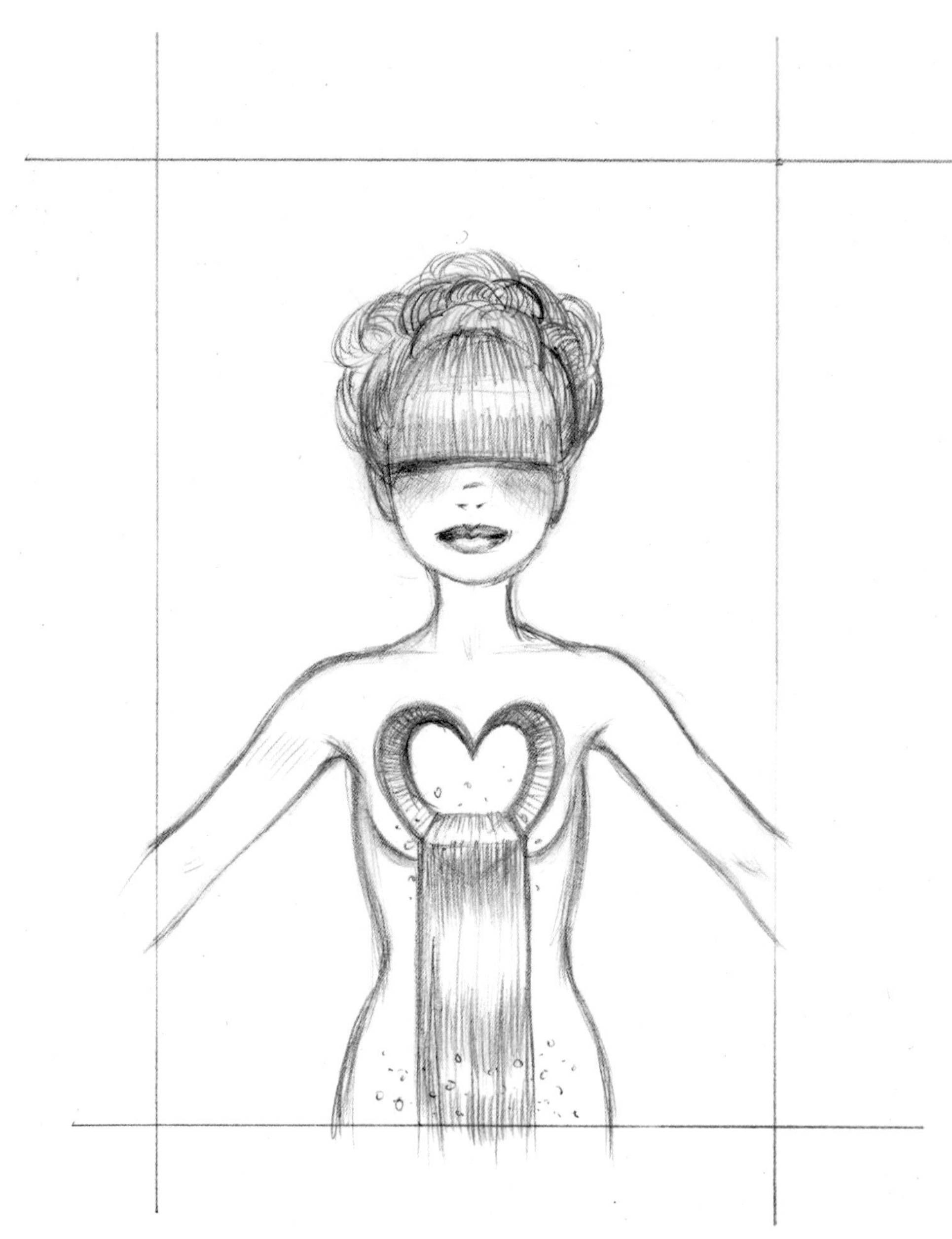

drawing
graphite on paper
6" x 8"

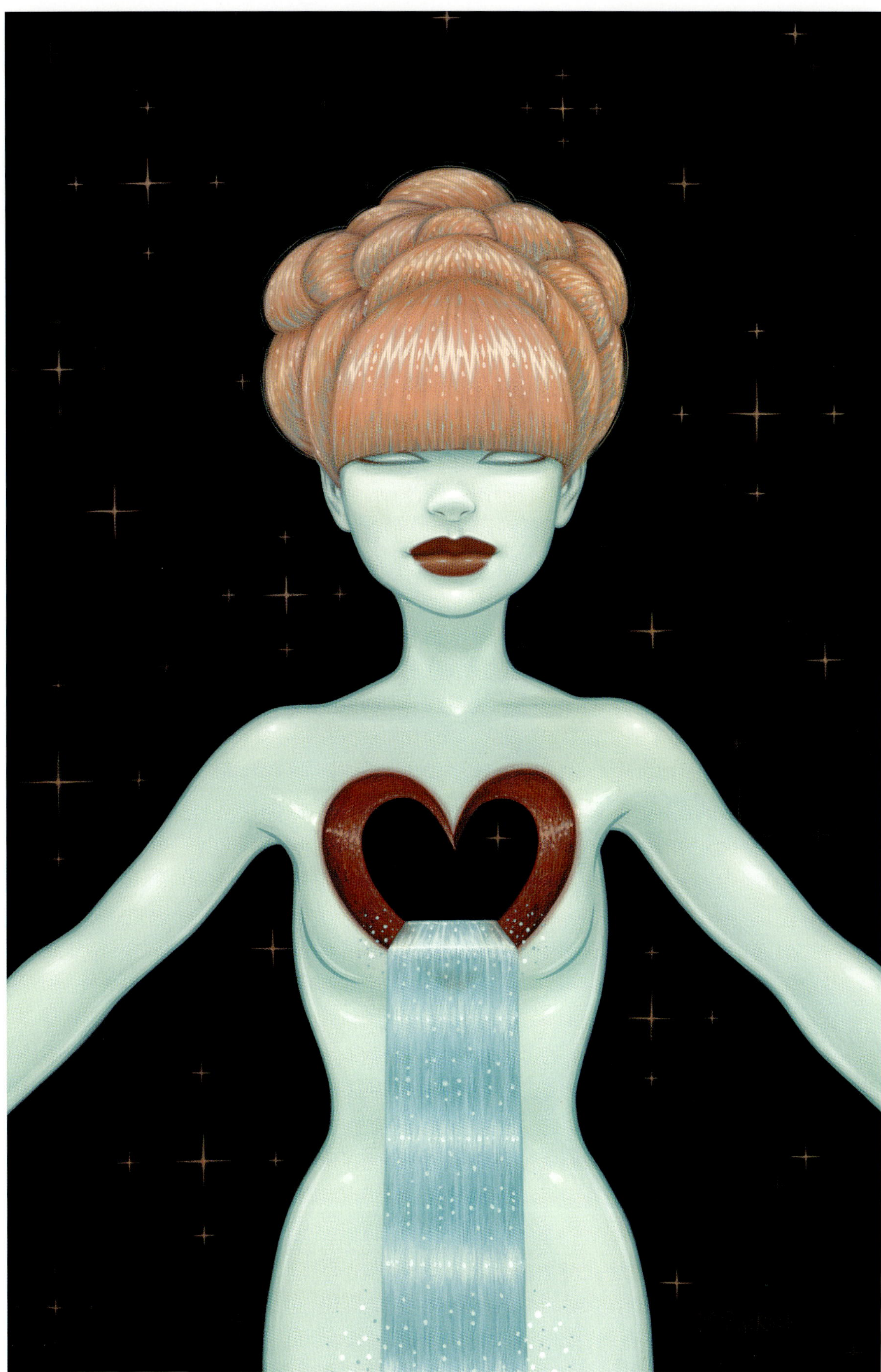

Hey, We All Die Sometimes

oil on birch
36" x 24"
2008

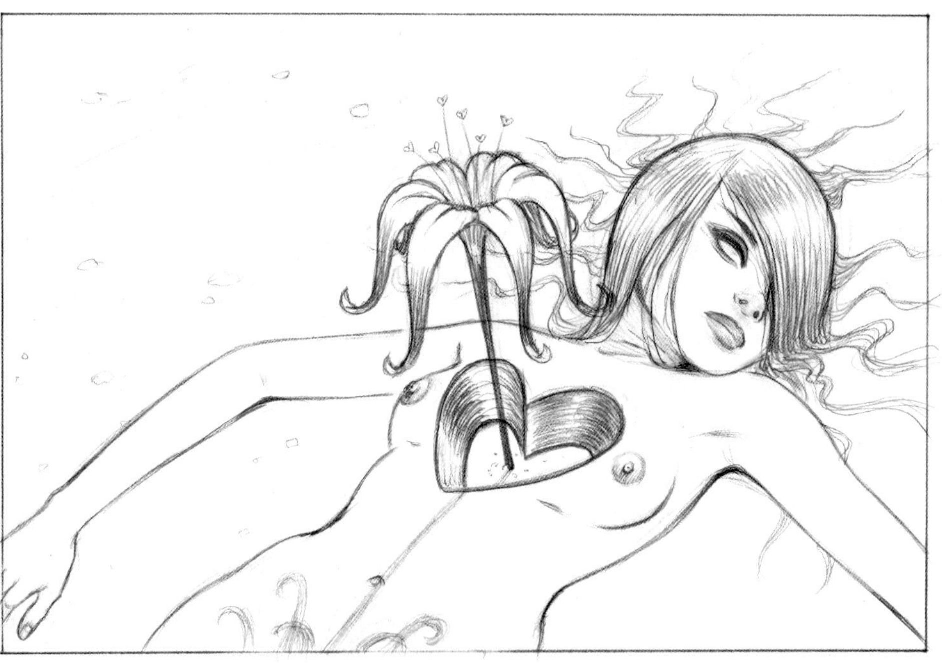

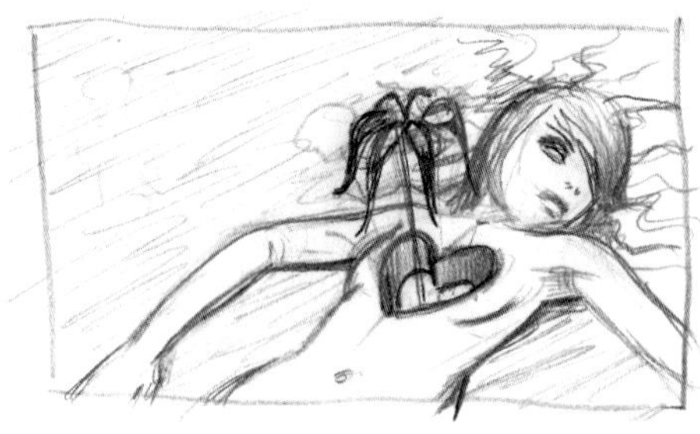

rough
graphite on paper
3" x 2"

drawing
graphite on bristol
10" x 7"

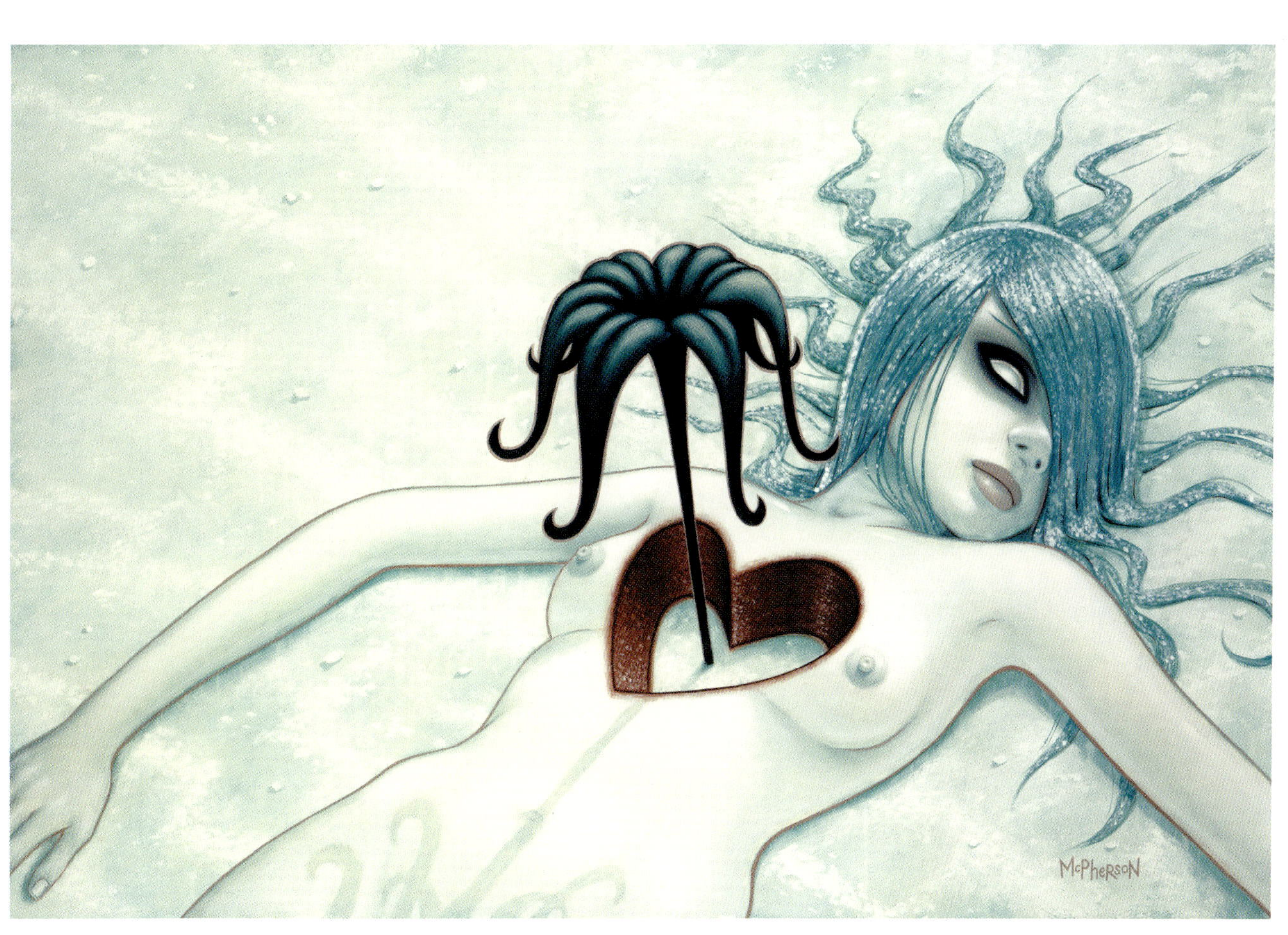
McPherson

The Guilt Will Eat You Alive . . . If You Let It

oil on birch
30" x 36"
2008

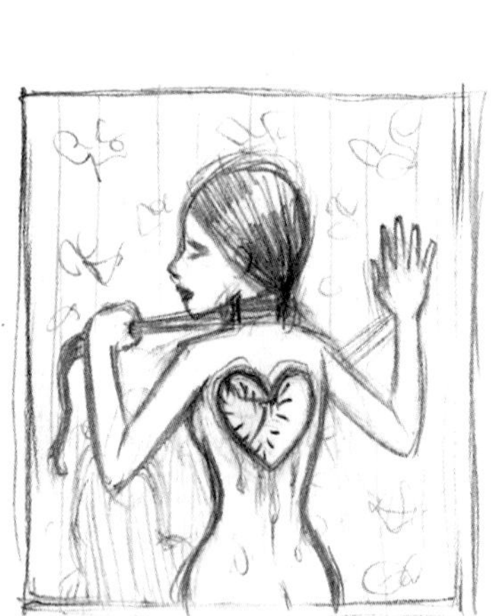

rough
graphite on paper
2.5" x 2.5"

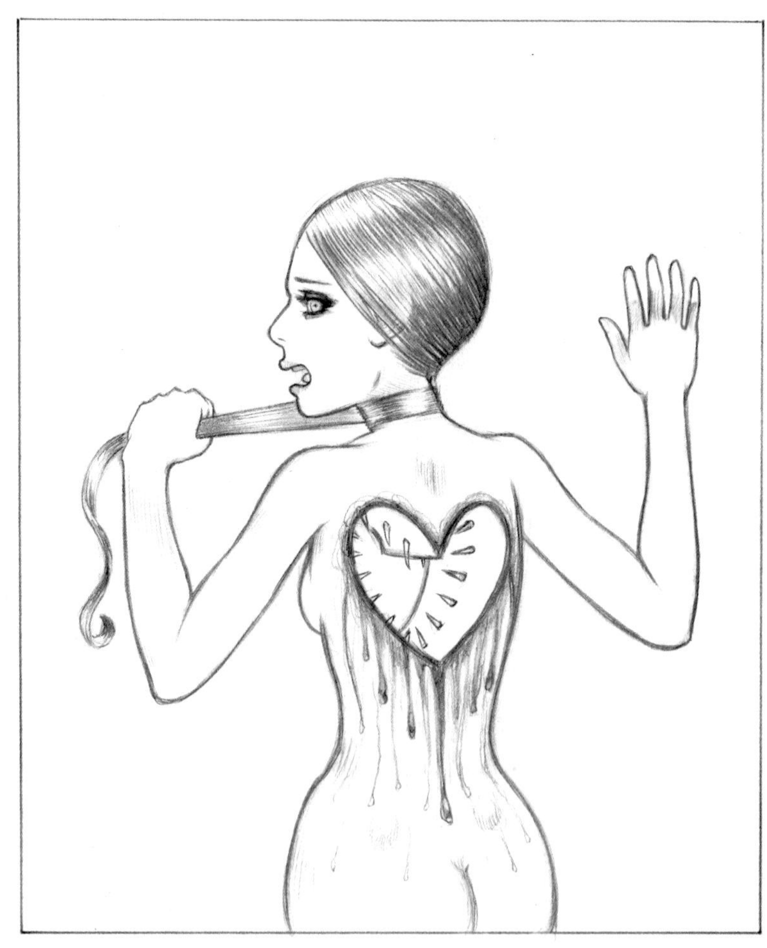

drawing
graphite on bristol
7" x 8"

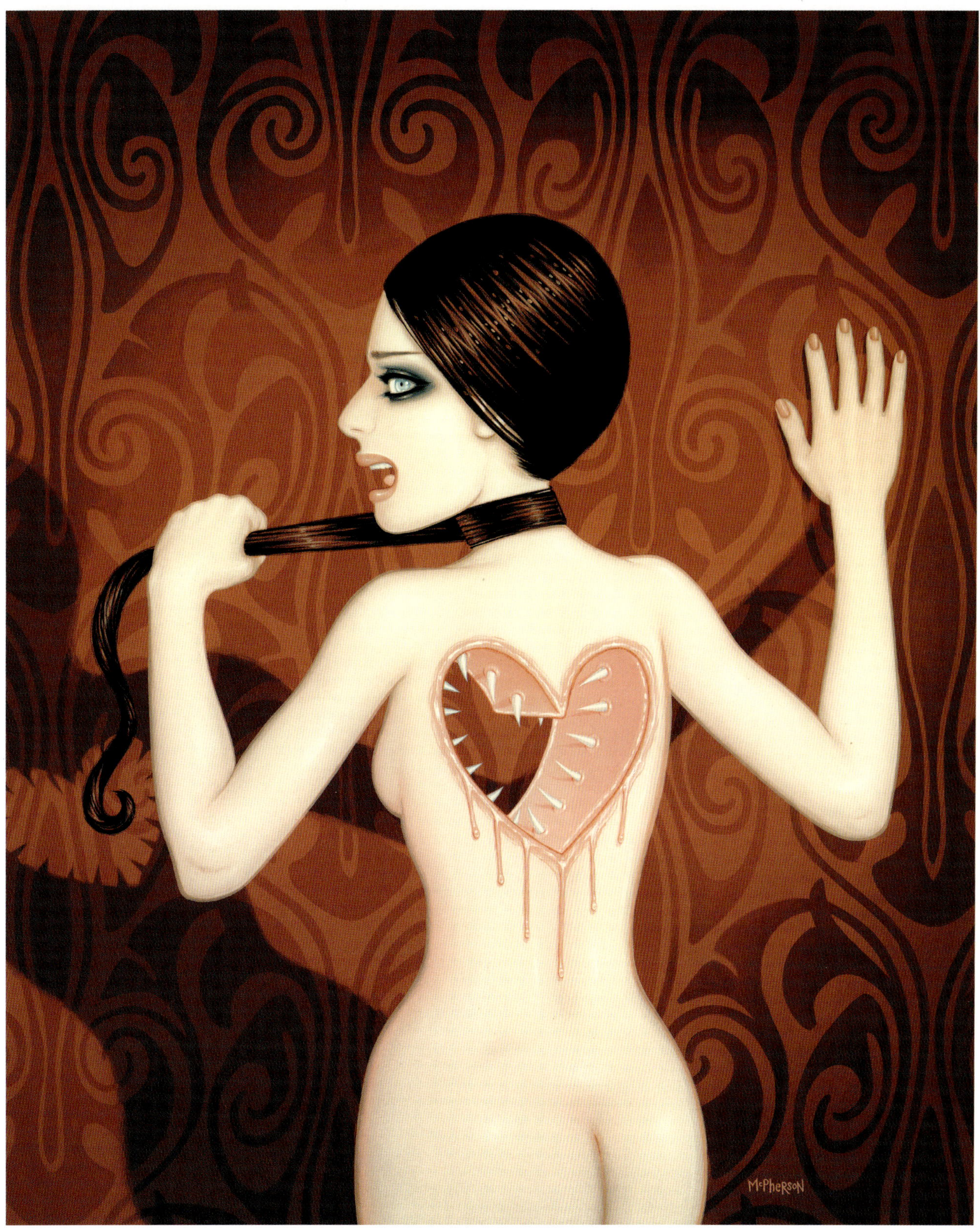
McPHERSON

This World Turned Upside Down

oil on birch
20" x 24"
2008

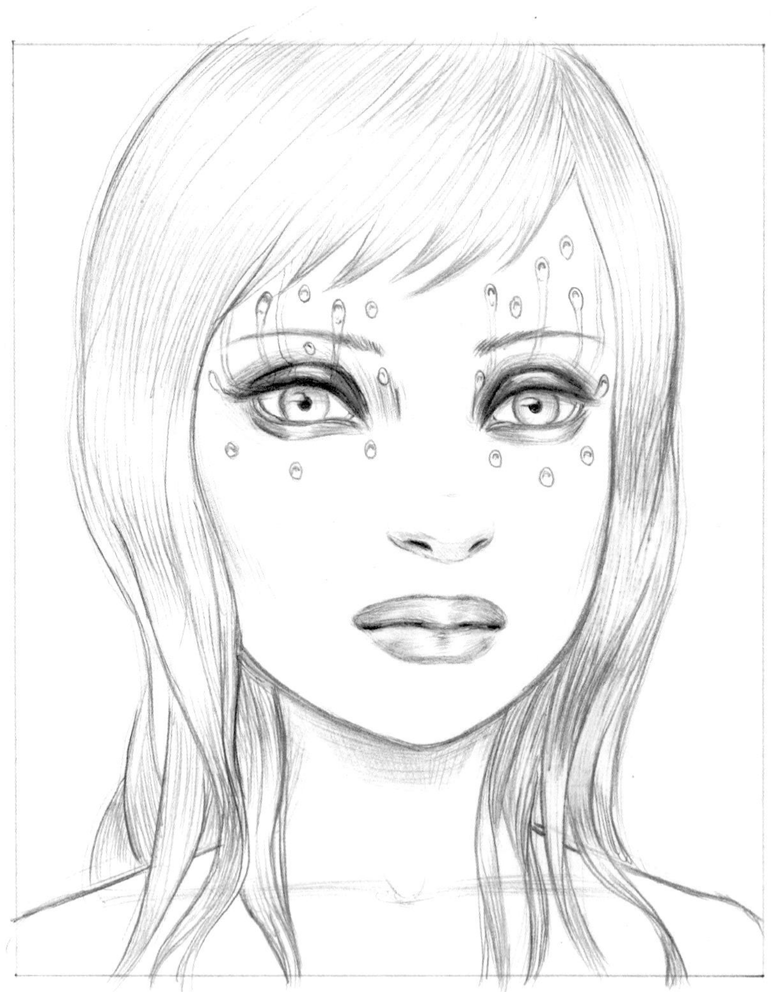

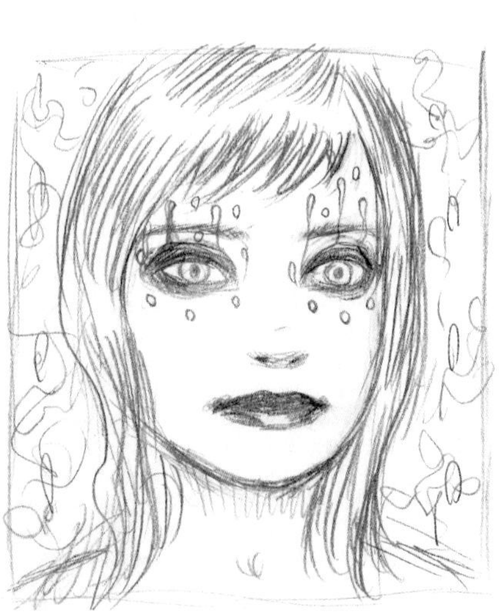

rough
graphite on paper
3" x 4"

drawing
graphite on bristol
7.5" x 9"

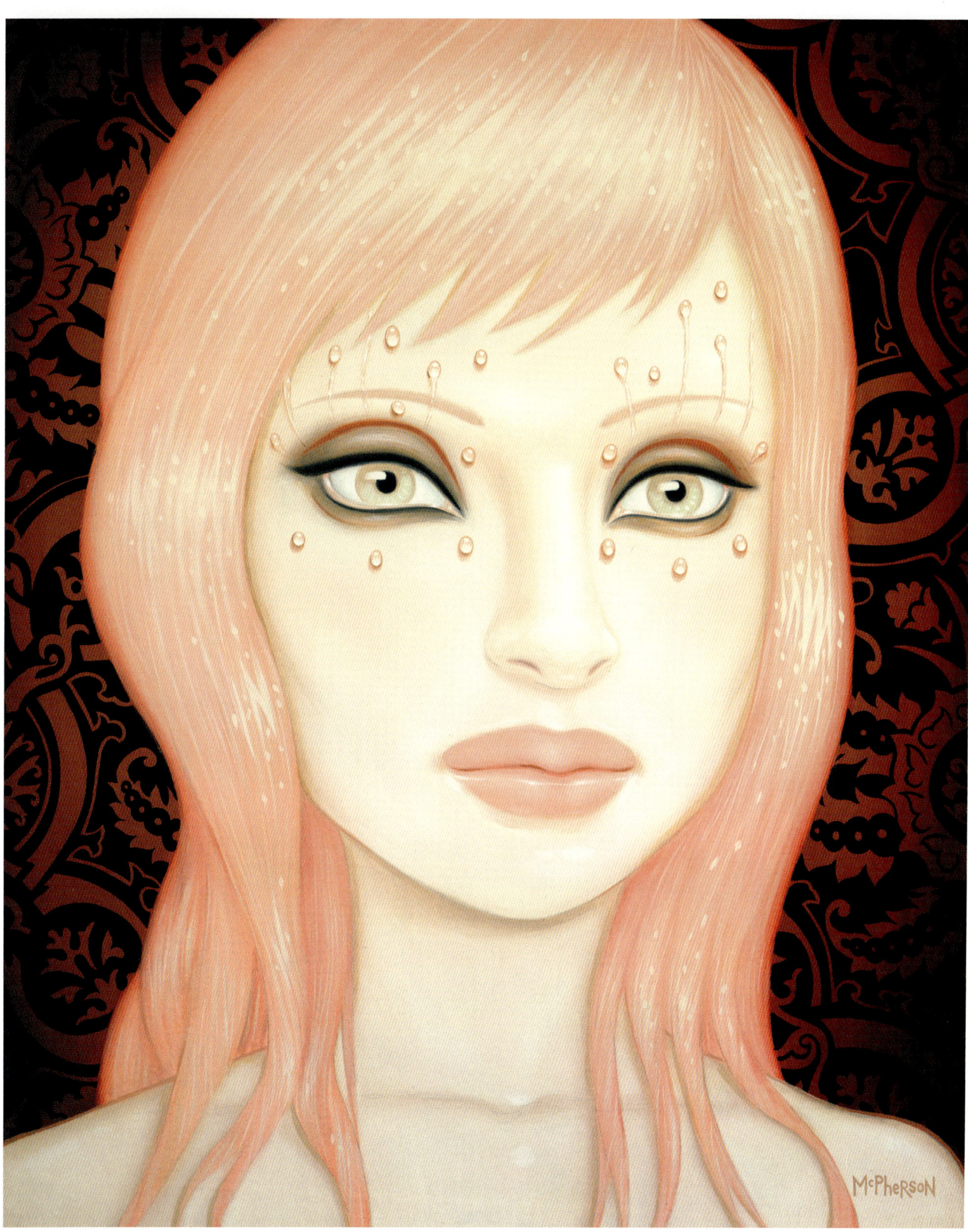
McPherson

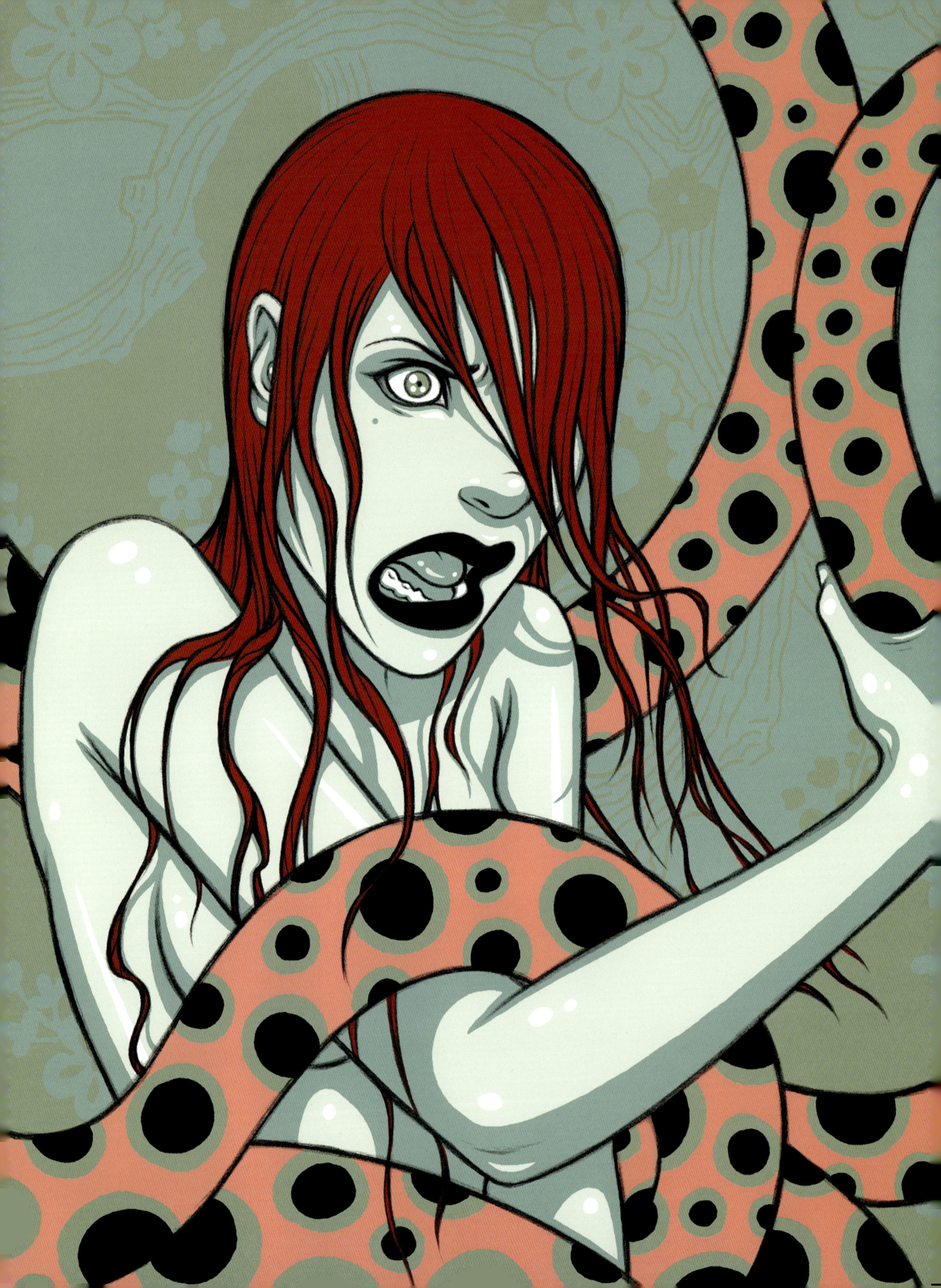

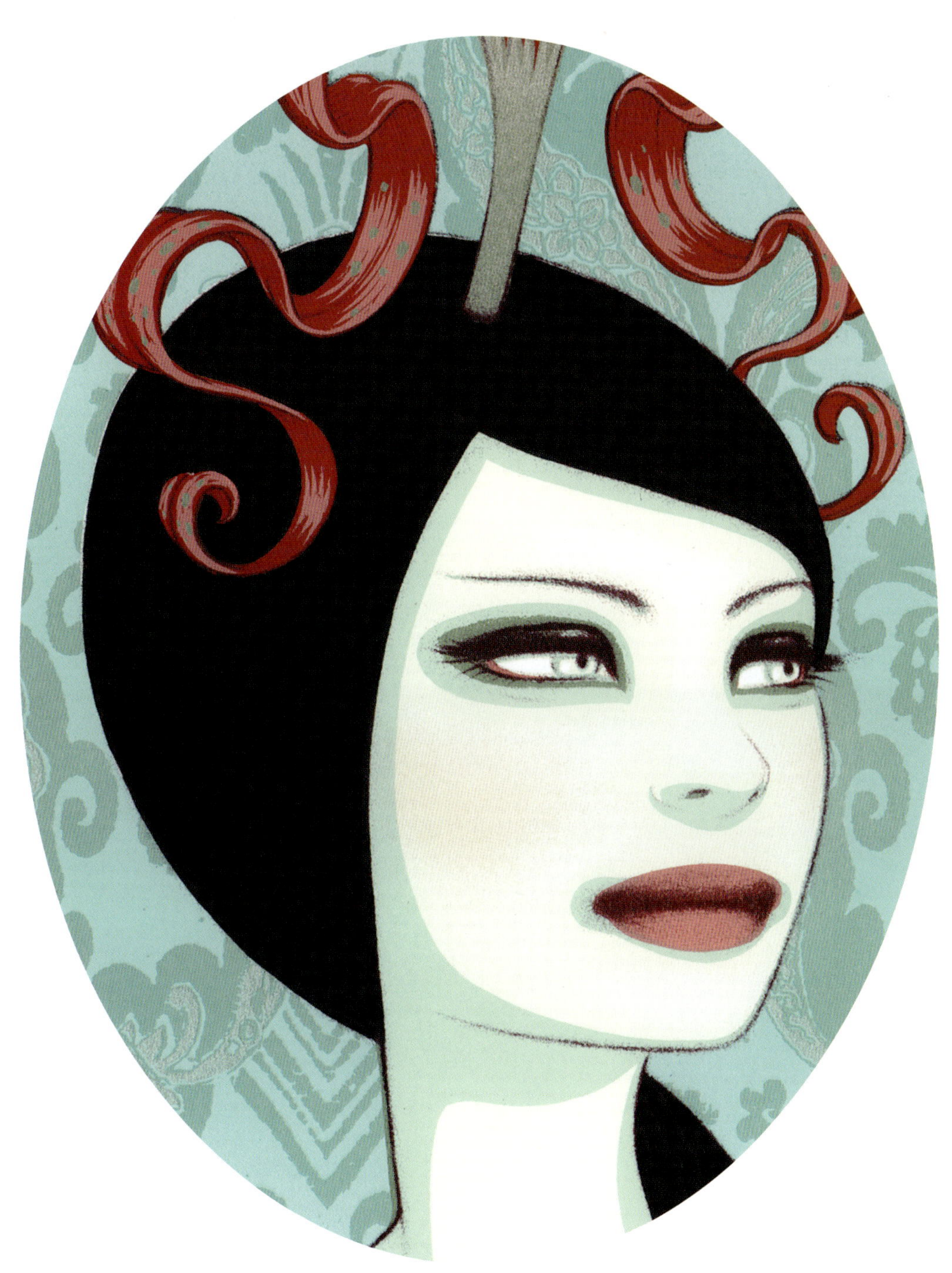

Art Prints

Oops!

three-color silkscreen
11" x 17"
edition of 100
2007

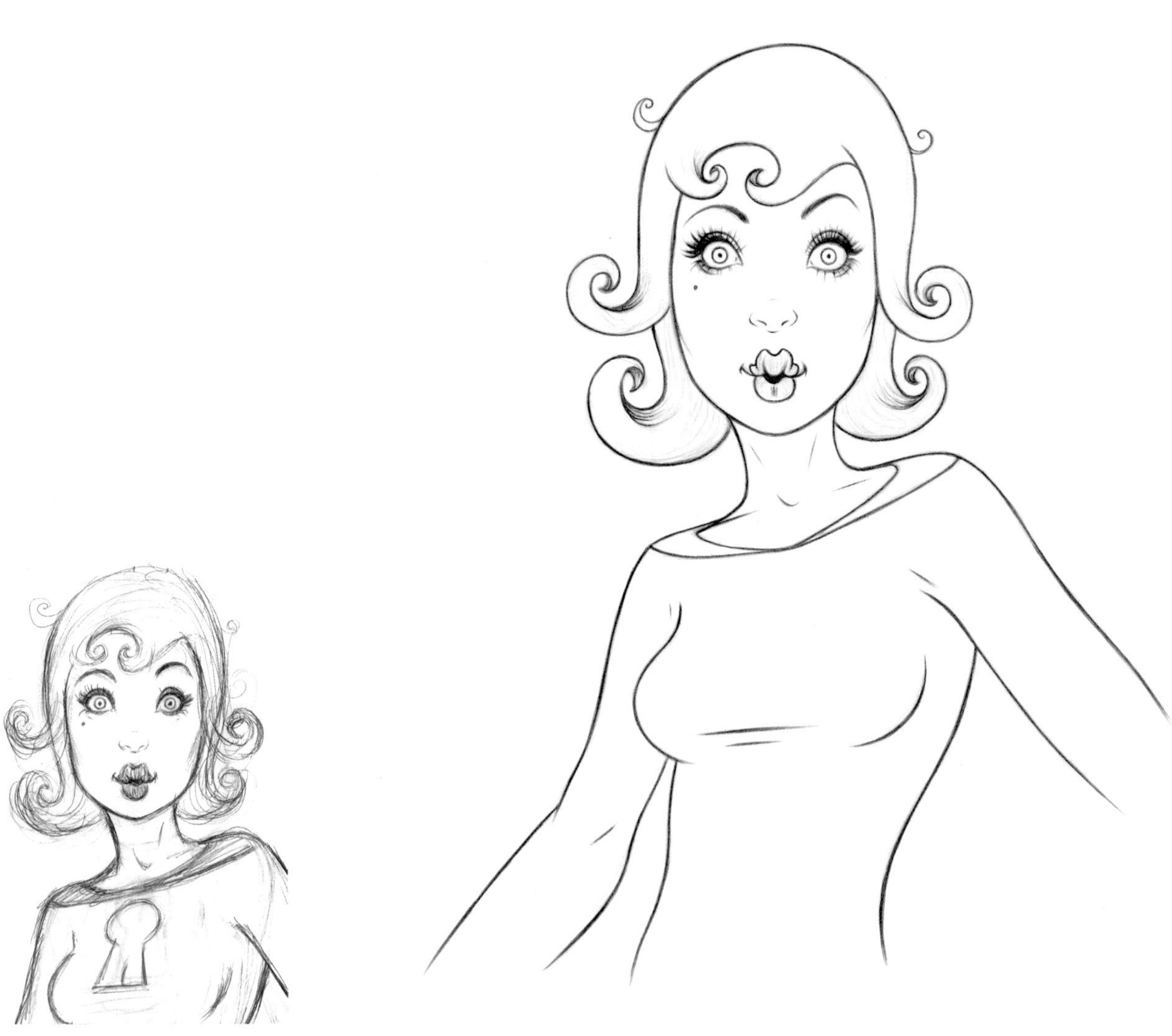

rough
graphite on paper
6" x 9"

drawing
graphite on bristol
14" x 17"

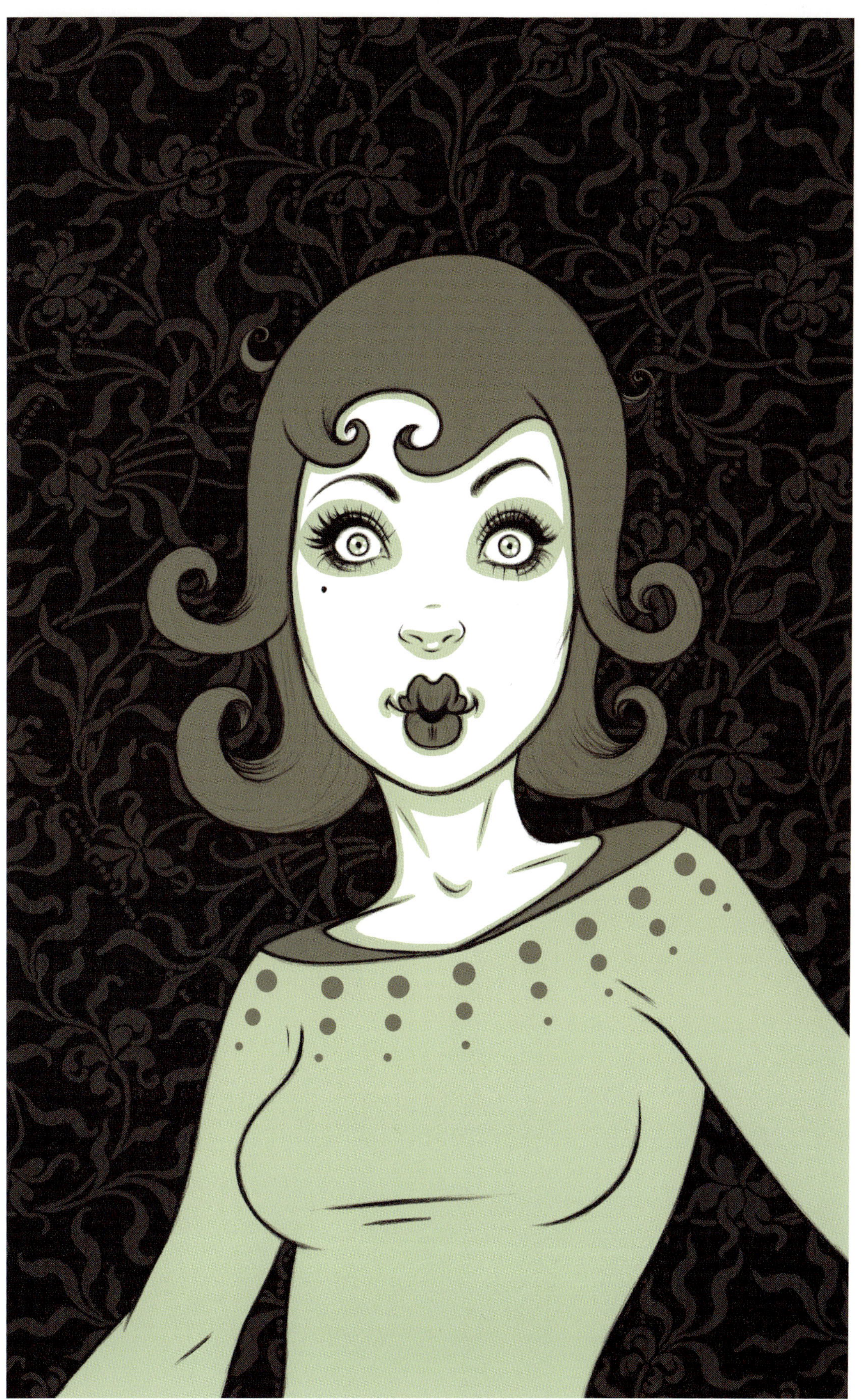

Pink Metal Lover

five-color silkscreen
16" x 23"
edition of 100
2006

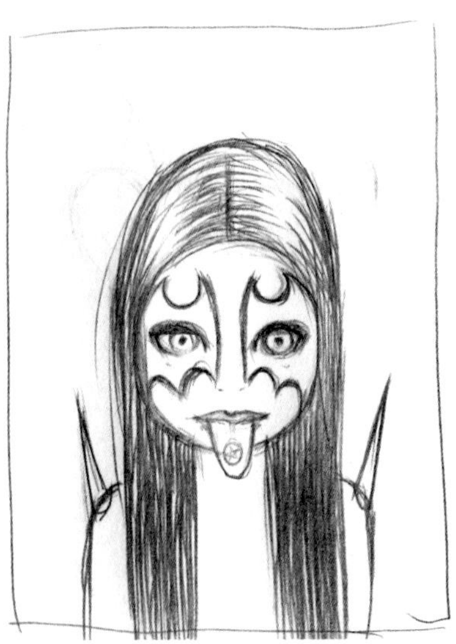

rough
graphite on paper
2.5" x 3"

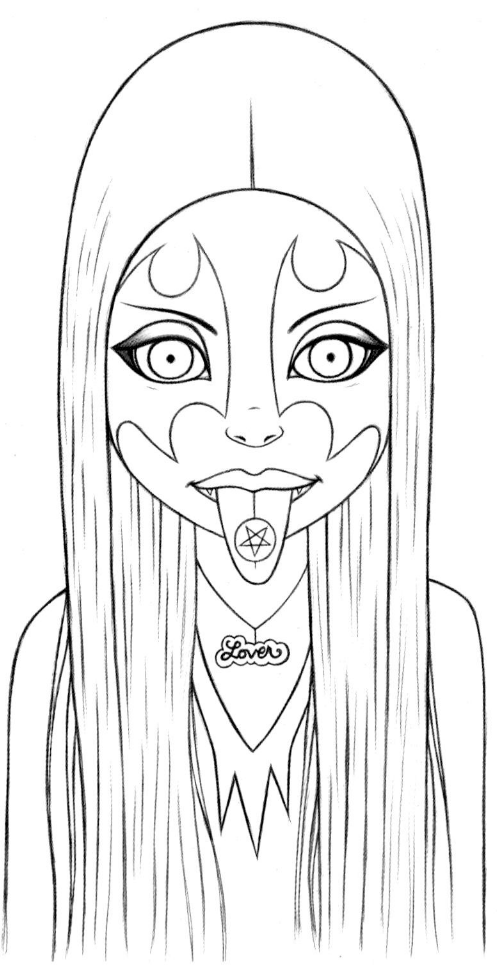

drawing
graphite on bristol
14" x 17"

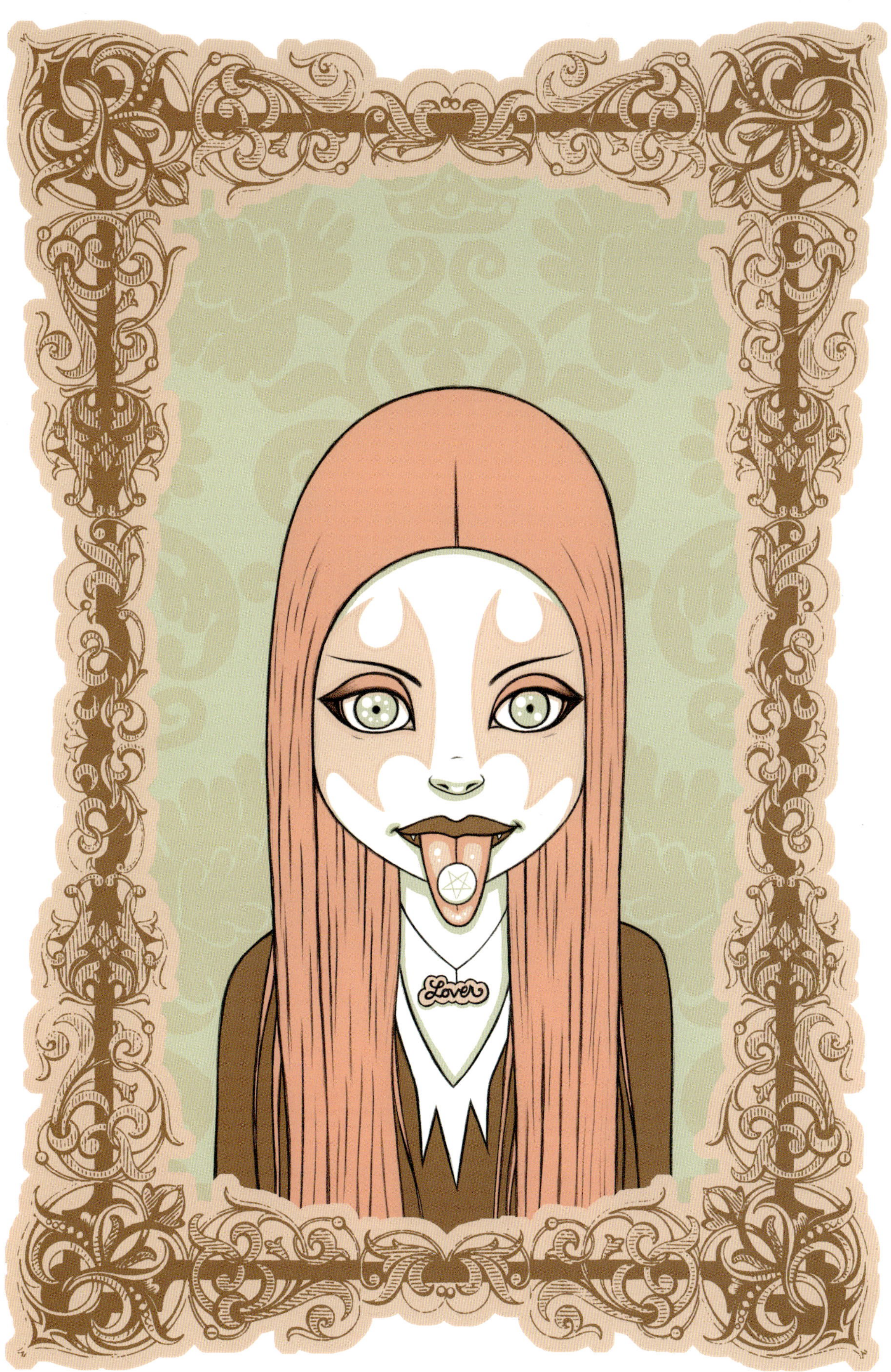
Lover

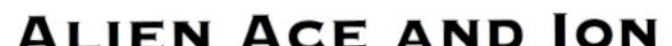

Alien Ace and Ion

six-color silkscreen
16" x 23"
edition of 200
2006

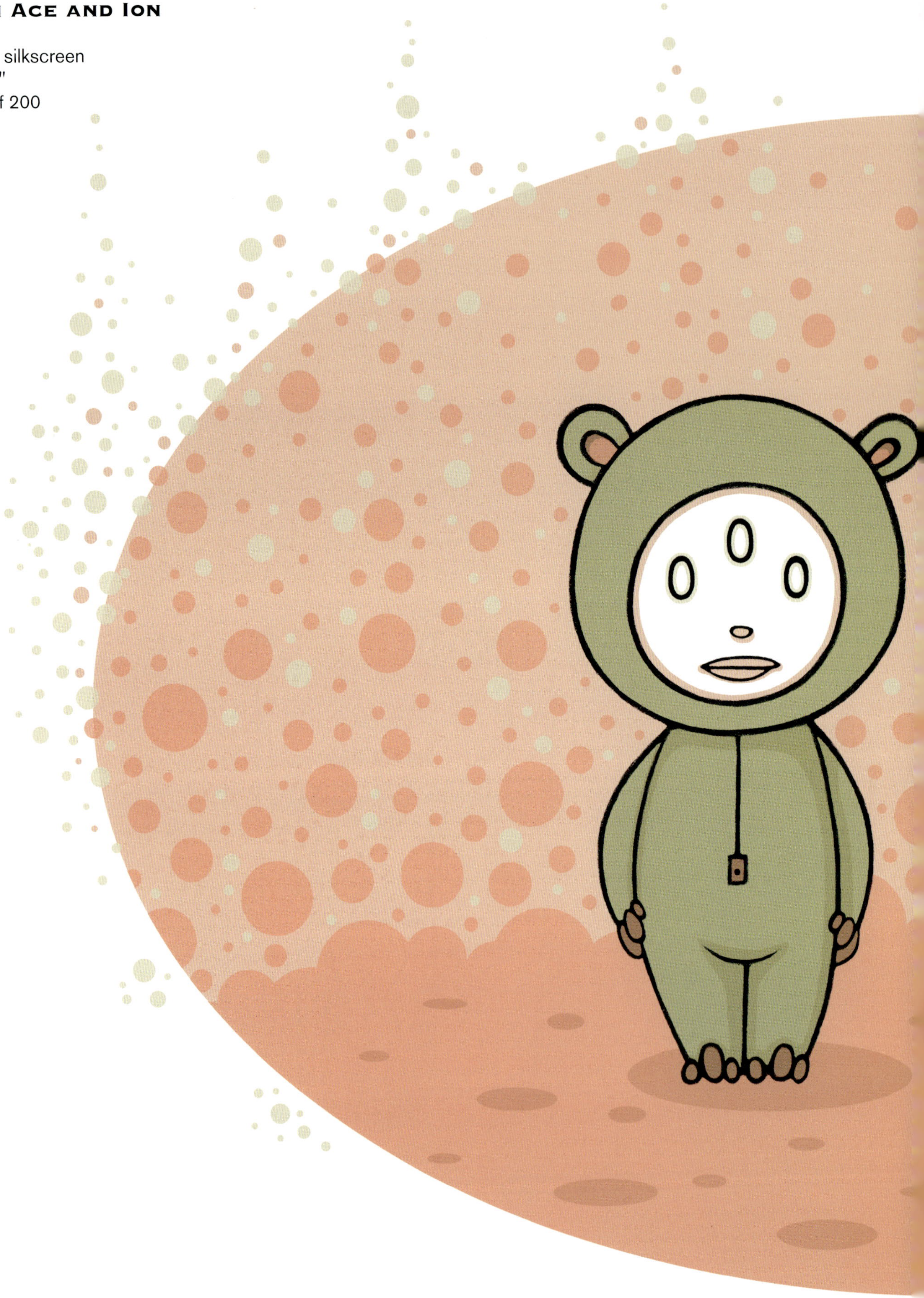

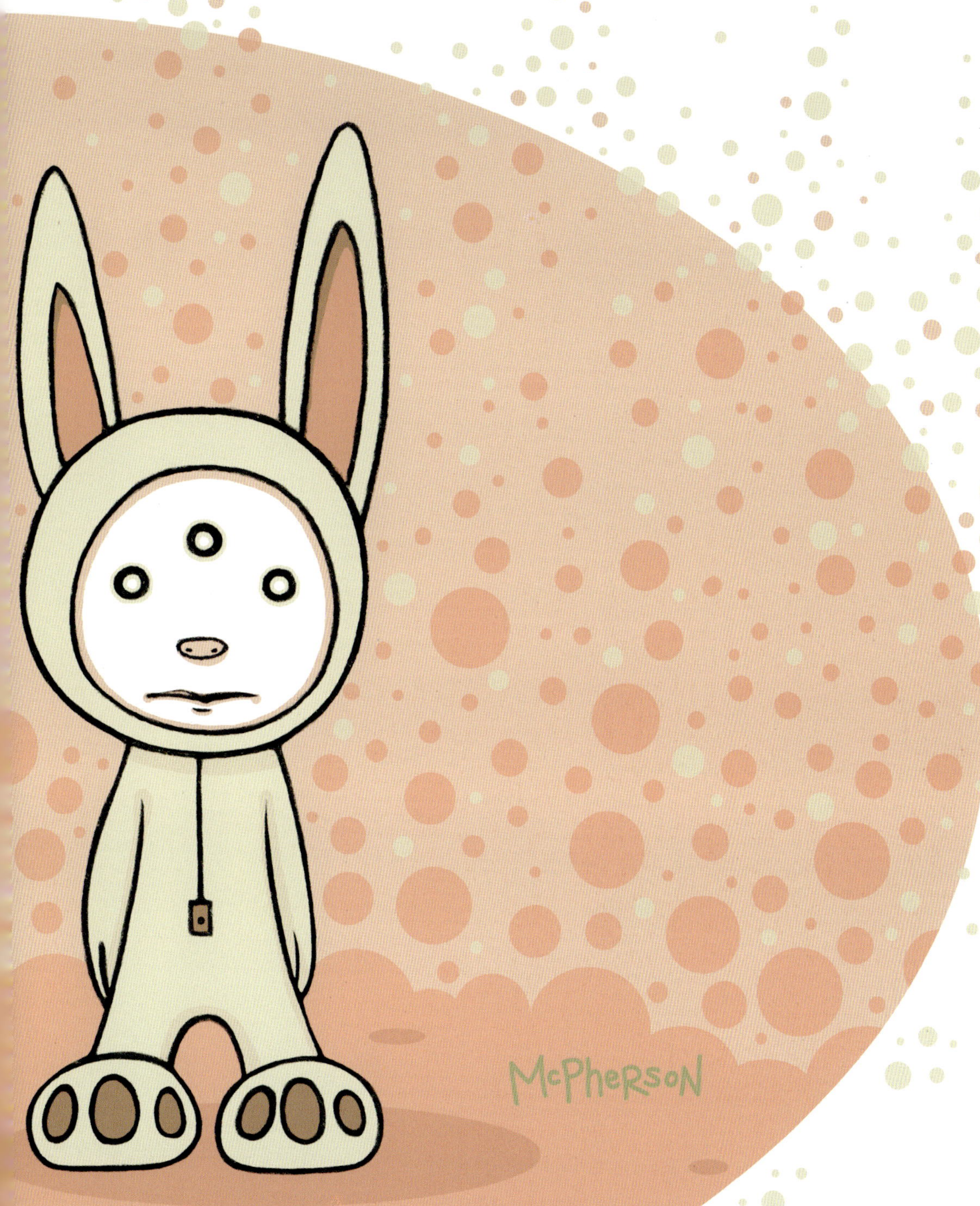
McPherson

ACE AND ION GO SPACE MINING

six-color silkscreen
16" x 23"
edition of 200
2006

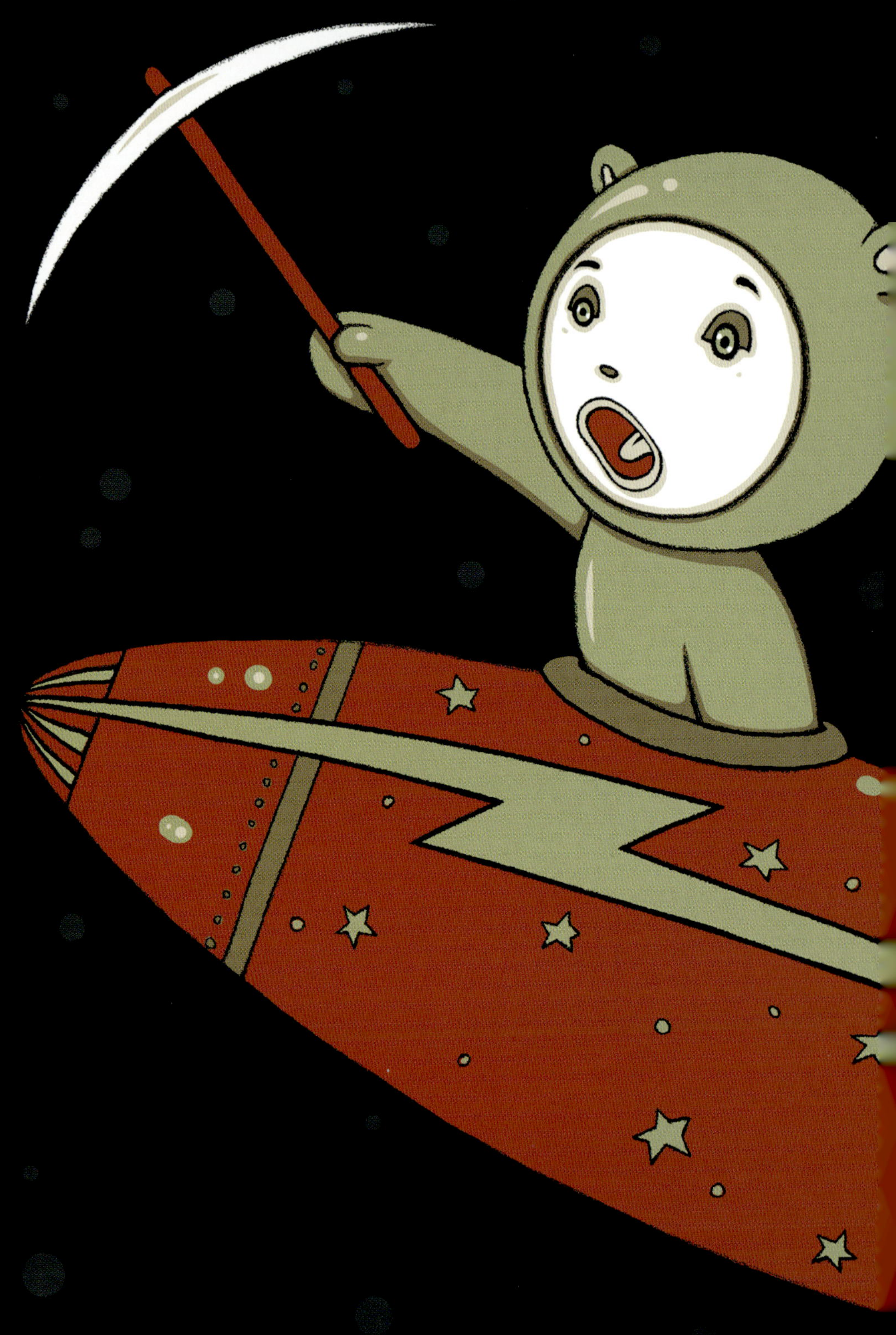

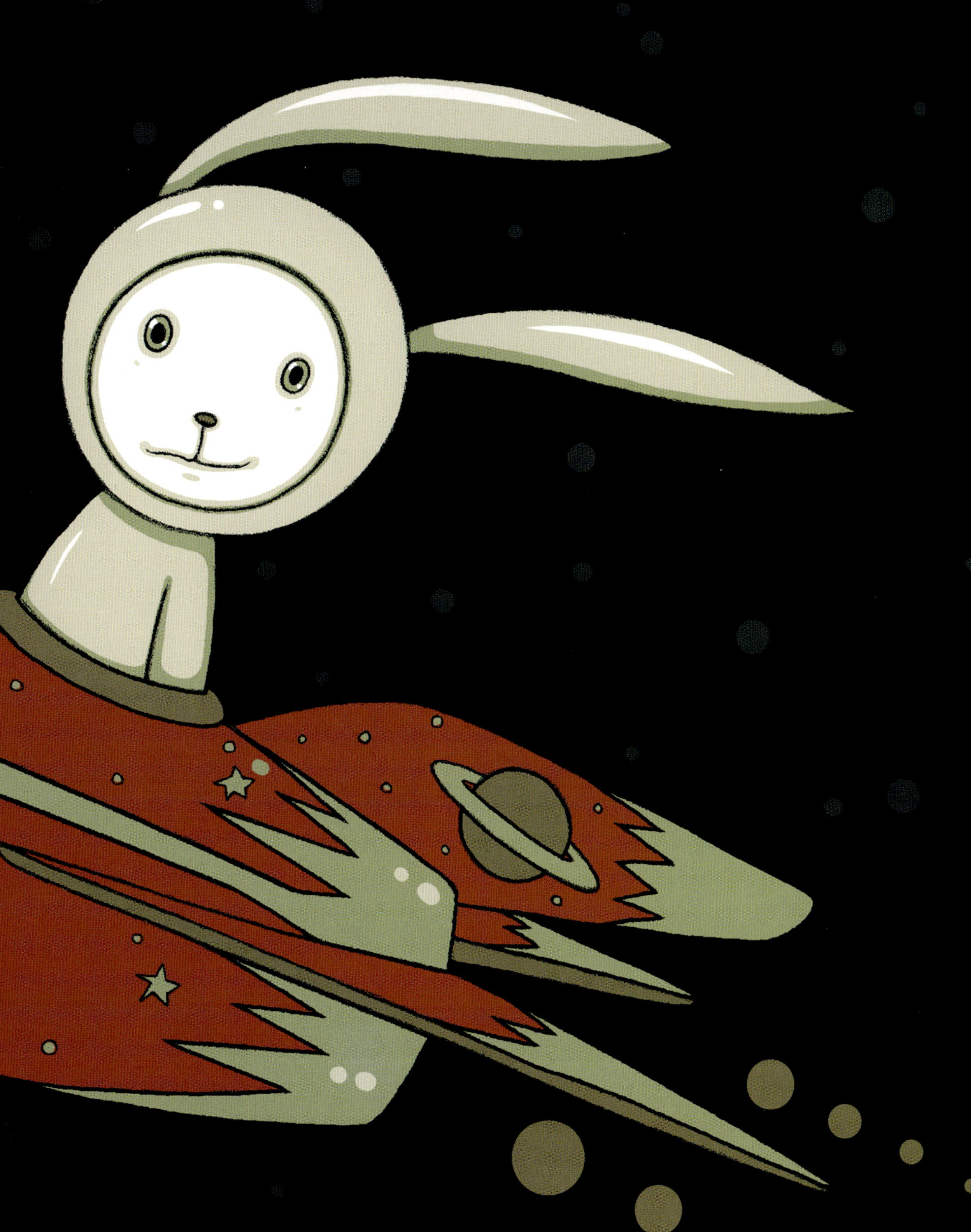

Unicorn Girl

six-color silkscreen
20" x 20"
edition of 75
2006

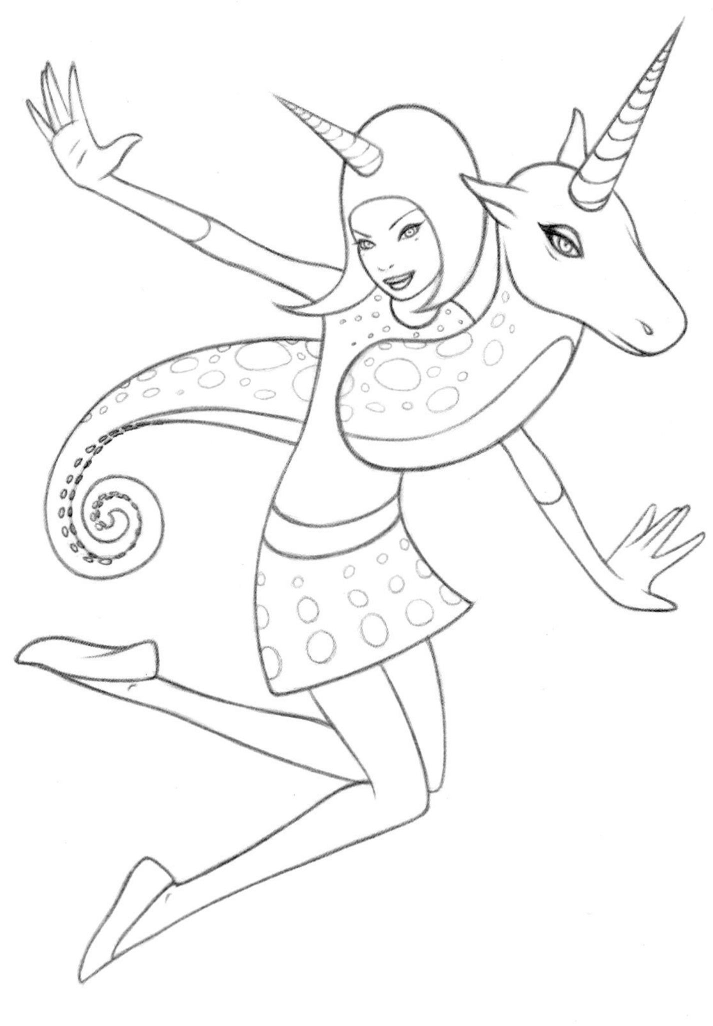

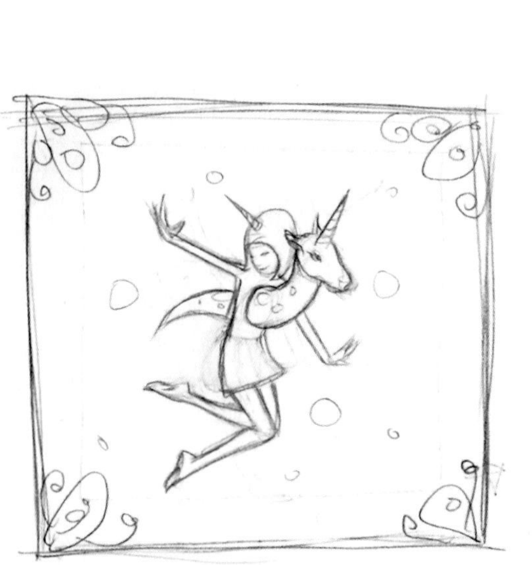

rough
graphite on paper
3" x 3"

drawing
graphite on bristol
10" x 10"

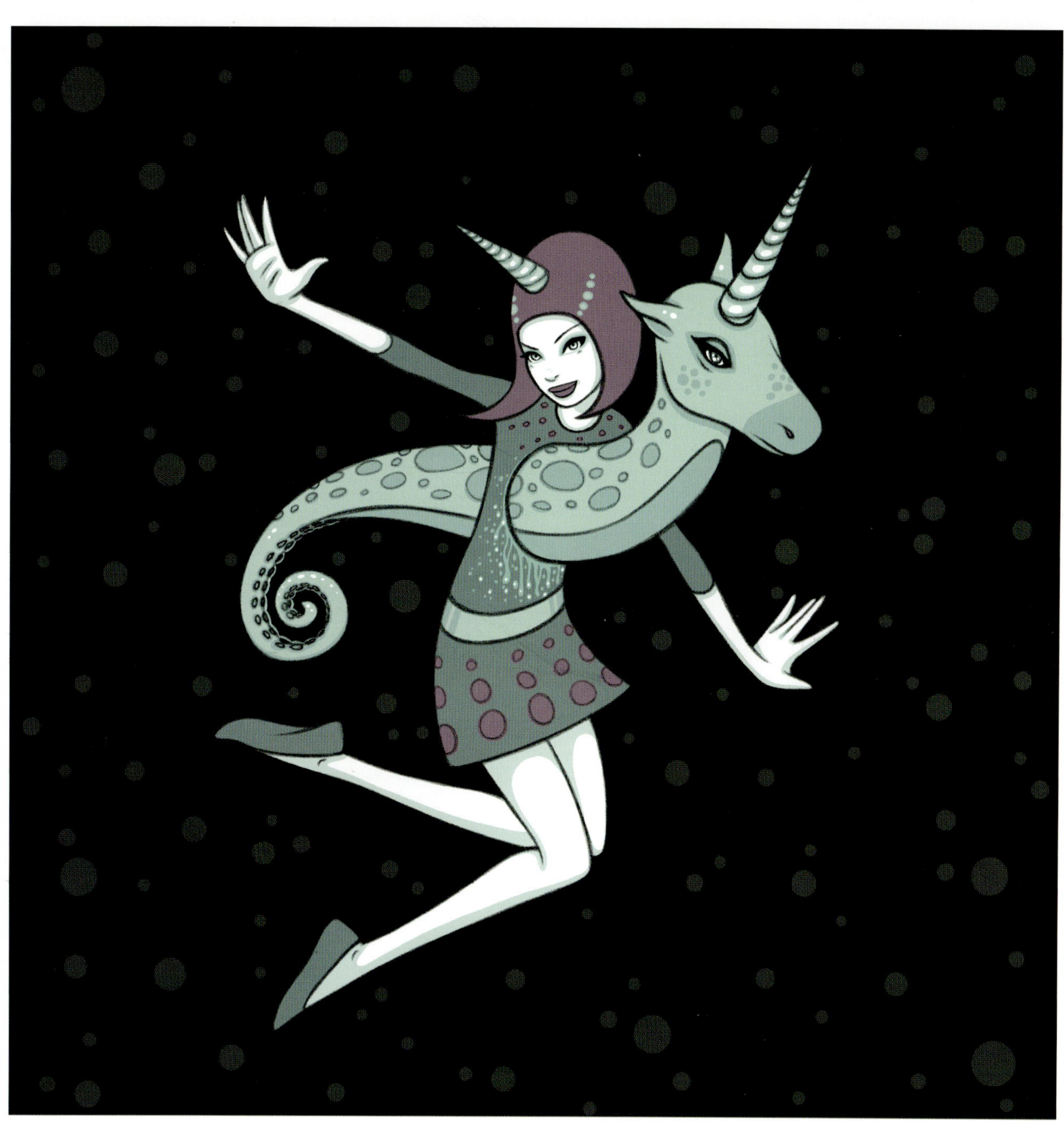

How to Heal a Broken Heart: Method 37

sixteen-color silkscreen
16" x 22"
edition of 100
2009

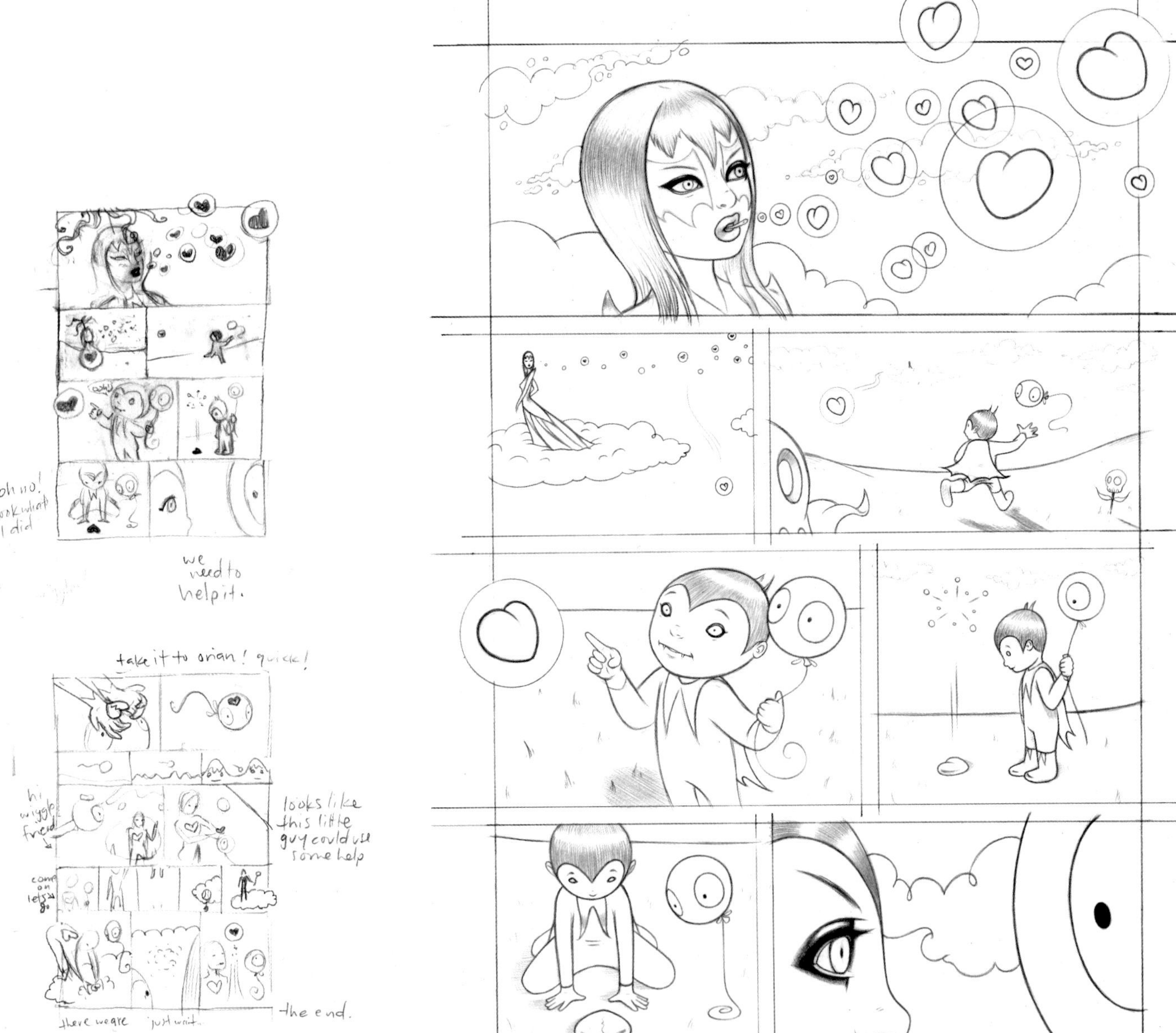

roughs
graphite on paper
3" x 5"

drawing (page 1)
graphite on bristol
14" x 17"

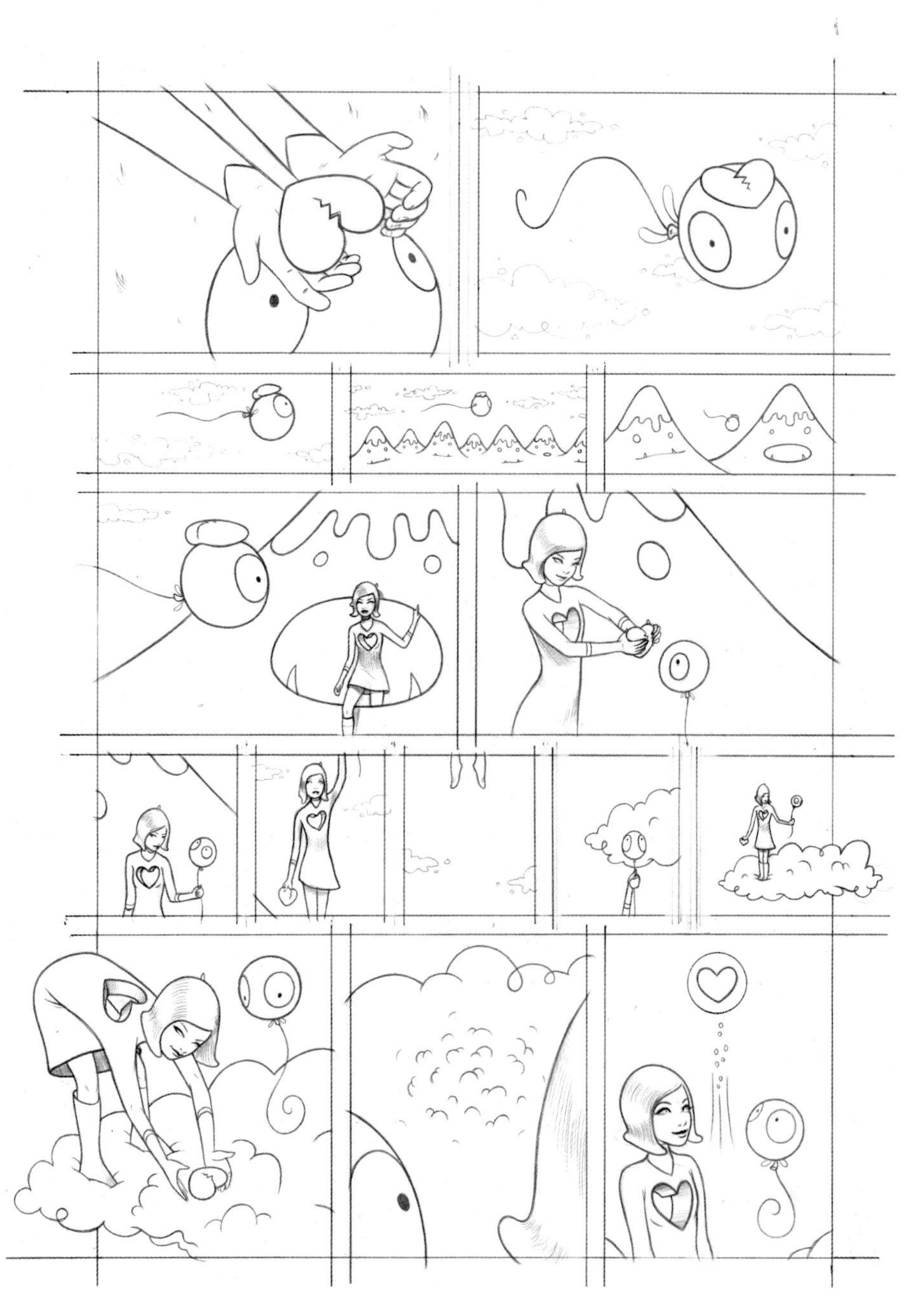

drawing (page 2)
graphite on bristol
14" x 17"

How to Heal a Broken Heart: Method 37

by Tara McPherson

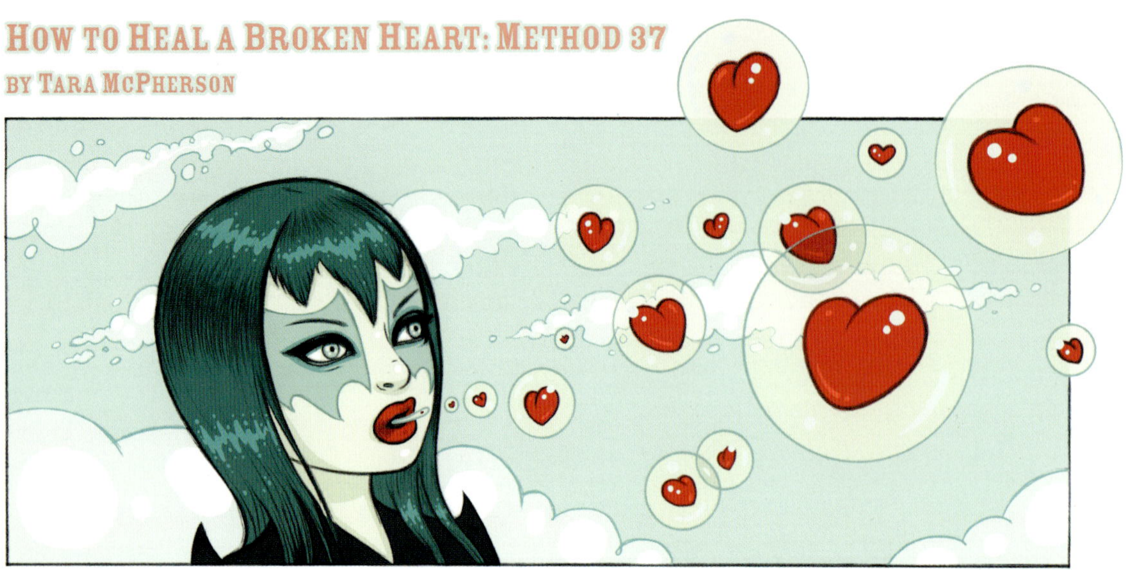

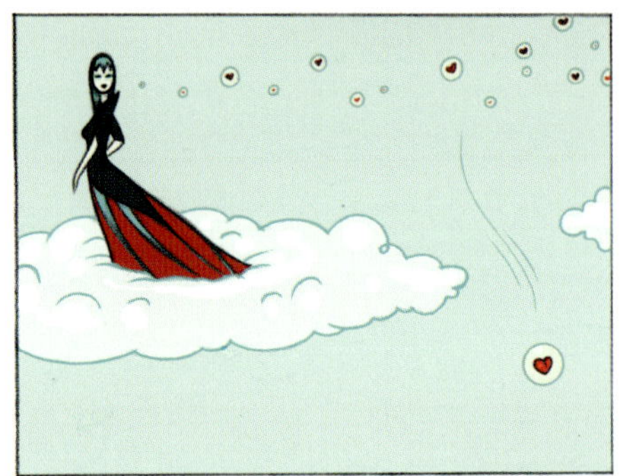

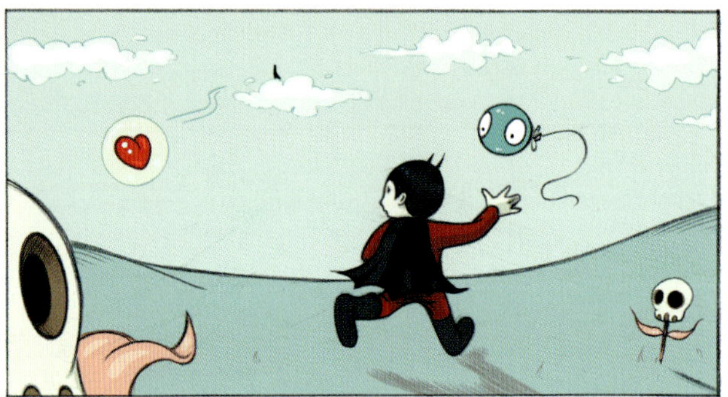

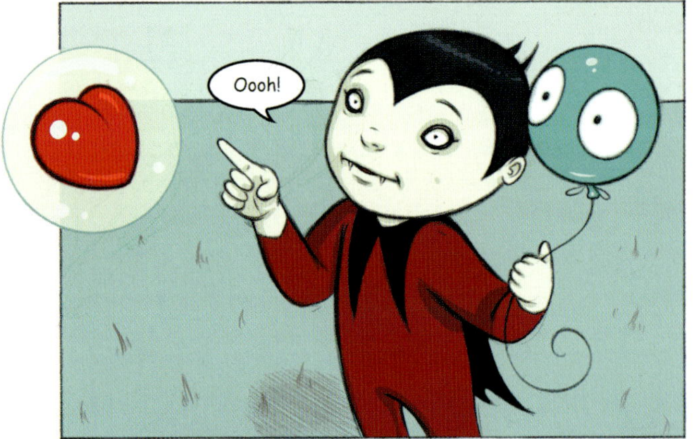

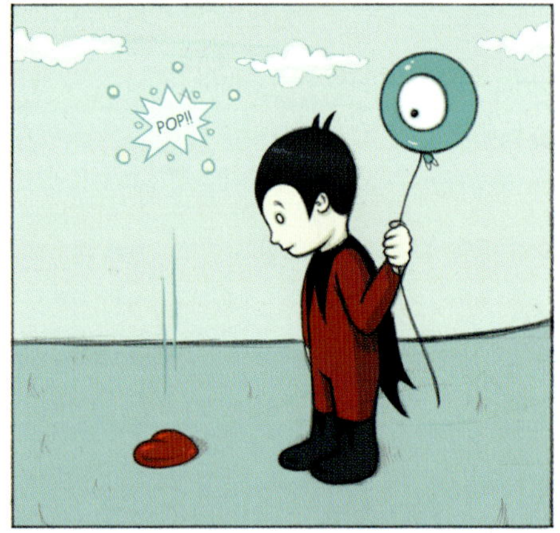

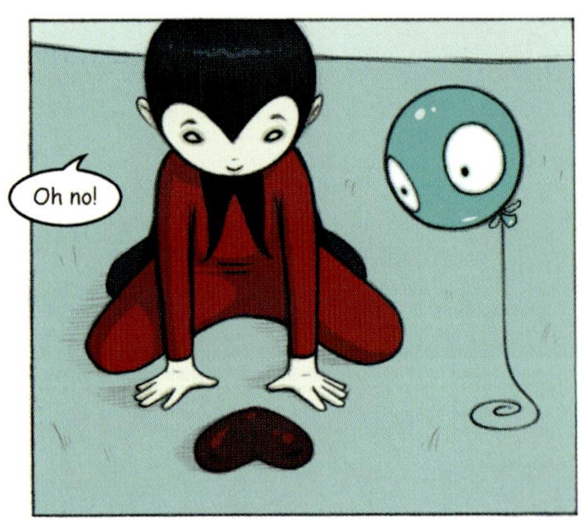

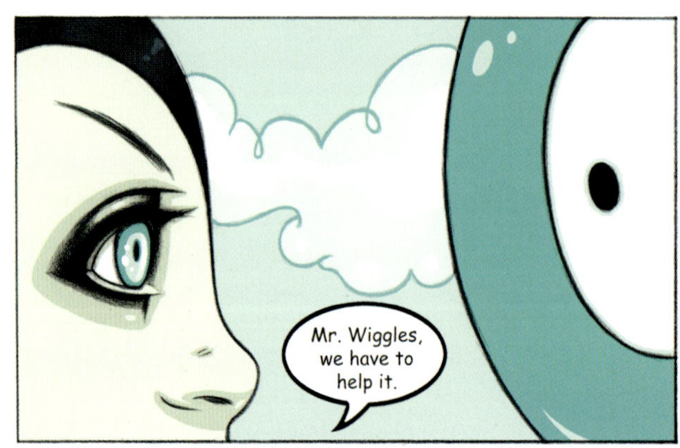

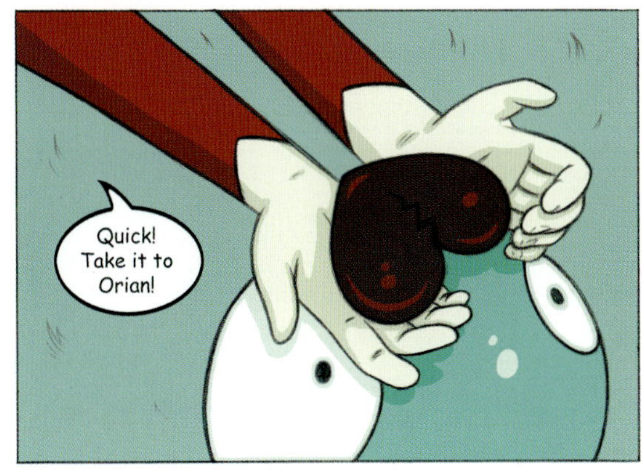
Quick! Take it to Orian!

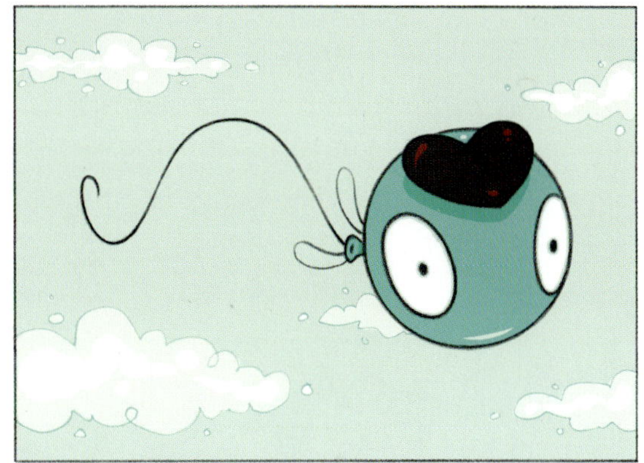

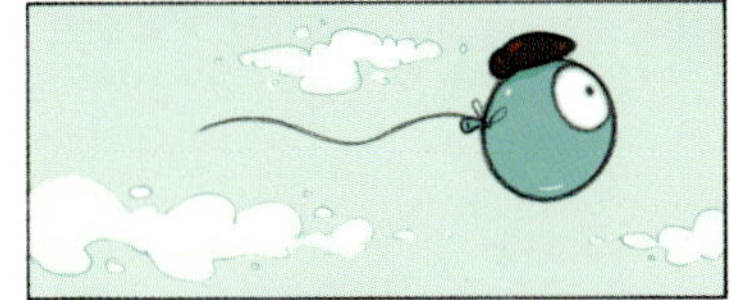

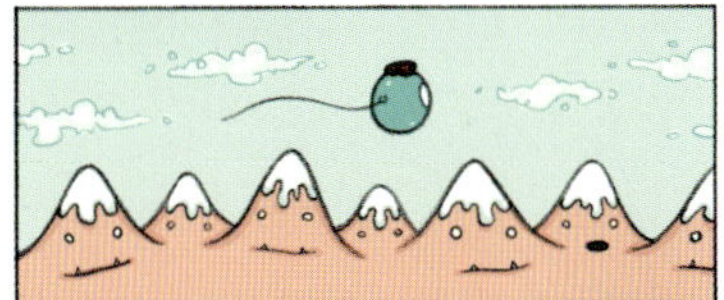

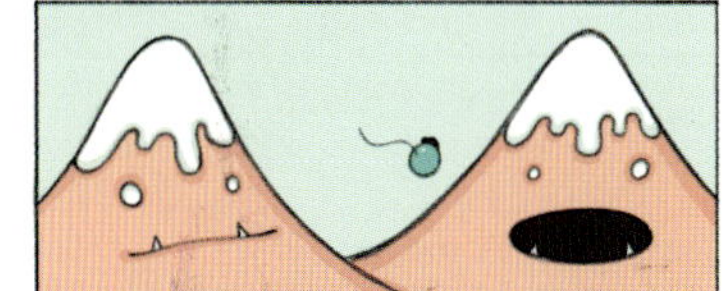

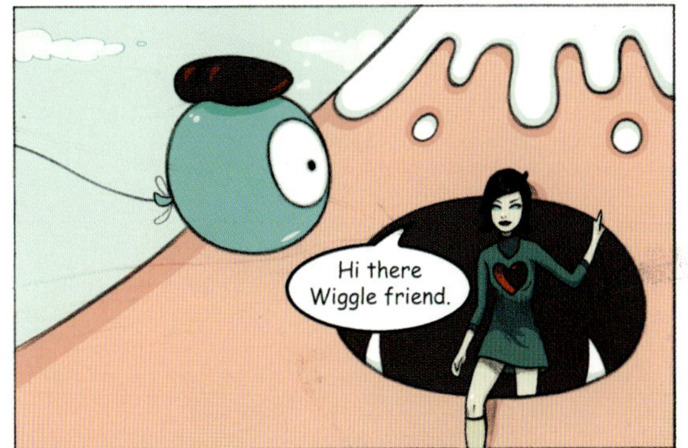
Hi there Wiggle friend.

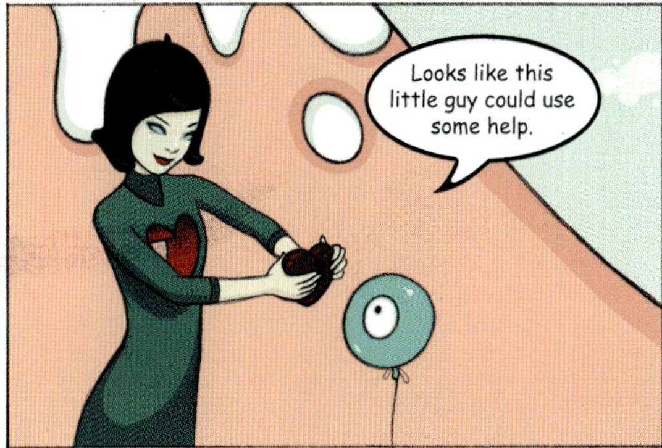
Looks like this little guy could use some help.

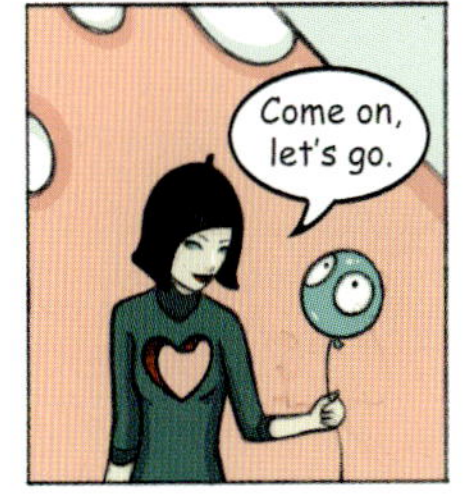
Come on, let's go.

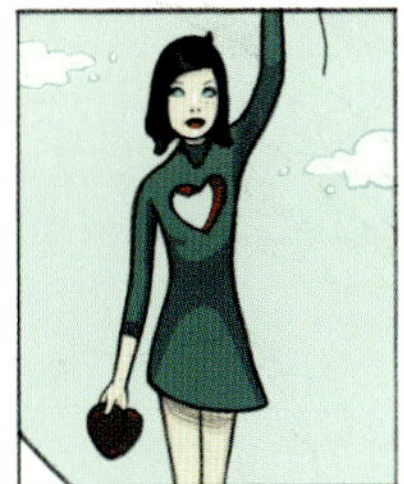

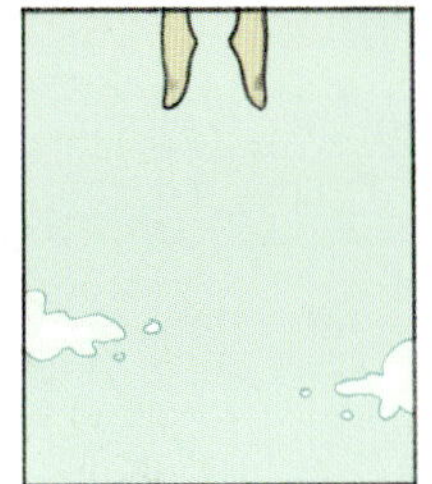

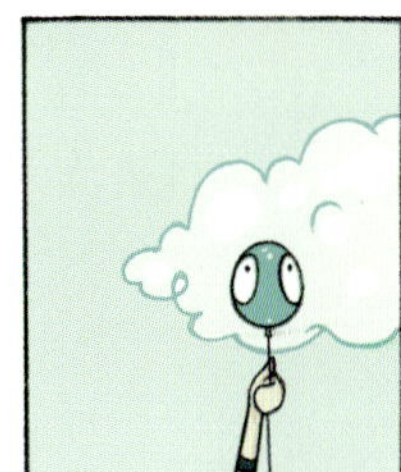

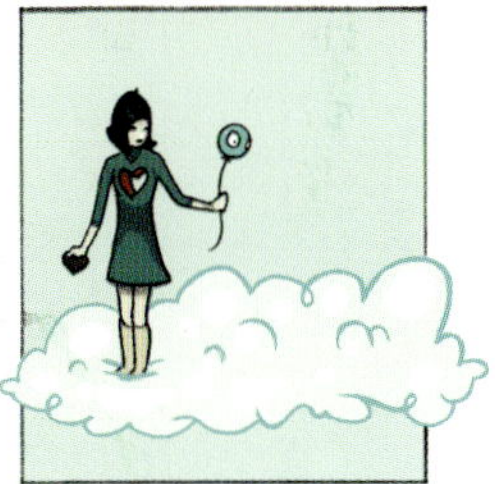

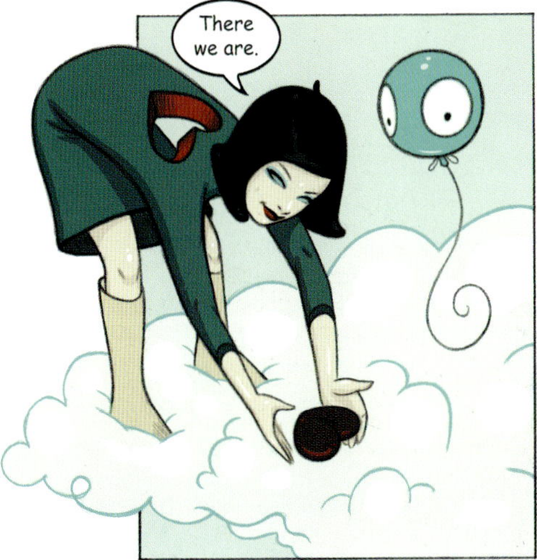
There we are.

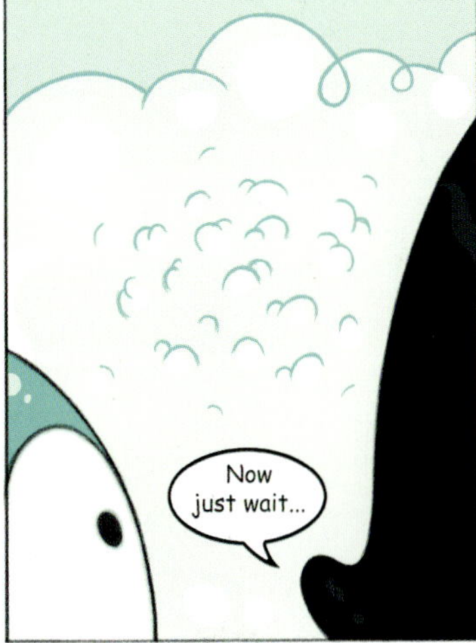
Now just wait...

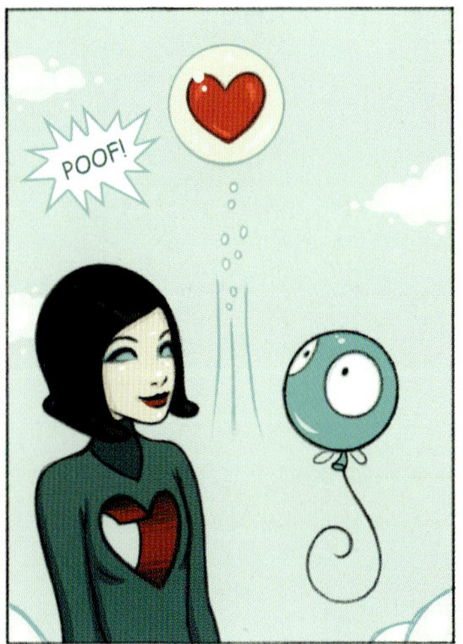
POOF!

THE END

Death Metal Girl

five-color silkscreen
18" x 25"
edition of 100
2007

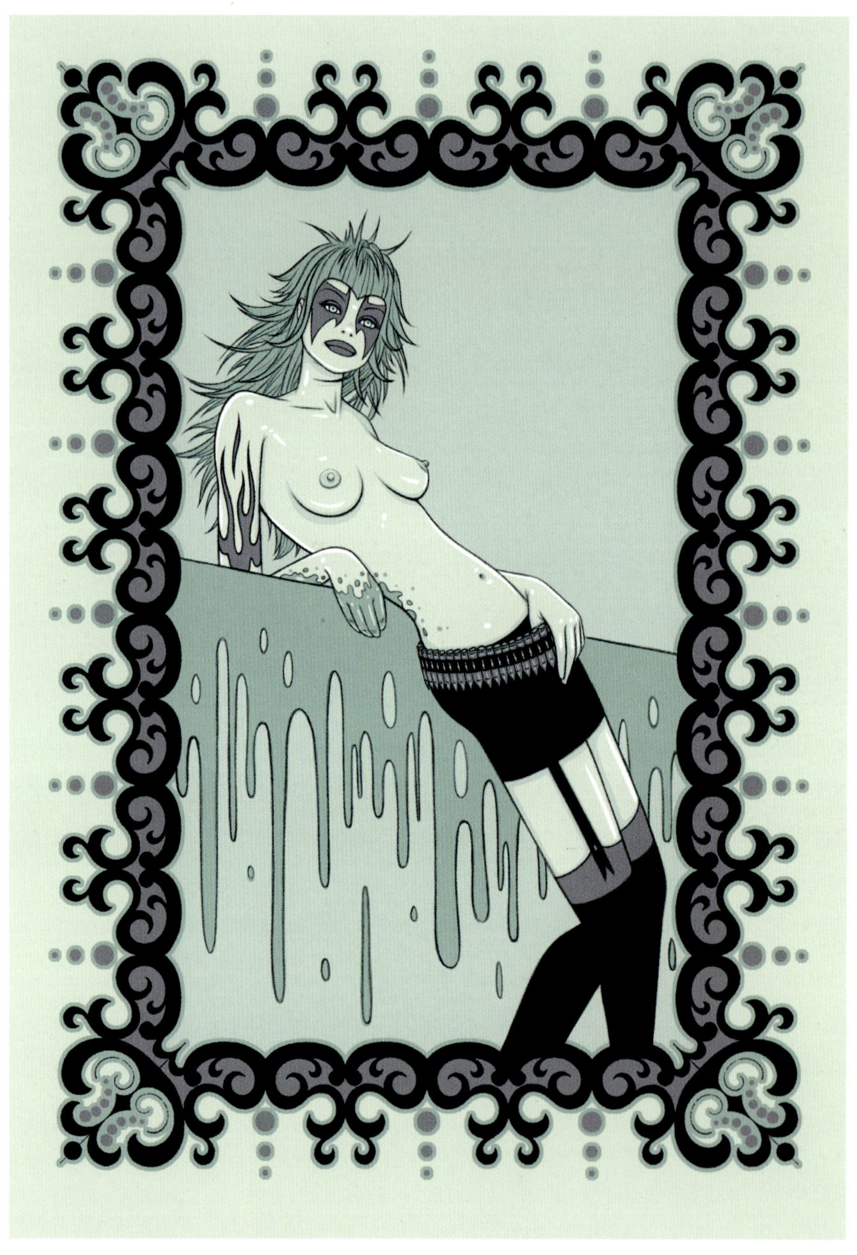

The Weight of Water 1

five-color serigraph
15" x 20"
edition of 100
2008

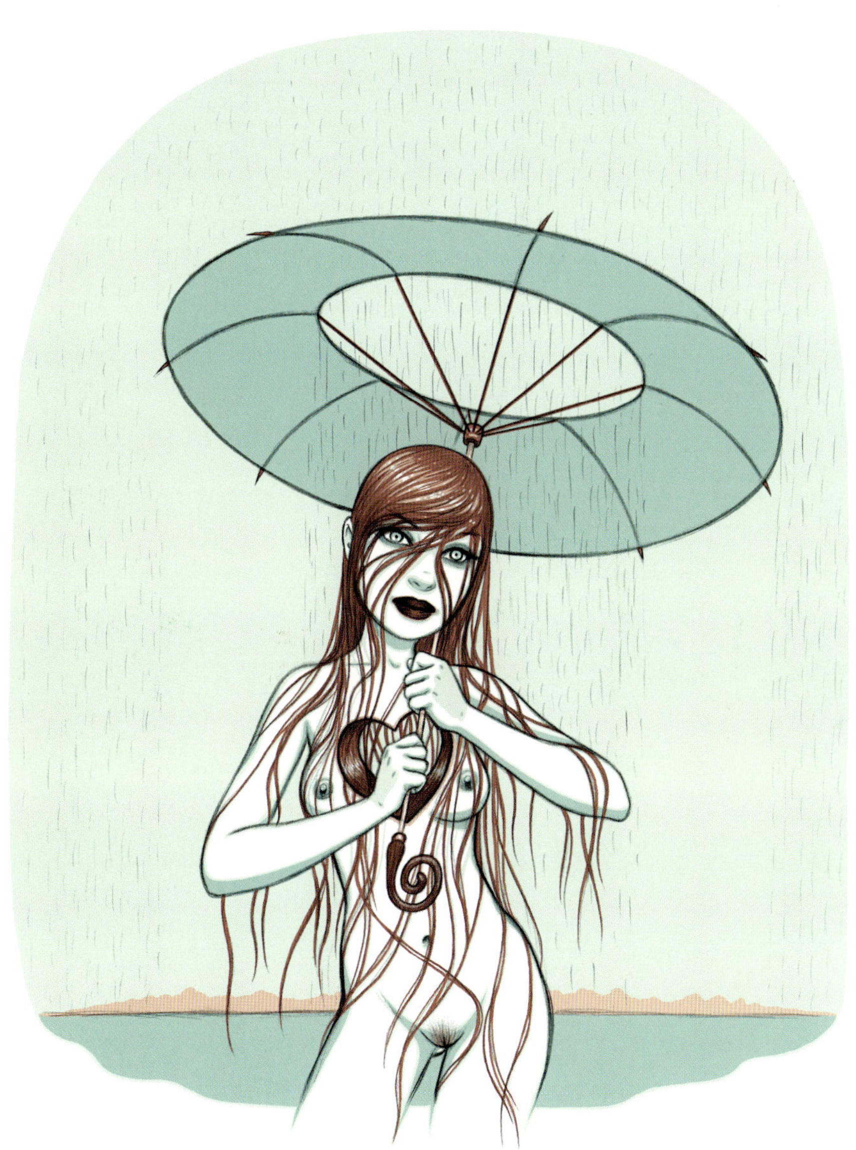

The Weight of Water 1
or
"A donut umbrella will never line up with the eye of a storm"

THE WEIGHT OF WATER 2

five-color serigraph
15" x 20"
edition of 100
2008

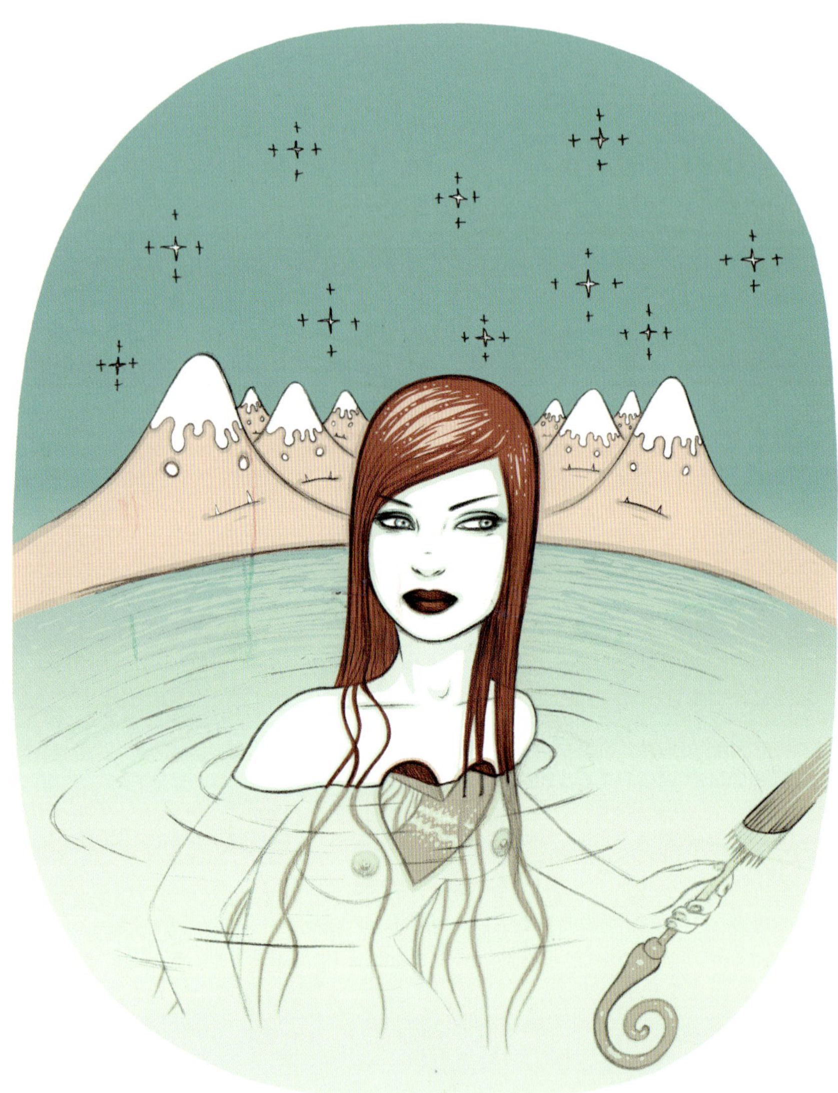

The Weight of Water II
or
"The Planet has cried and now I'm swimming in a pool of its tears"

THE WEIGHT OF WATER 3

five-color serigraph
15" x 20"
edition of 100
2008

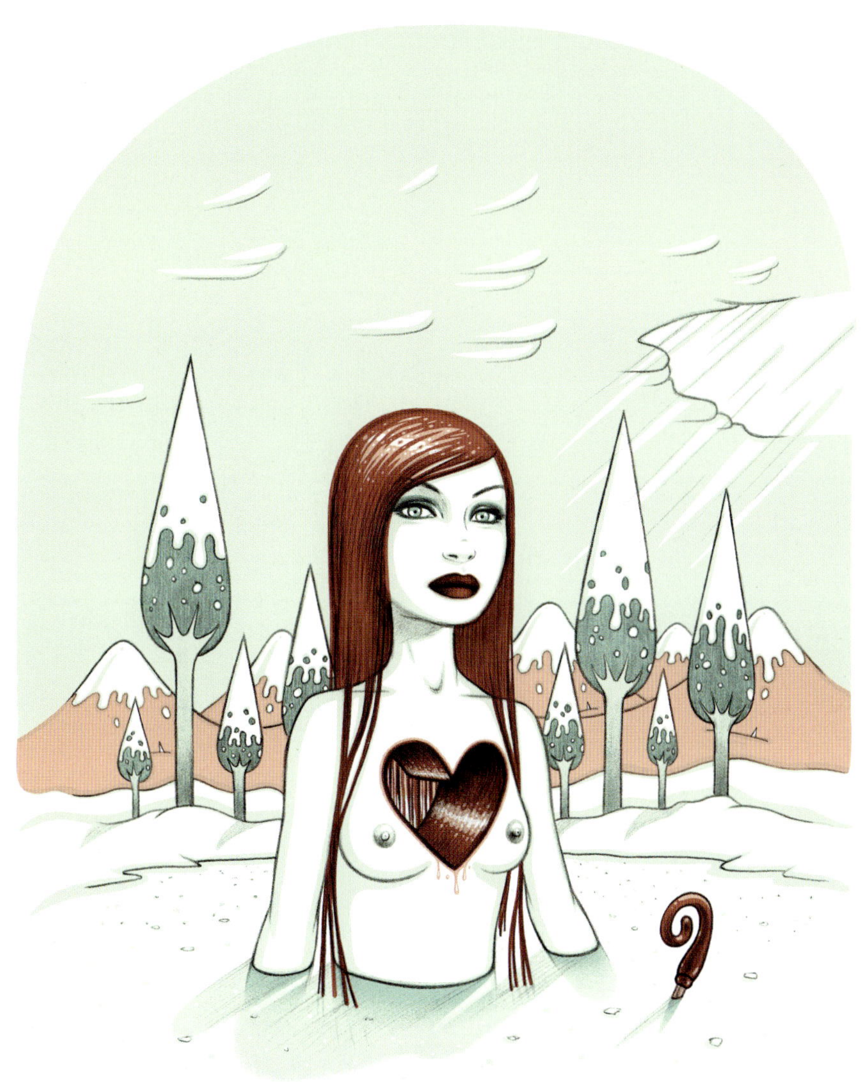

The Weight of Water III
or
"I have always dreamt of being naked and frozen on another planet"

THE IDEALIZATION OF ASYMMETRICAL THOUGHT

eighteen-color silkscreen
22" x 30"
edition of 100
2007

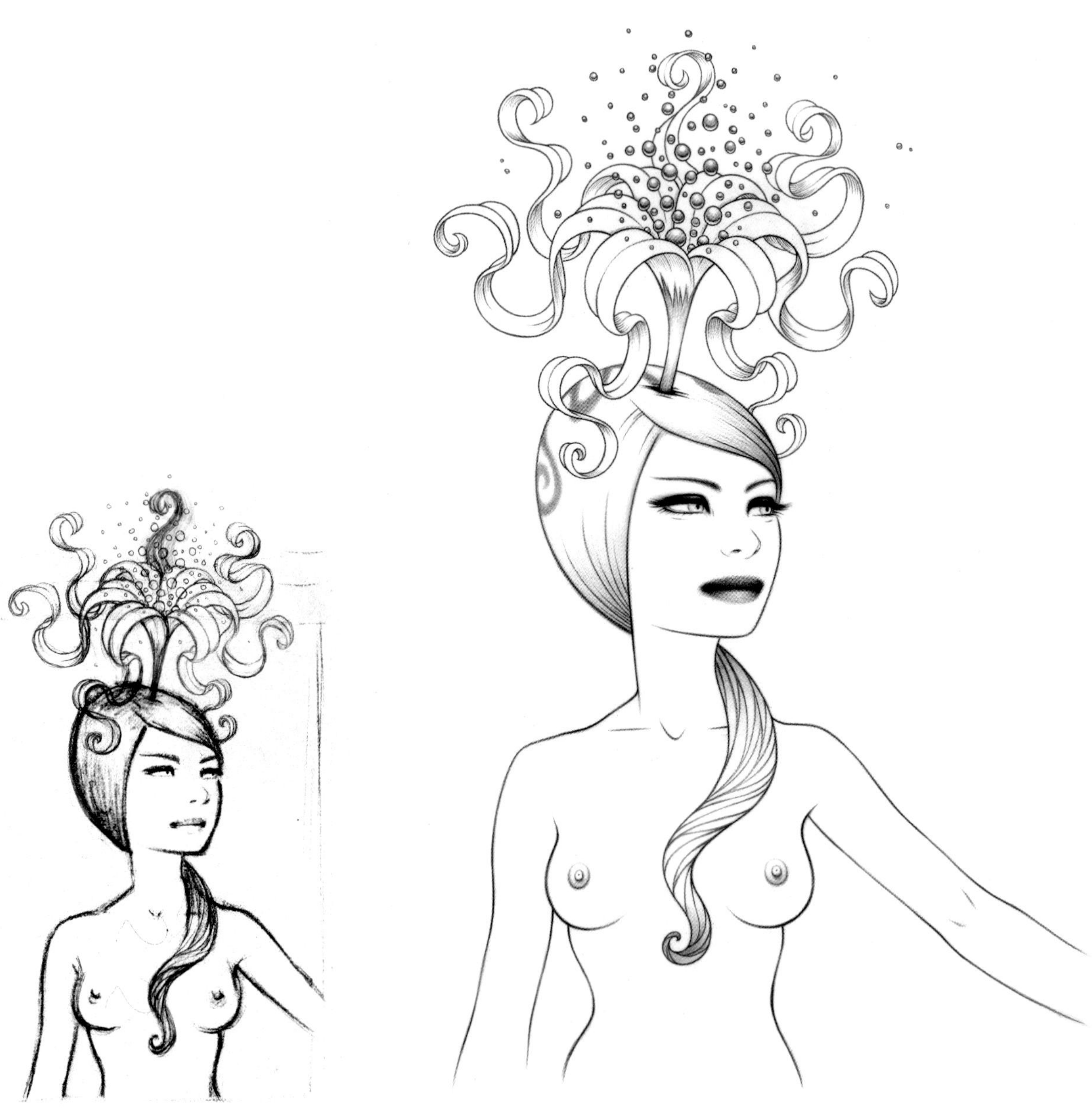

rough
graphite on paper
3" x 4"

drawing
graphite on watercolor paper
17" x 23"

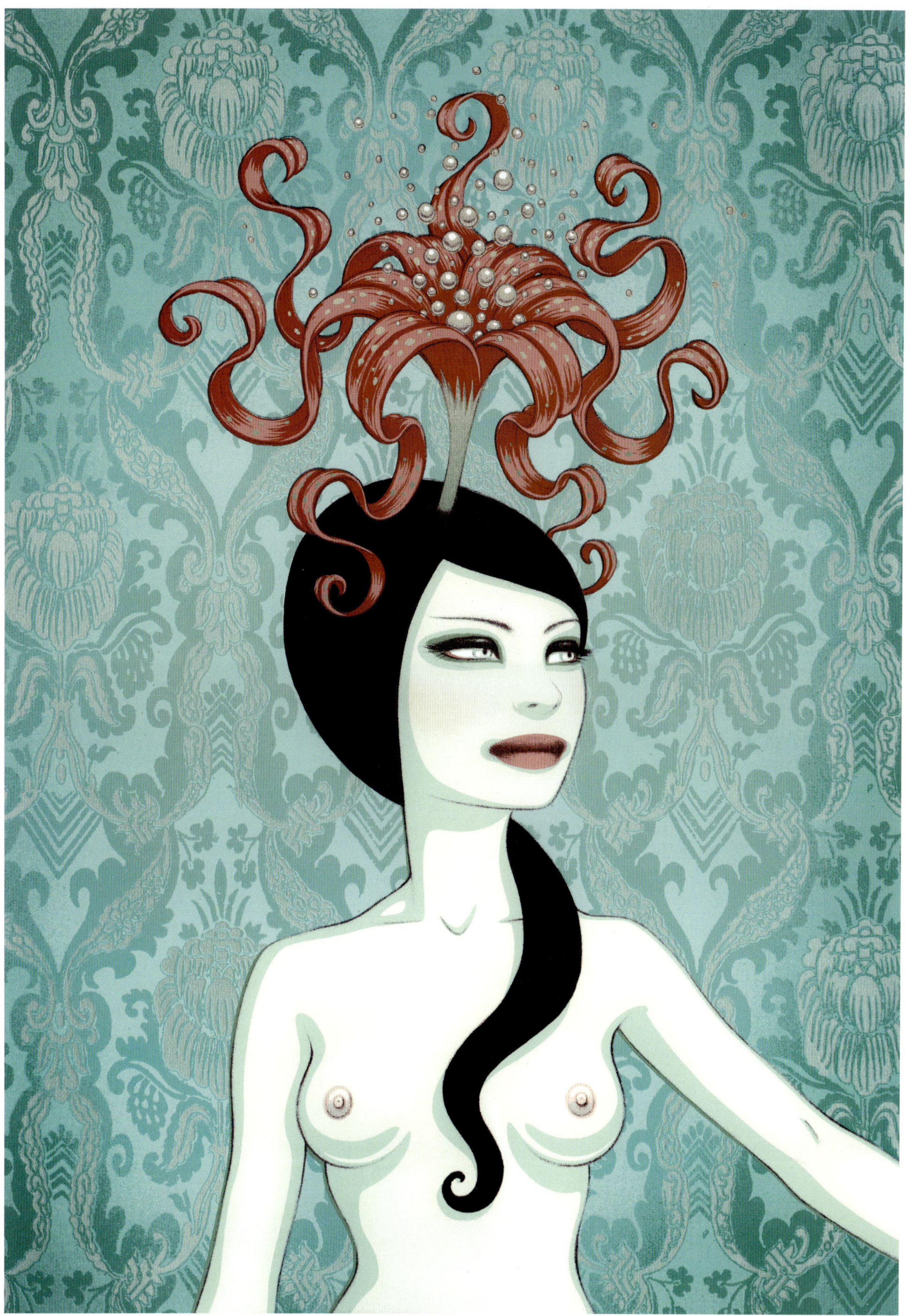

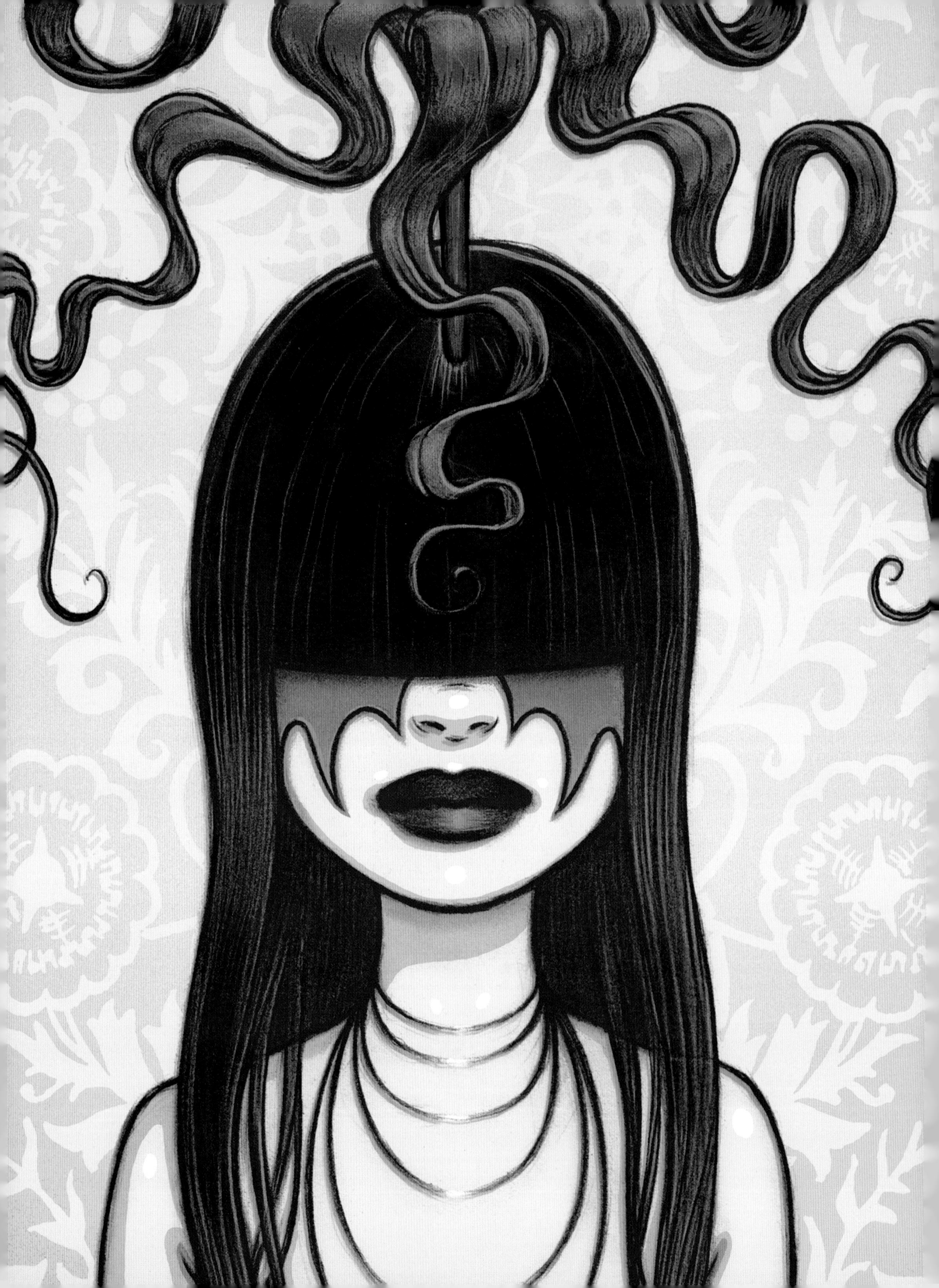

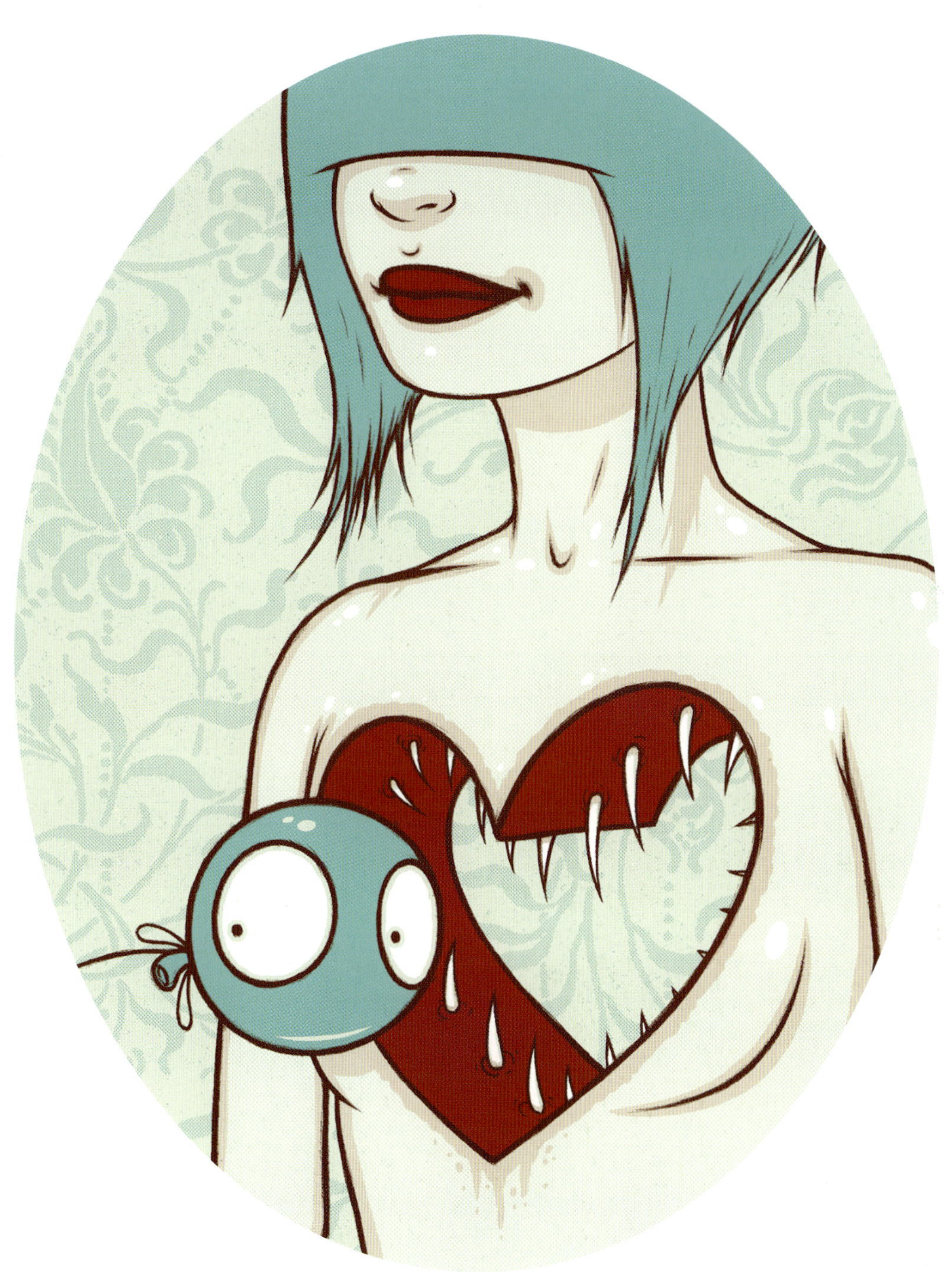

Posters

Kings of Leon

six-color silkscreen
16" x 23"
edition of 250
2007

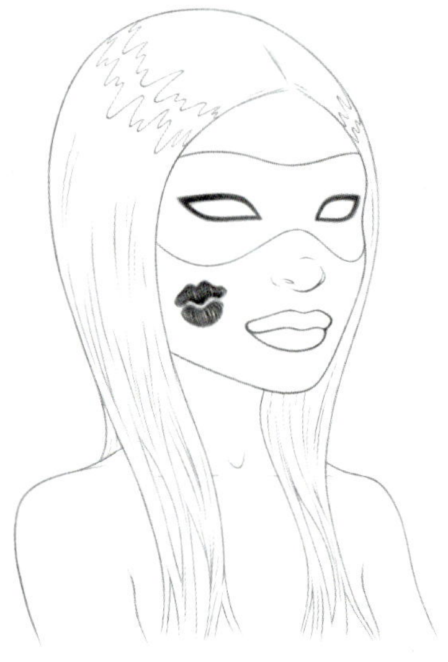

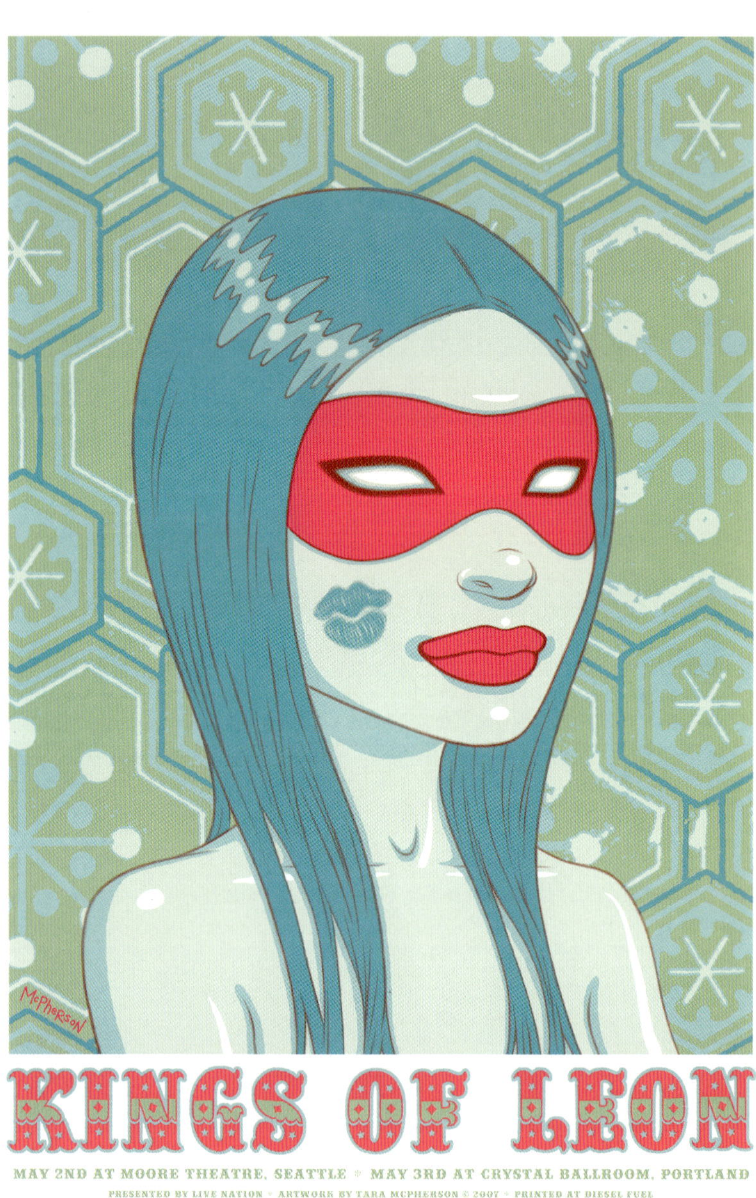

drawing
graphite on bristol
14" x 17"

blue variant
edition of 30

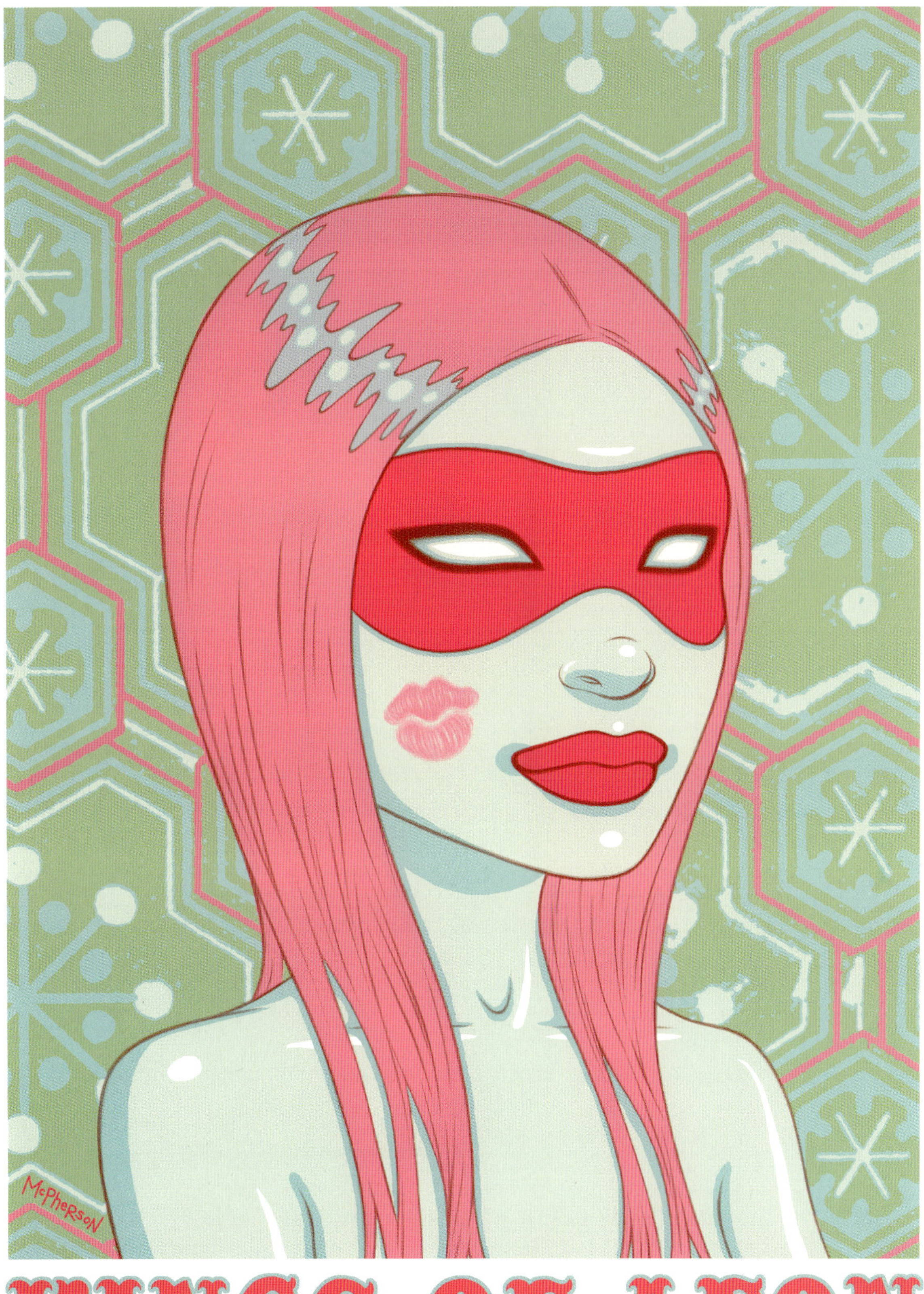

KINGS OF LEON

MAY 2ND AT MOORE THEATRE, SEATTLE * MAY 3RD AT CRYSTAL BALLROOM, PORTLAND

PRESENTED BY LIVE NATION * ARTWORK BY TARA MCPHERSON © 2007 * PRINTED AT DIESEL FUEL

Beck

five-color silkscreen
16" x 23"
edition of 500
2006

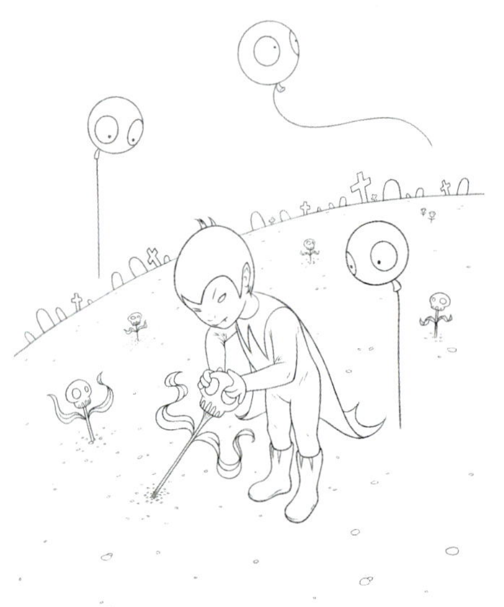

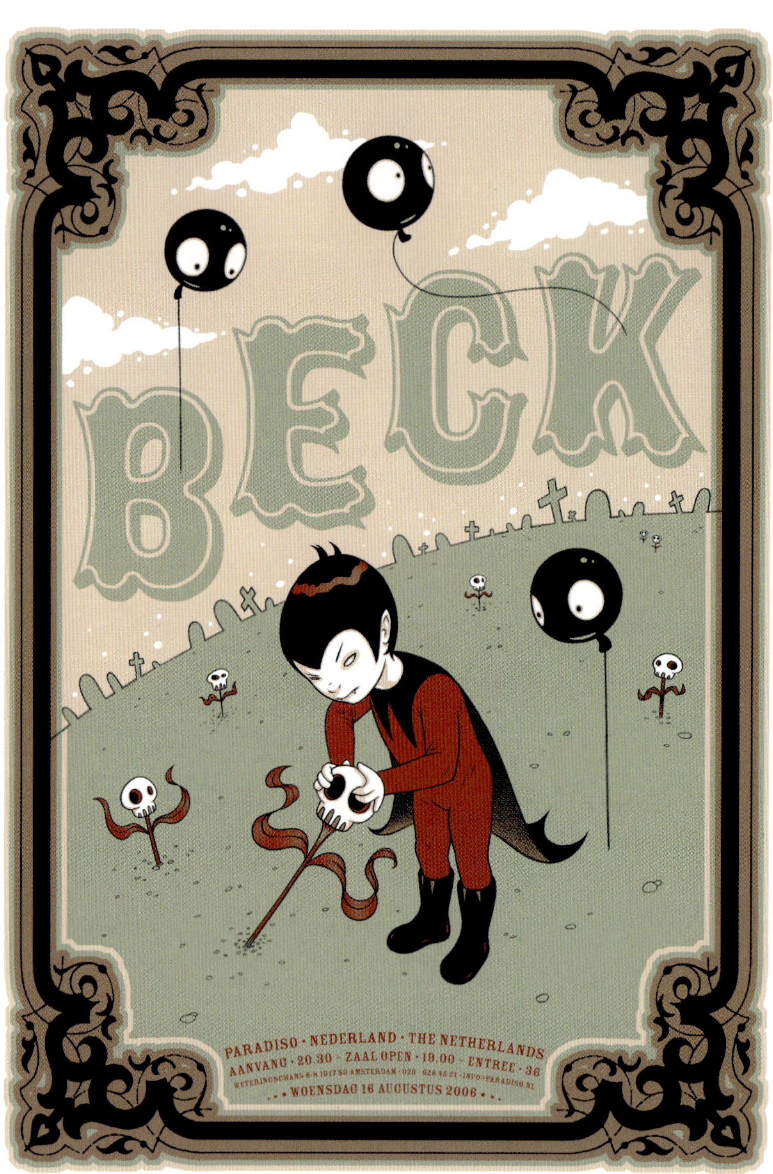

drawing
graphite on bristol
14" x 17"

green variant
edition of 45

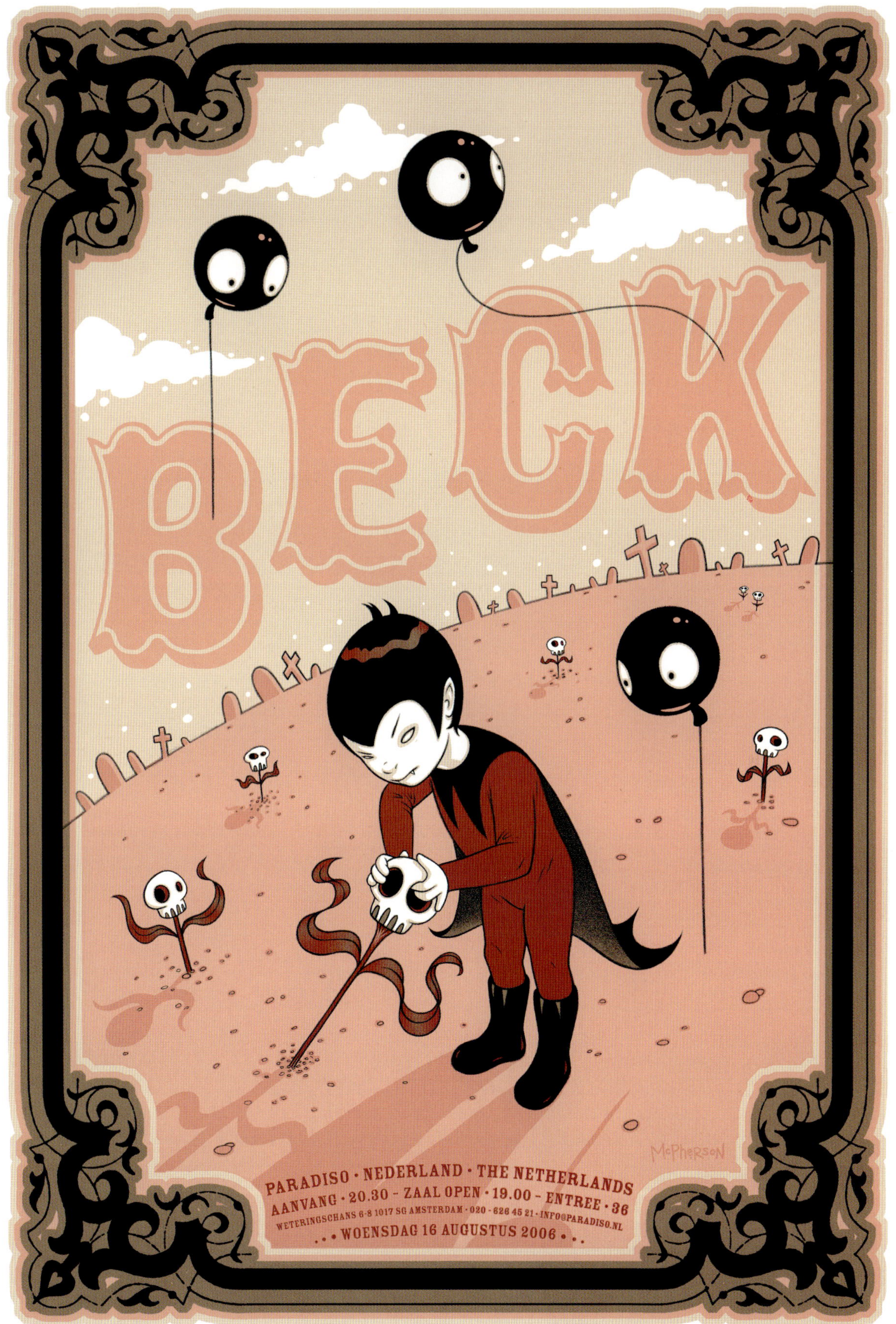
BECK
McPHERSON
PARADISO • NEDERLAND • THE NETHERLANDS
AANVANG • 20.30 – ZAAL OPEN • 19.00 – ENTREE • 36
WETERINGSCHANS 6-8 1017 SG AMSTERDAM • 020 - 626 45 21 • INFO@PARADISO.NL
• • • WOENSDAG 16 AUGUSTUS 2006 • • •
COPYRIGHT 2006 TARA MCPHERSON • WWW.TARAMCPHERSON.COM • WWW.IDEALPOSTERS.COM • DEDICATED TO PEACE • JC 37

The Decemberists

four-color silkscreen
16" x 23"
edition of 300
2006

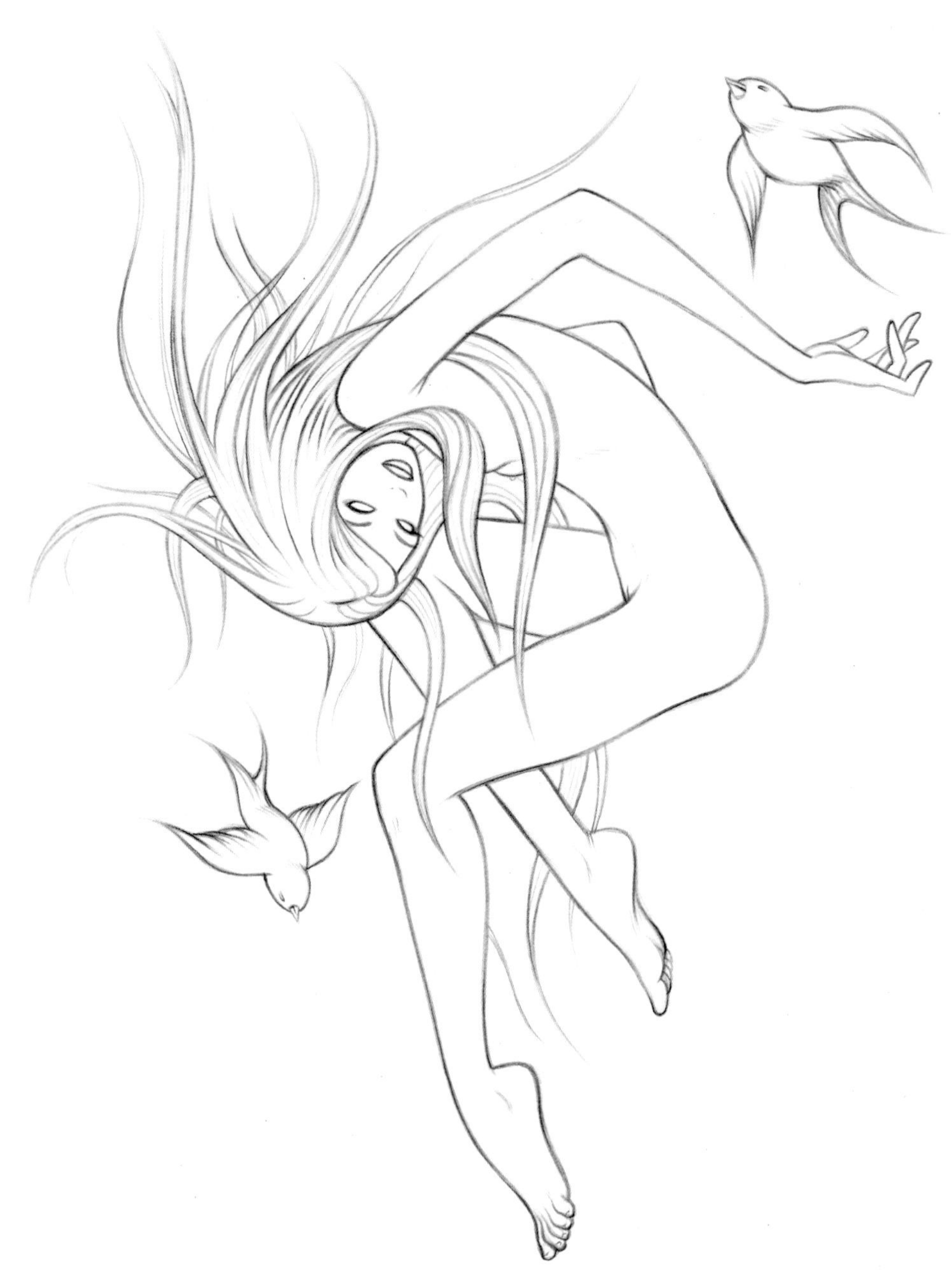

drawing
graphite on bristol
14" x 17"

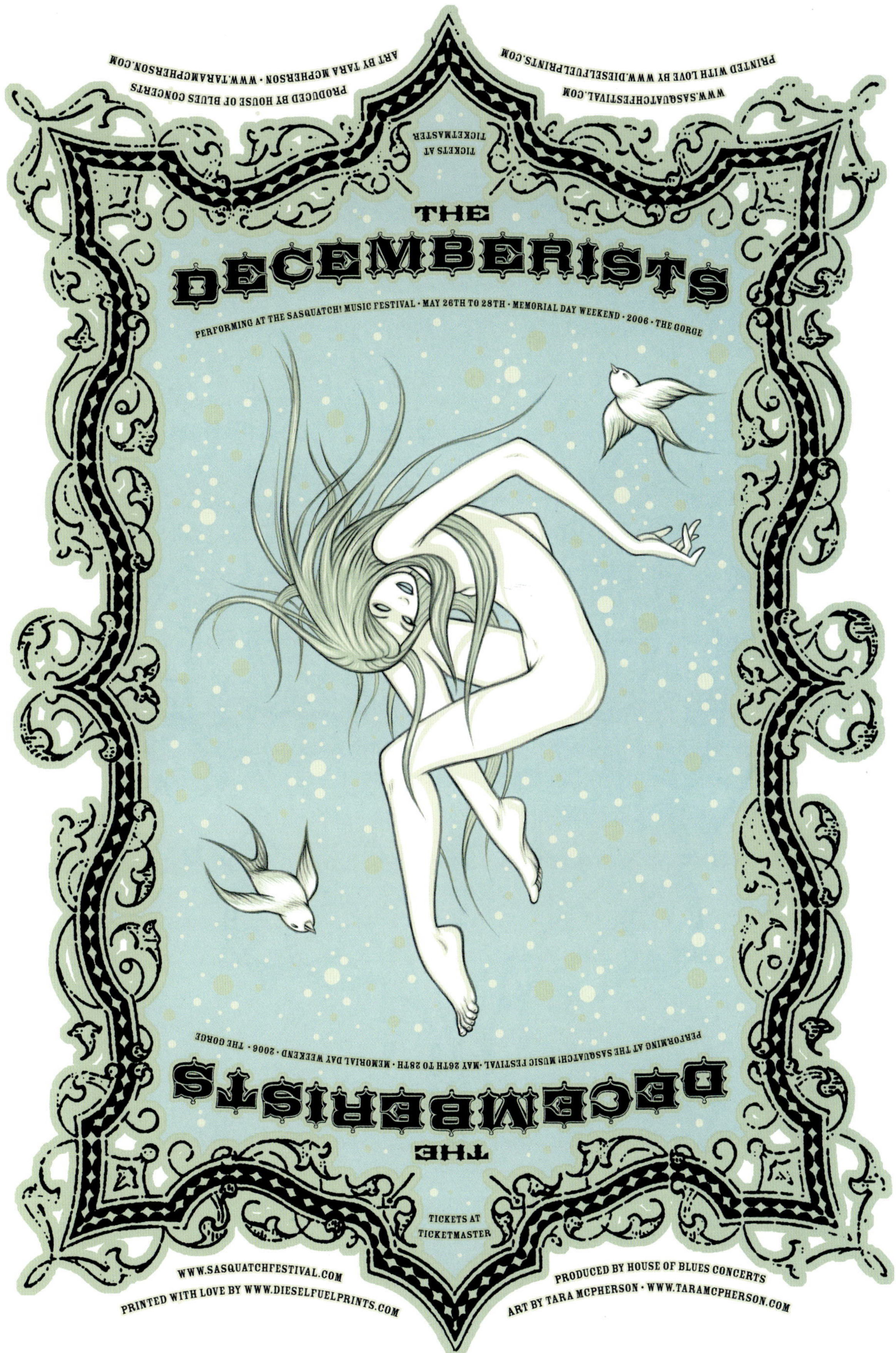
THE
DECEMBERISTS
PERFORMING AT THE SASQUATCH! MUSIC FESTIVAL · MAY 26TH TO 28TH · MEMORIAL DAY WEEKEND · 2006 · THE GORGE
TICKETS AT
TICKETMASTER
WWW.SASQUATCHFESTIVAL.COM
PRINTED WITH LOVE BY WWW.DIESELFUELPRINTS.COM
PRODUCED BY HOUSE OF BLUES CONCERTS
ART BY TARA MCPHERSON · WWW.TARAMCPHERSON.COM

Lonely Heart European Book Tour 2006

seven-color silkscreen
16" x 23"
open edition
2006

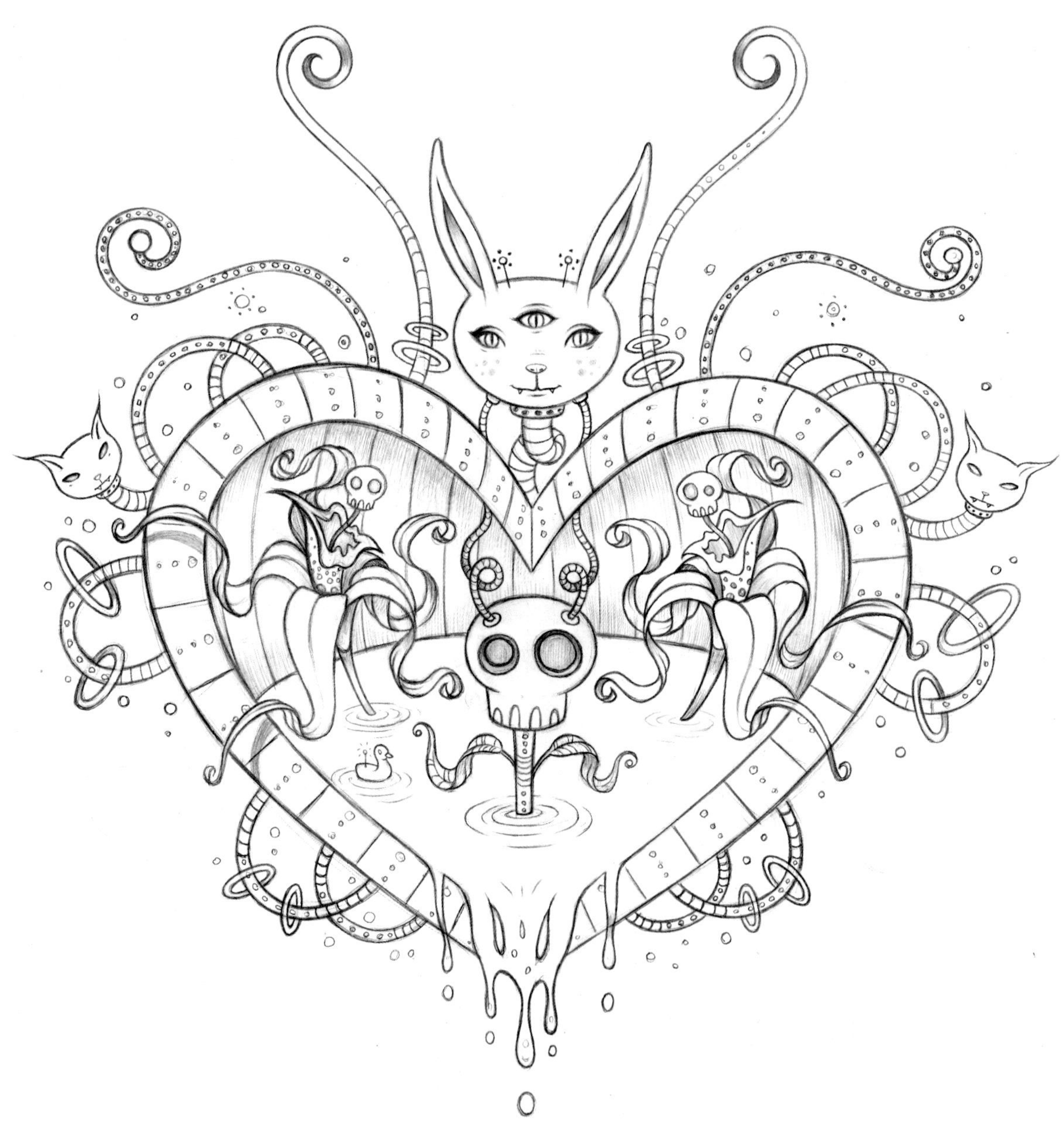

drawing
graphite on bristol
14" x 17"

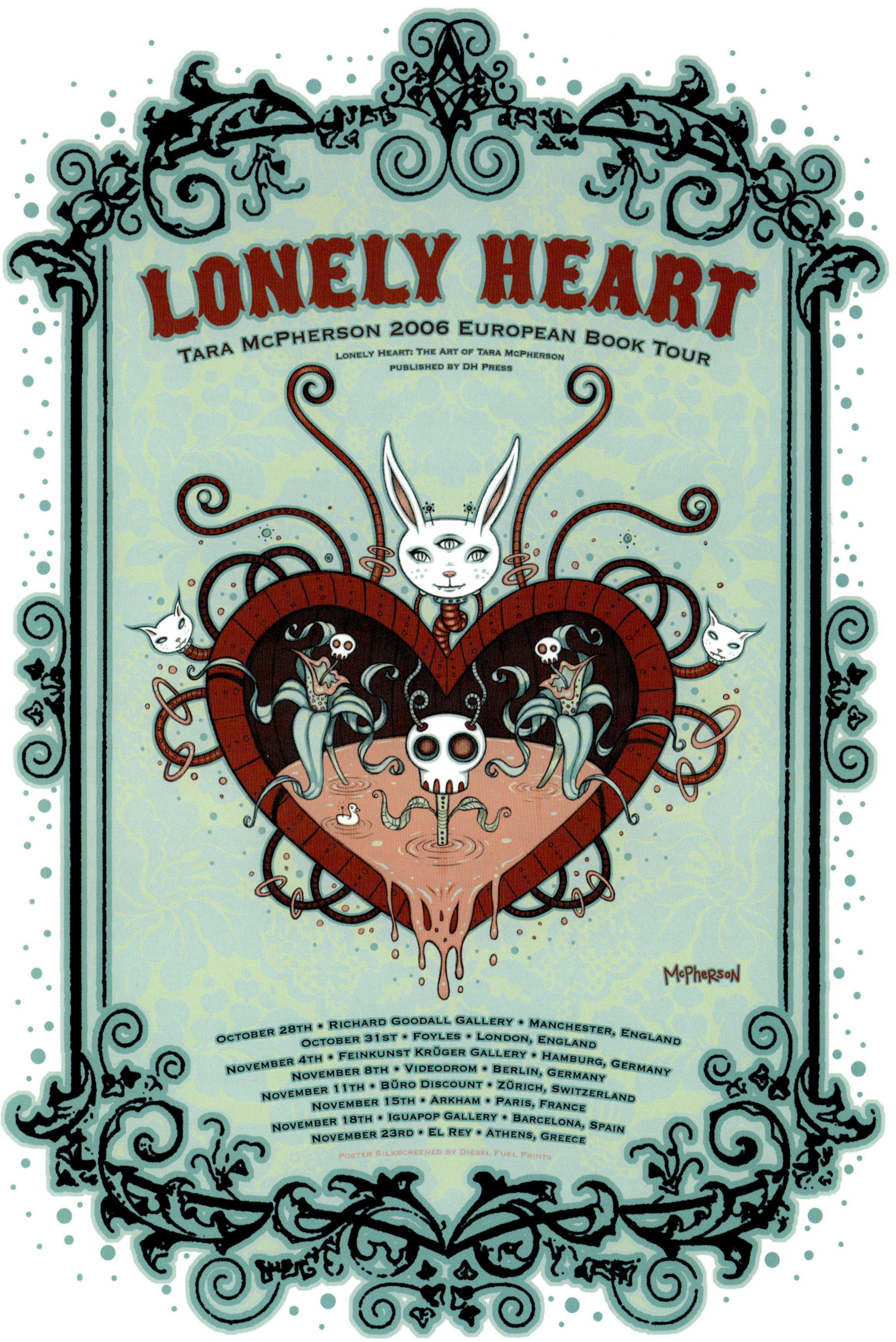

WWW.TARAMCPHERSON.COM WWW.DARKHORSE.COM WWW.DIESELFUELPRINTS.COM

Isis, Dälek, Zombi

six-color silkscreen
23" x 32"
edition of 300
2006

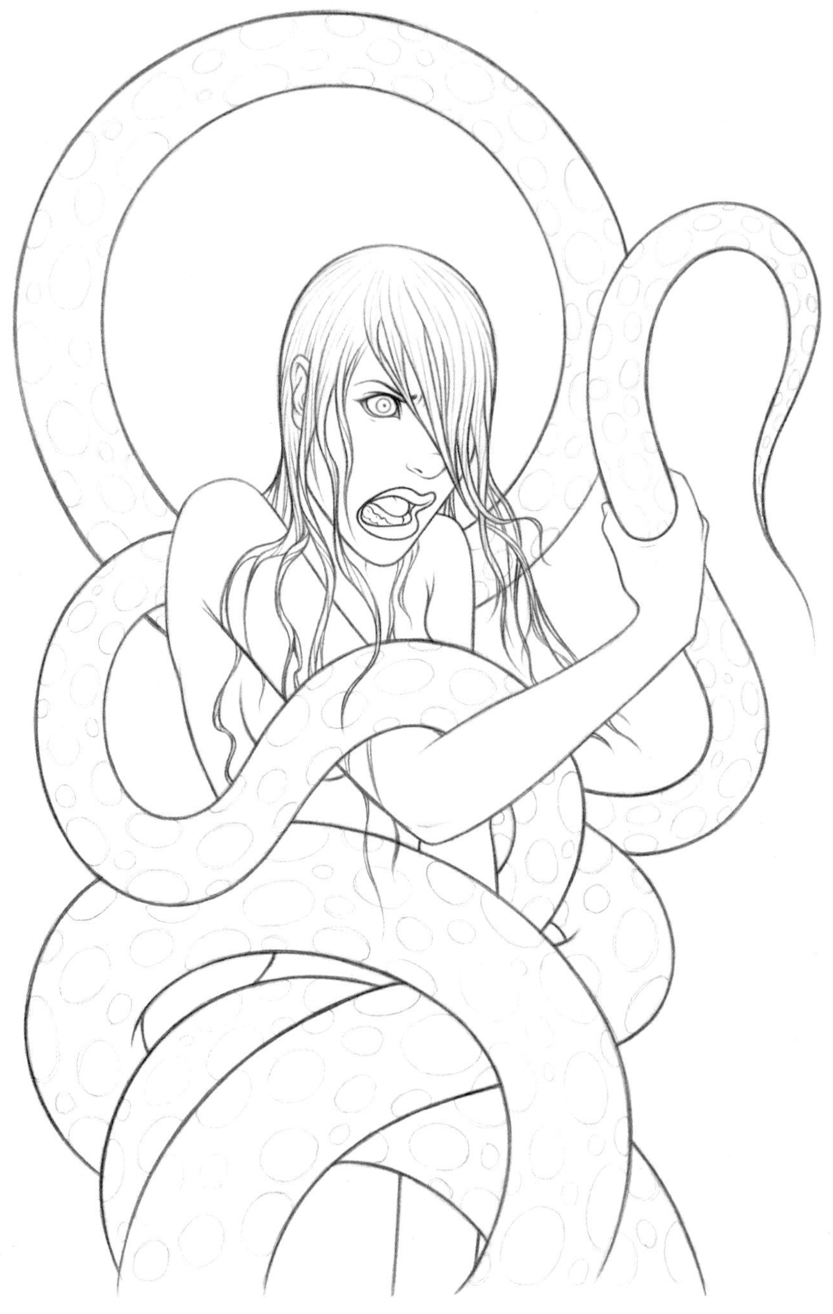

drawing
graphite on bristol
14" x 17"

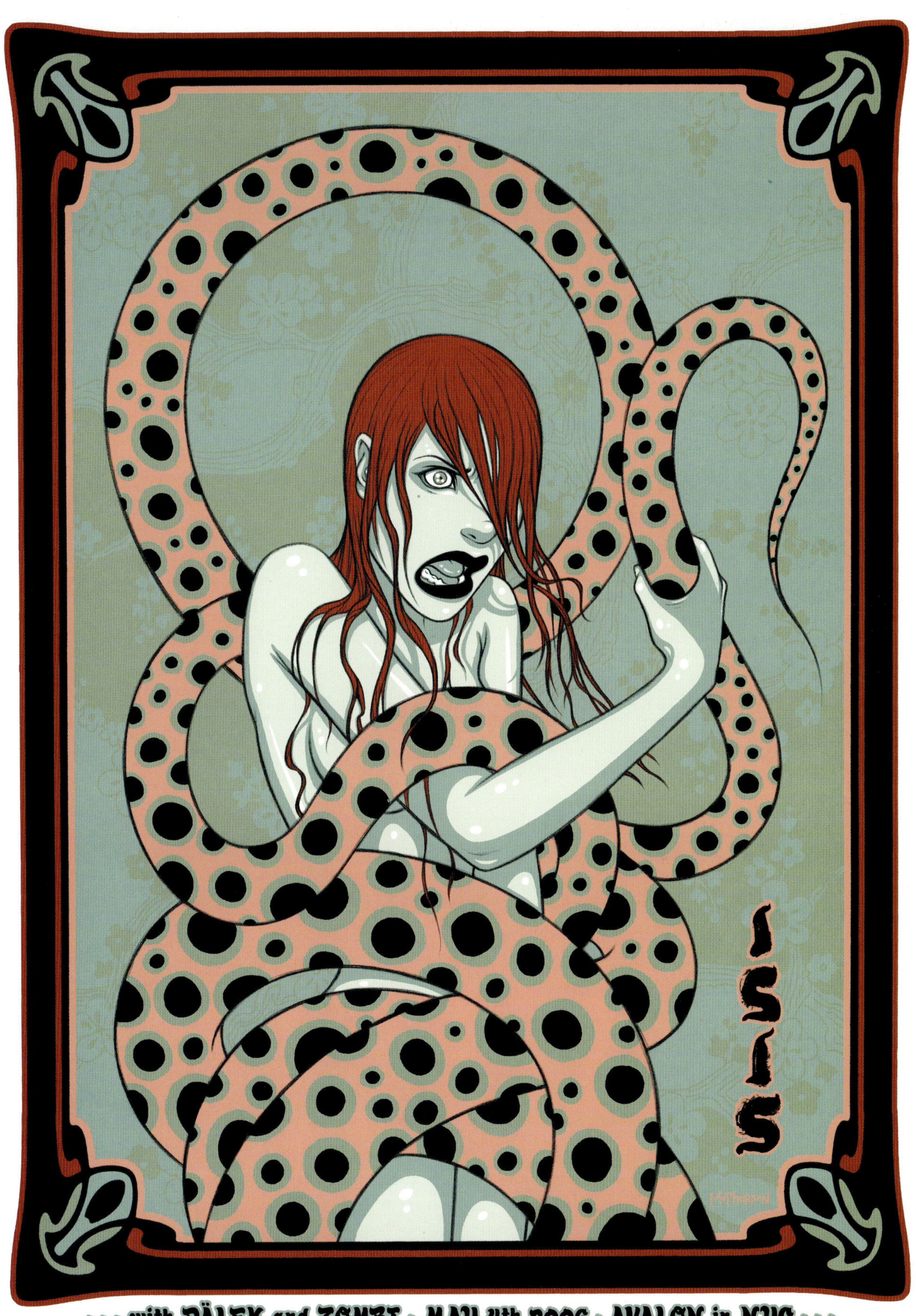

. . . with DÄLEK and ZOMBI · MAY 4th 2006 · AVALON in NYC . . .

Mastodon, Slayer, Lamb of God, Children of Bodom, Thine Eyes Bleed

four-color silkscreen
17" x 21"
edition of 200
2006

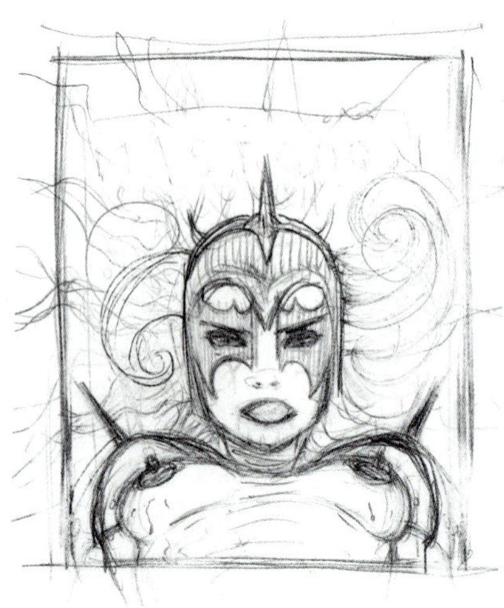

rough
graphite on paper
4" x 4"

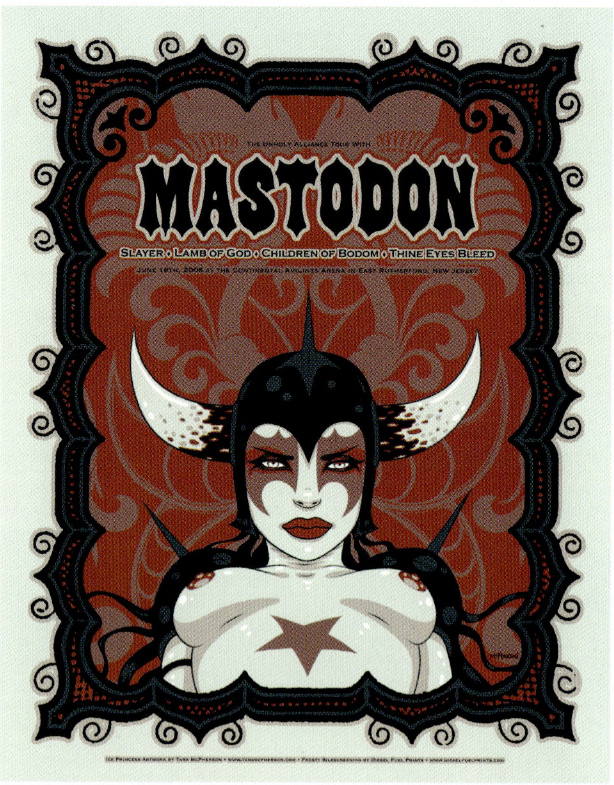

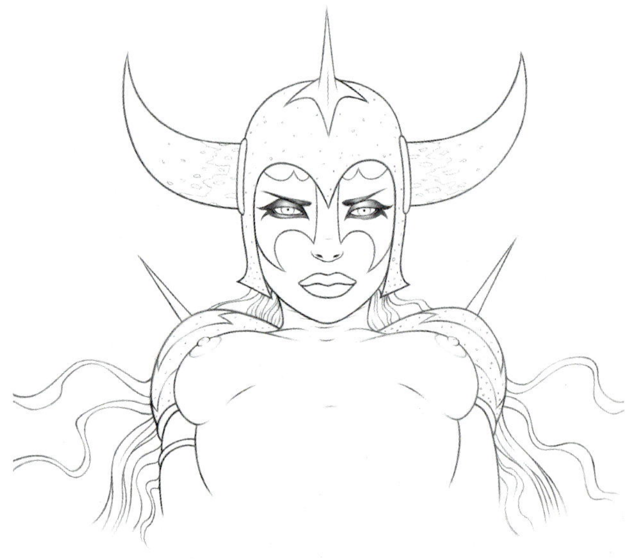

drawing
graphite on bristol
14" x 14"

red variant
edition of 40

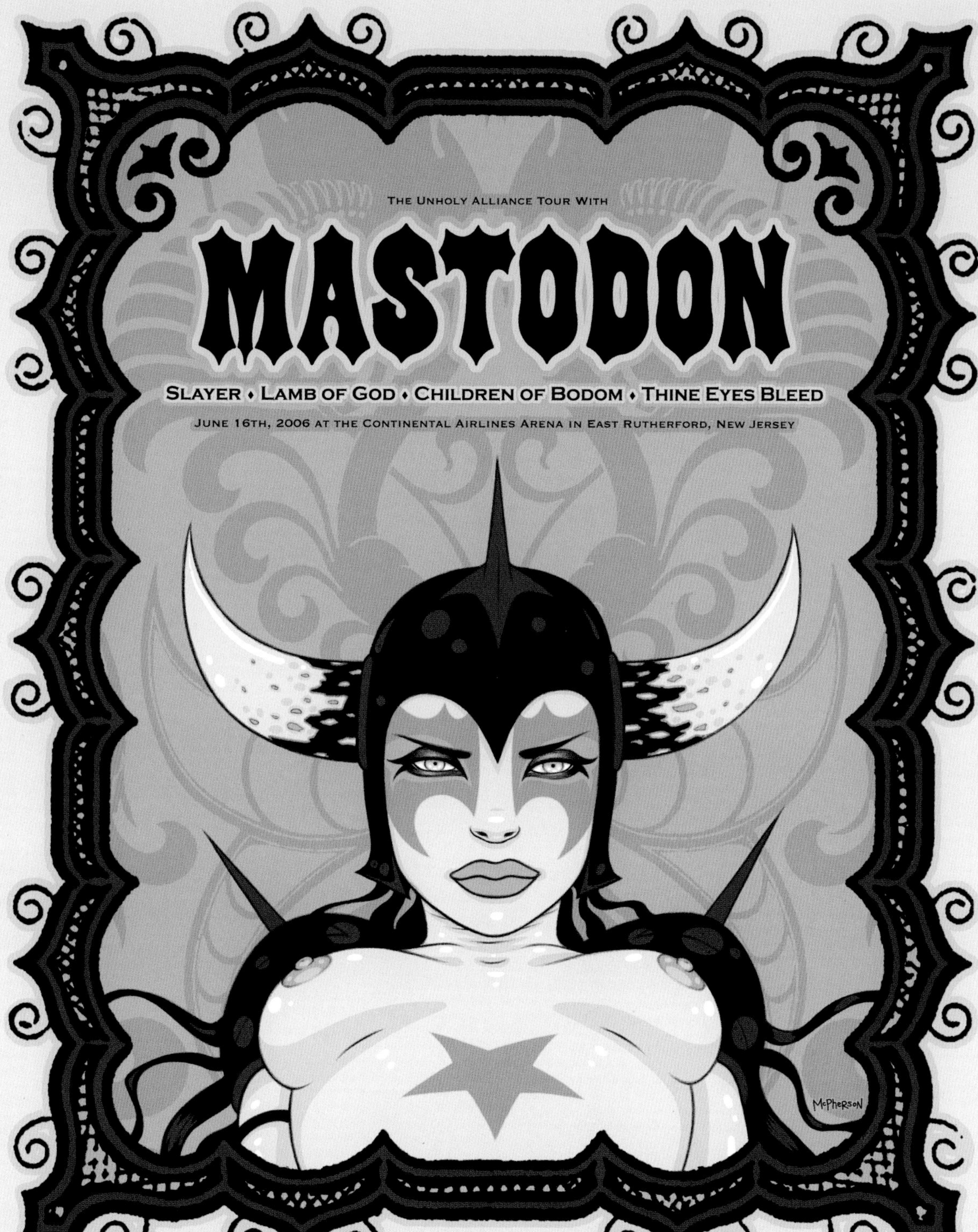

The Unholy Alliance Tour With
MASTODON
Slayer • Lamb of God • Children of Bodom • Thine Eyes Bleed
June 16th, 2006 at the Continental Airlines Arena in East Rutherford, New Jersey
McPherson
Ice Princess Artwork by Tara McPherson • www.taramcpherson.com • Frosty Silkscreening by Diesel Fuel Prints • www.dieselfuelprints.com

NEUROSIS AND MASTODON, WHITE

seven-color silkscreen
21.5" x 32"
edition of 200
2008

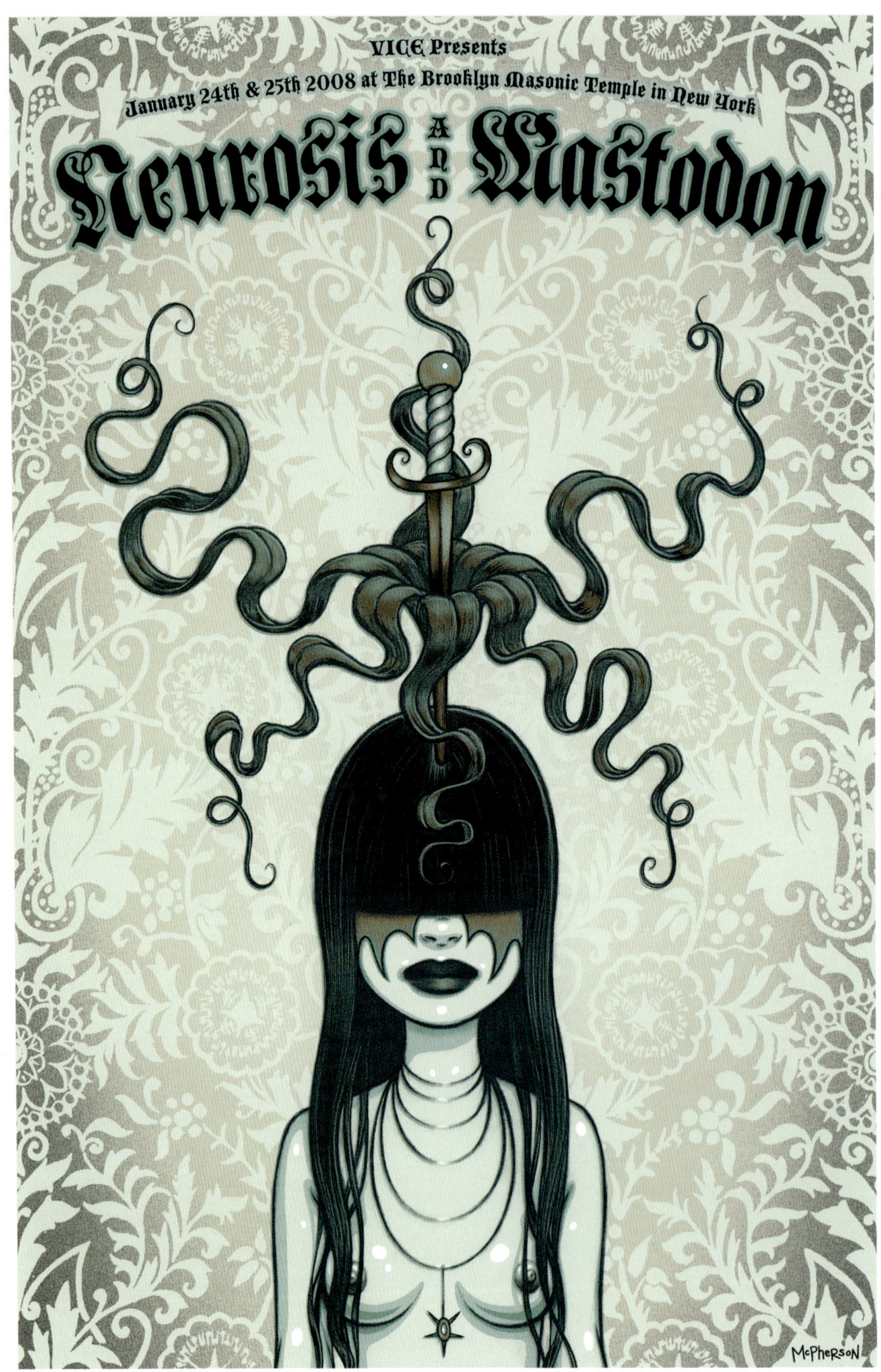

Neurosis and Mastodon, Black

eight-color silkscreen
21.5" x 32"
edition of 200
2008

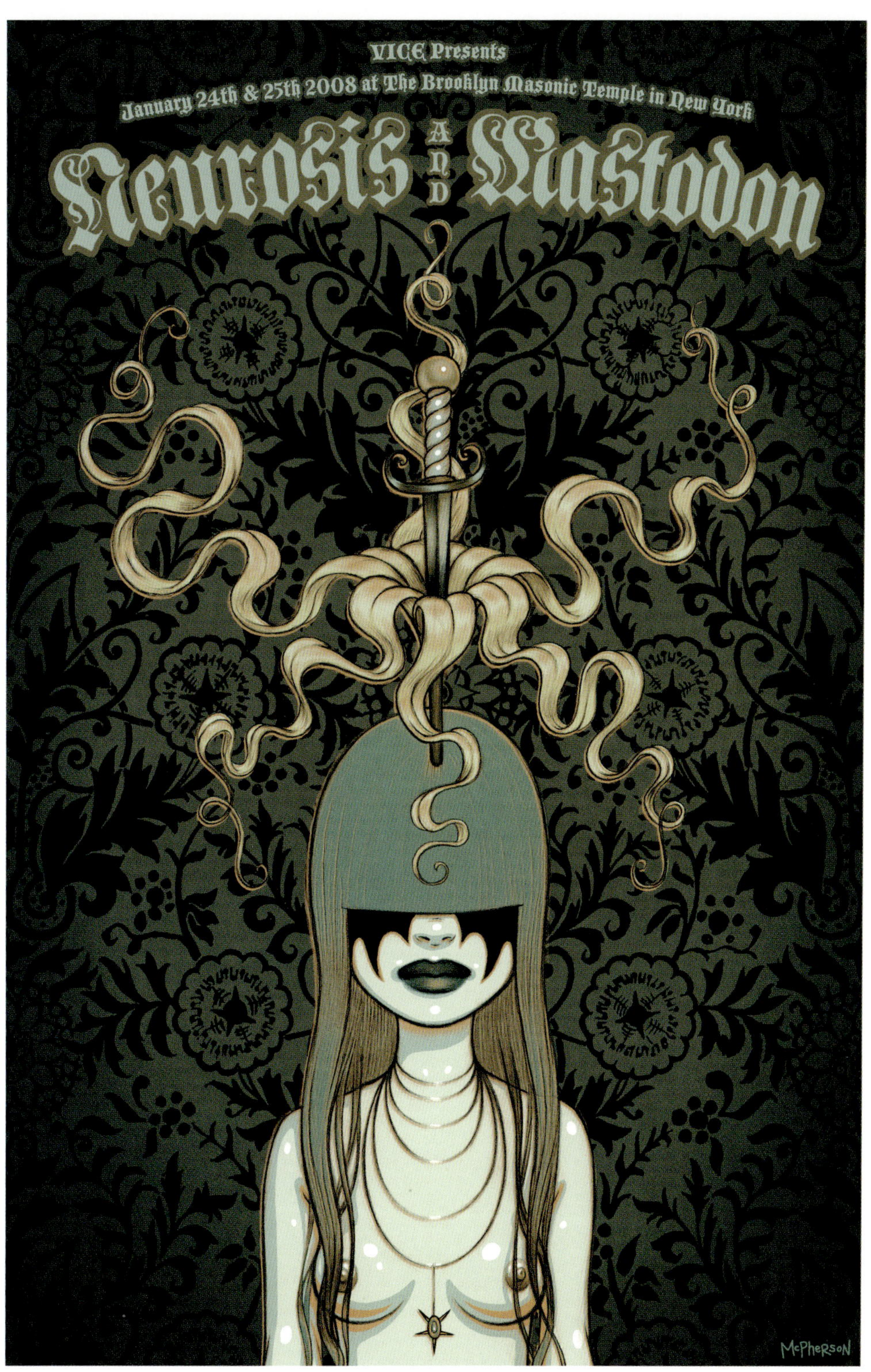

Melvins, Big Business, Porn, Altamont

five-color silkscreen
17" x 22"
edition of 200
2006

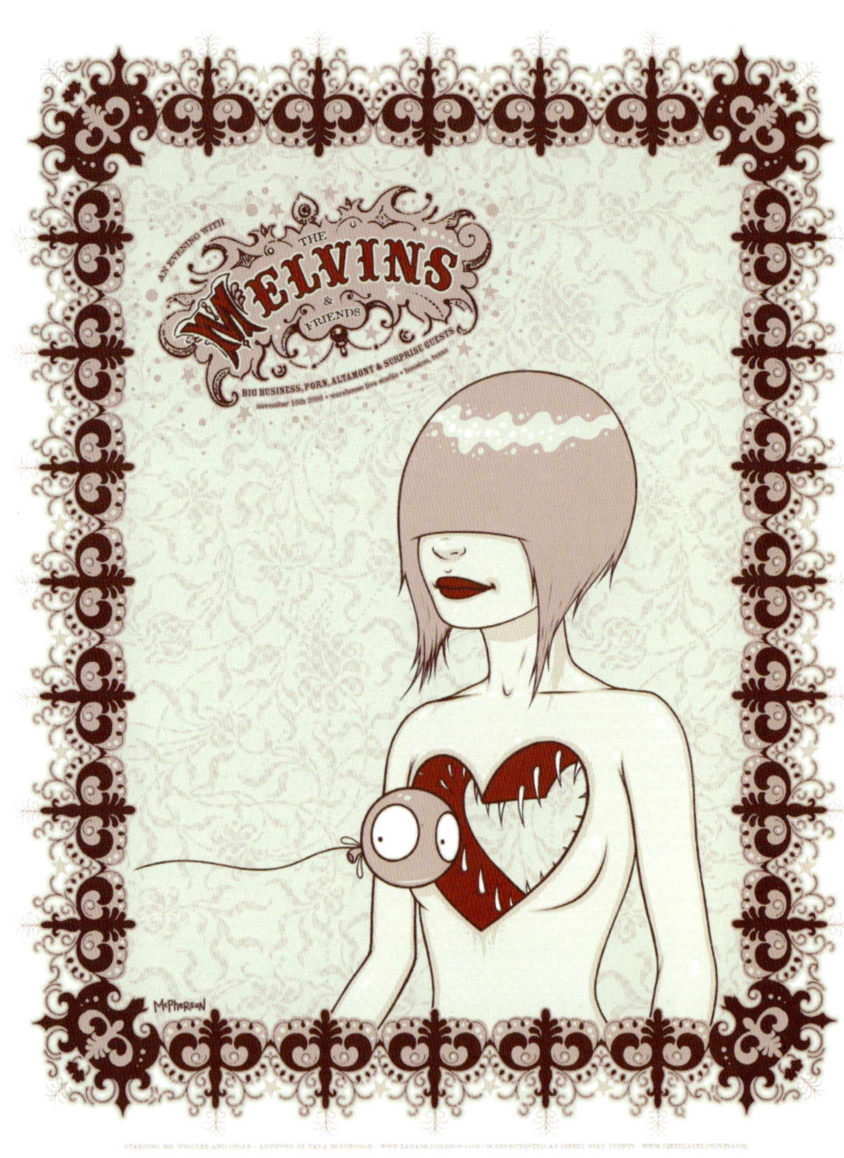

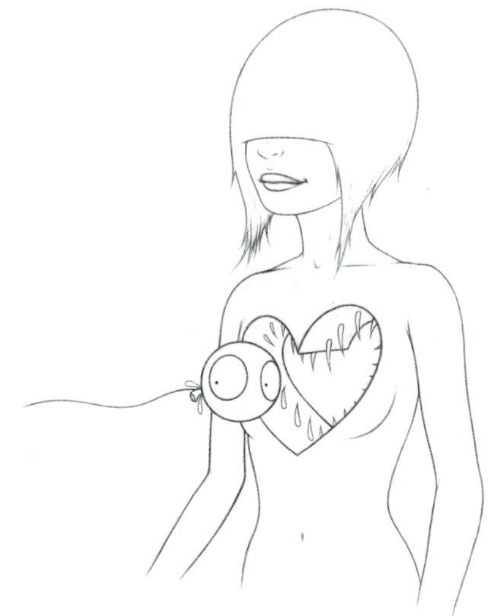

drawing
graphite on bristol
14" x 17"

pink variant
edition of 18

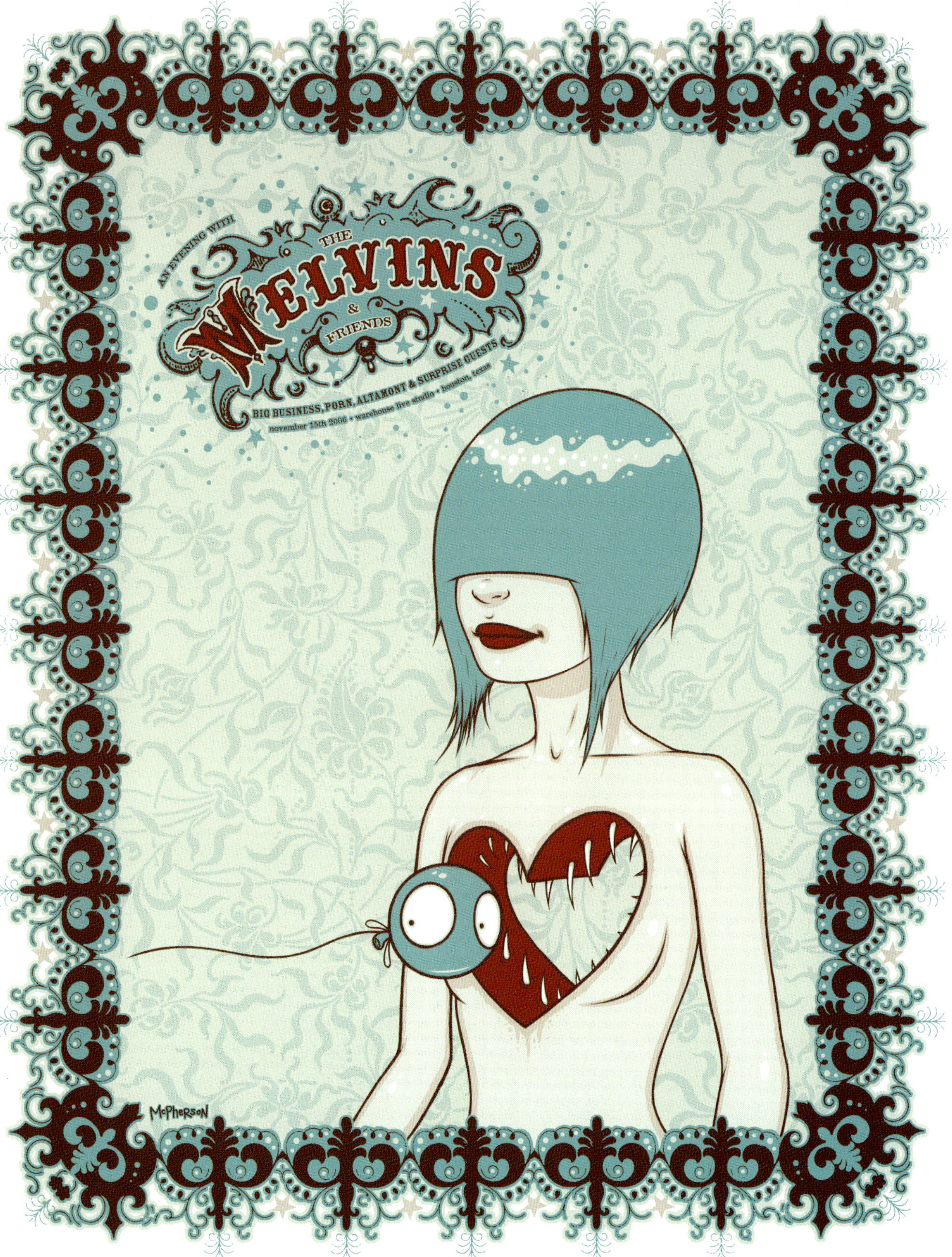

STARRING MR. WIGGLES AND ORIAN • ARTWORK BY TARA MCPHERSON • WWW.TARAMCPHERSON.COM • SCREENPRINTED AT DIESEL FUEL PRINTS • WWW.DIESELFUELPRINTS.COM

Melvins, Big Business, Shocker

six-color silkscreen
16" x 23"
edition of 350
2008

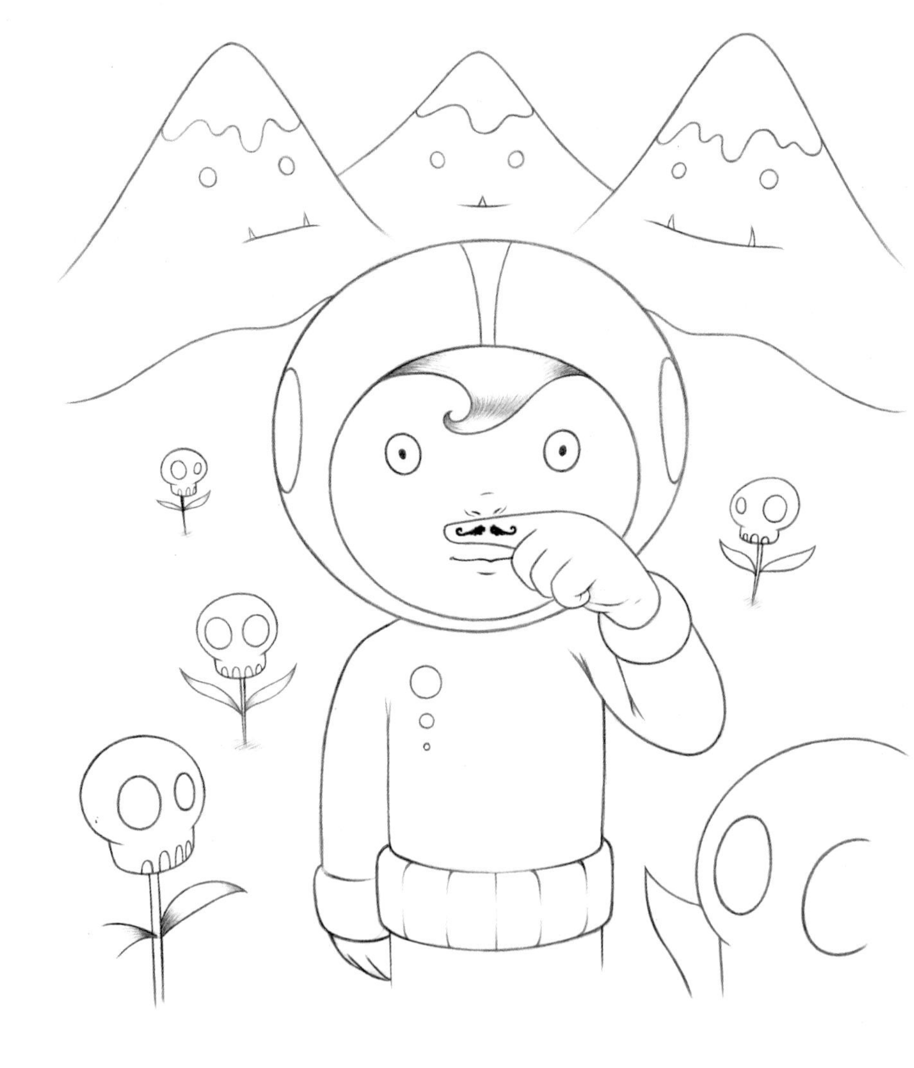

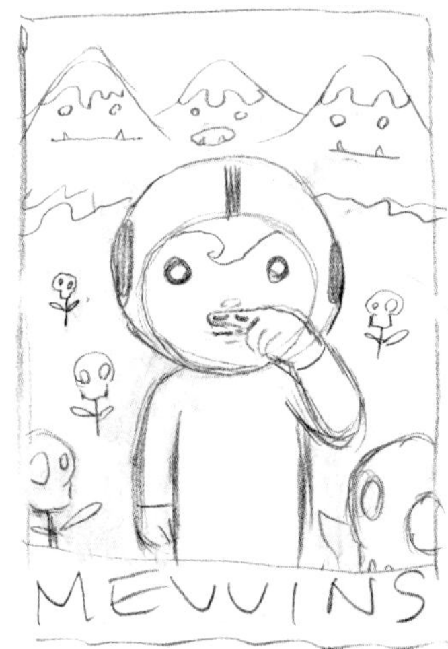

rough
graphite on paper
3" x 4"

drawing
graphite on bristol
11" x 17"

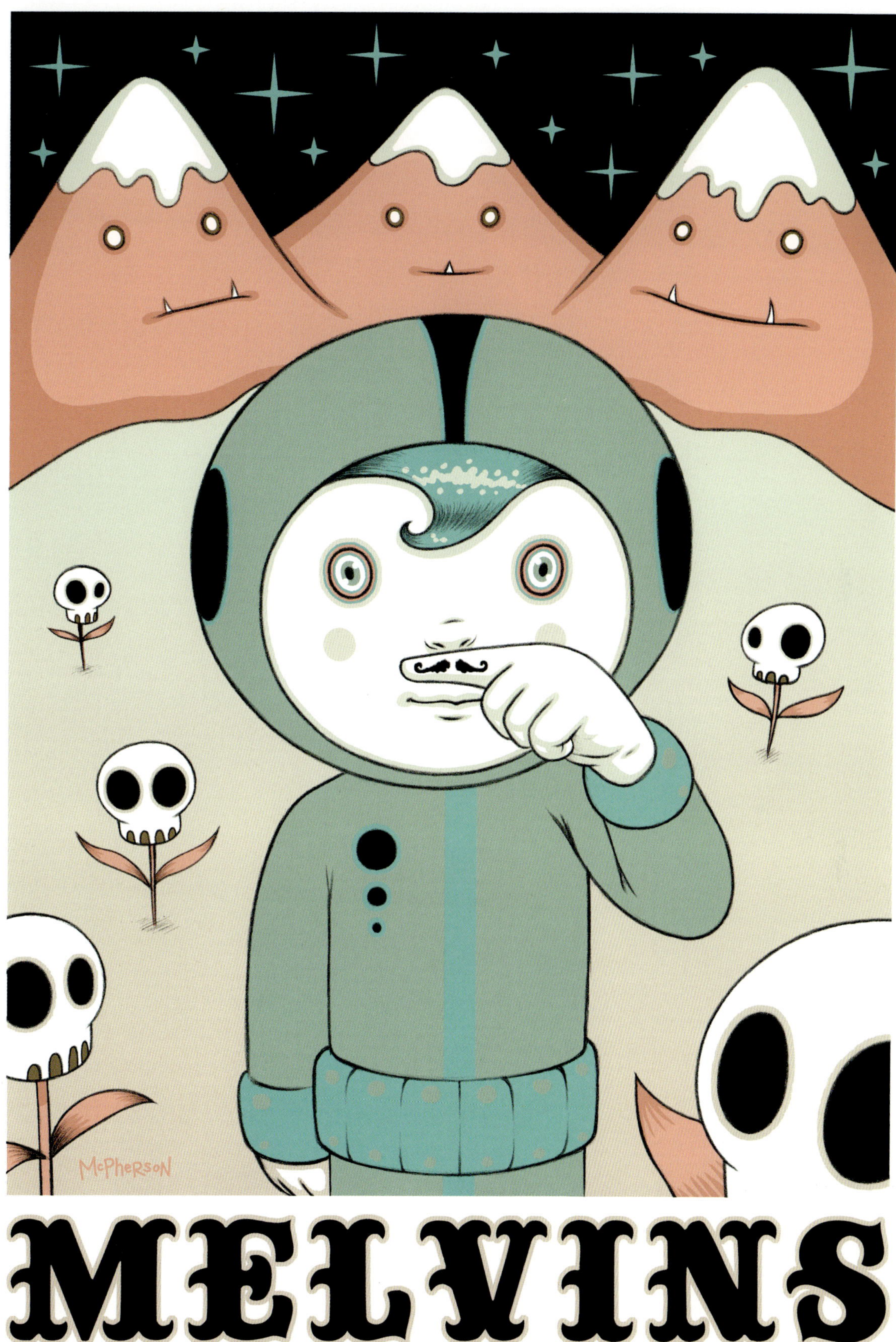

BIG BUSINESS AND SHOCKER 8•13•08 MUSIC HALL OF WILLIAMSBURG, BROOKLYN NY

• LUCIUS AND HIS FIRST MUSTACHE FINGER • POSTER ART © TARA MCPHERSON • PRINTED BY DIESEL FUEL PRINTS •

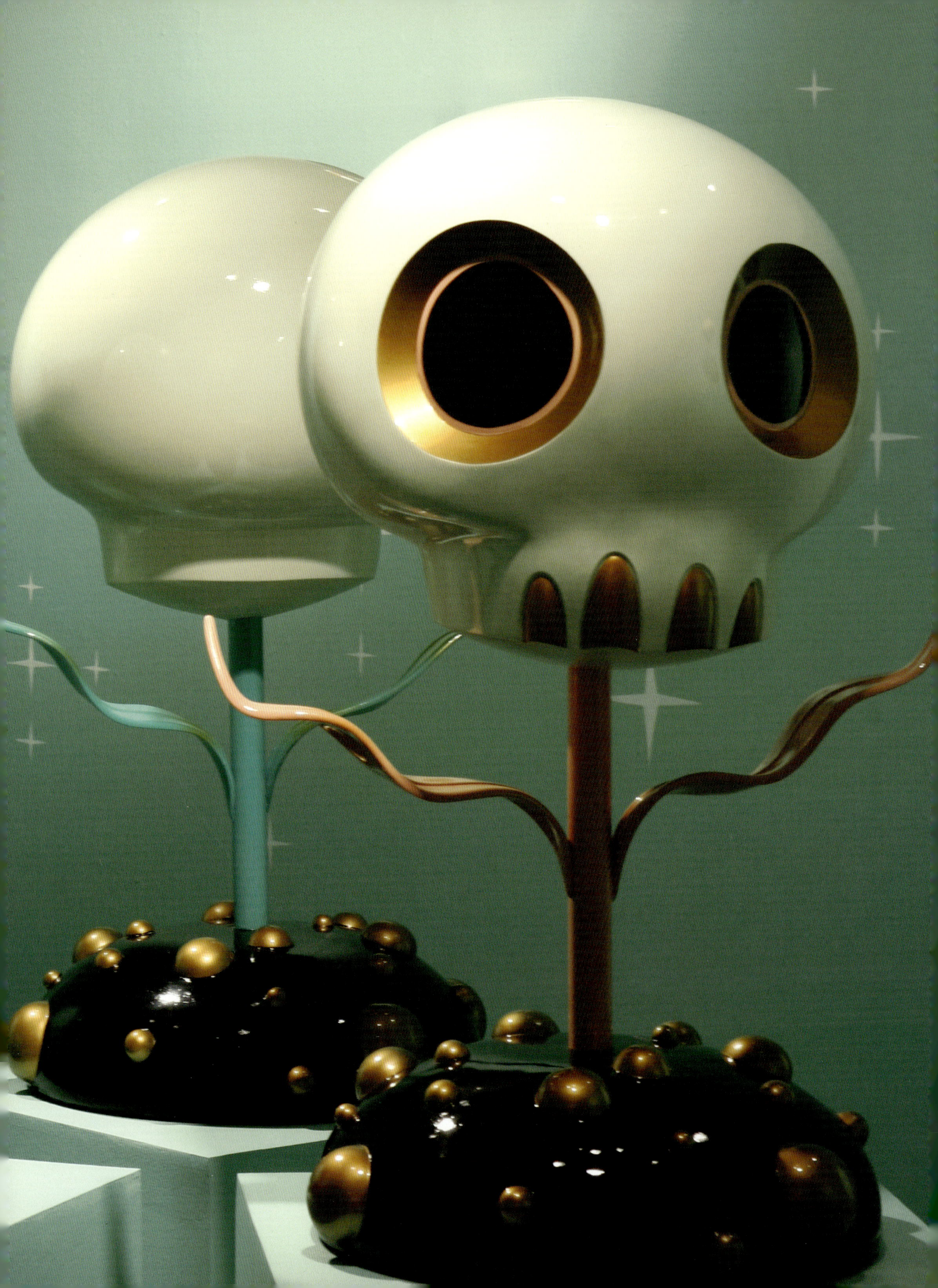

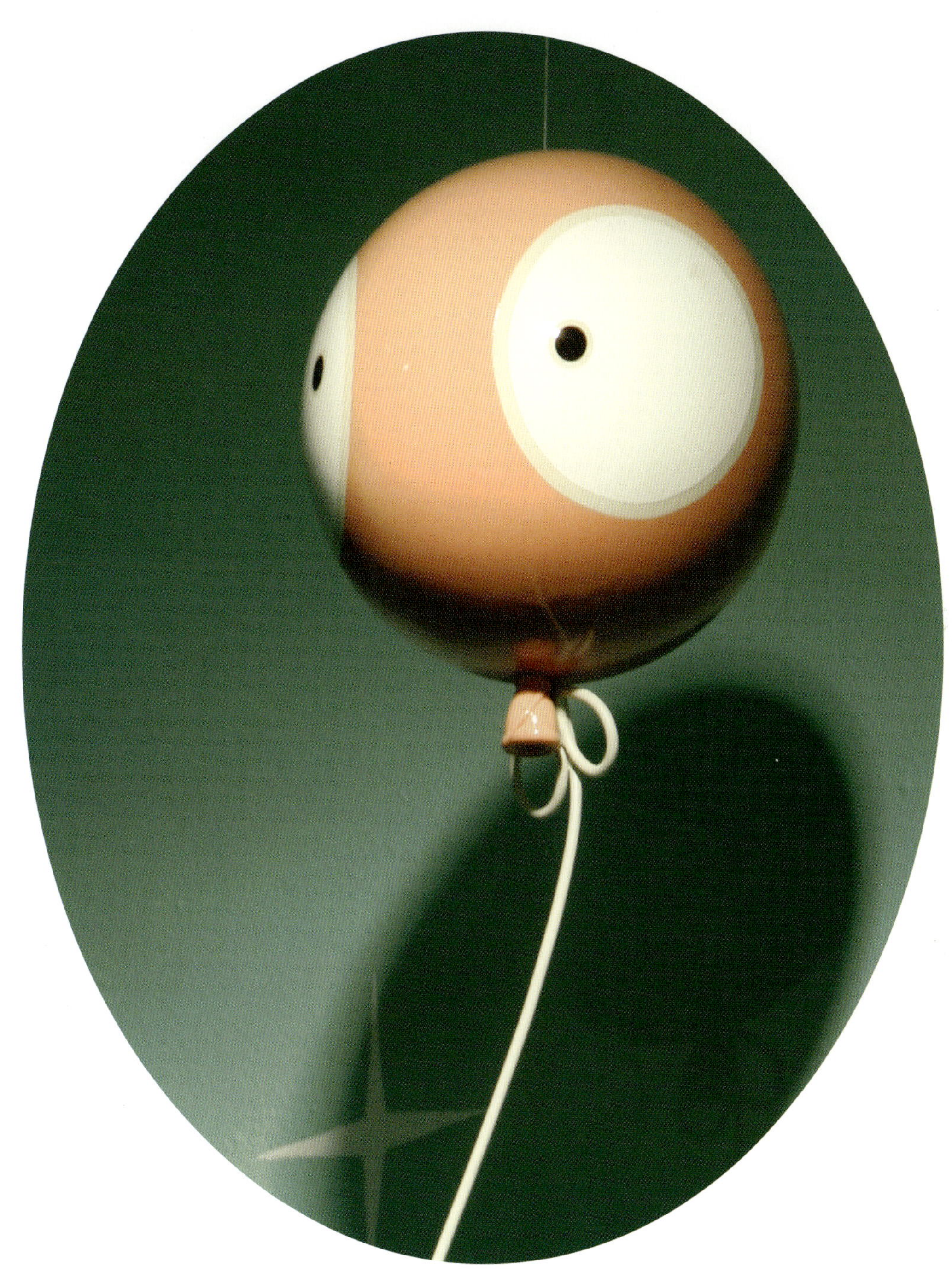

Sculptures

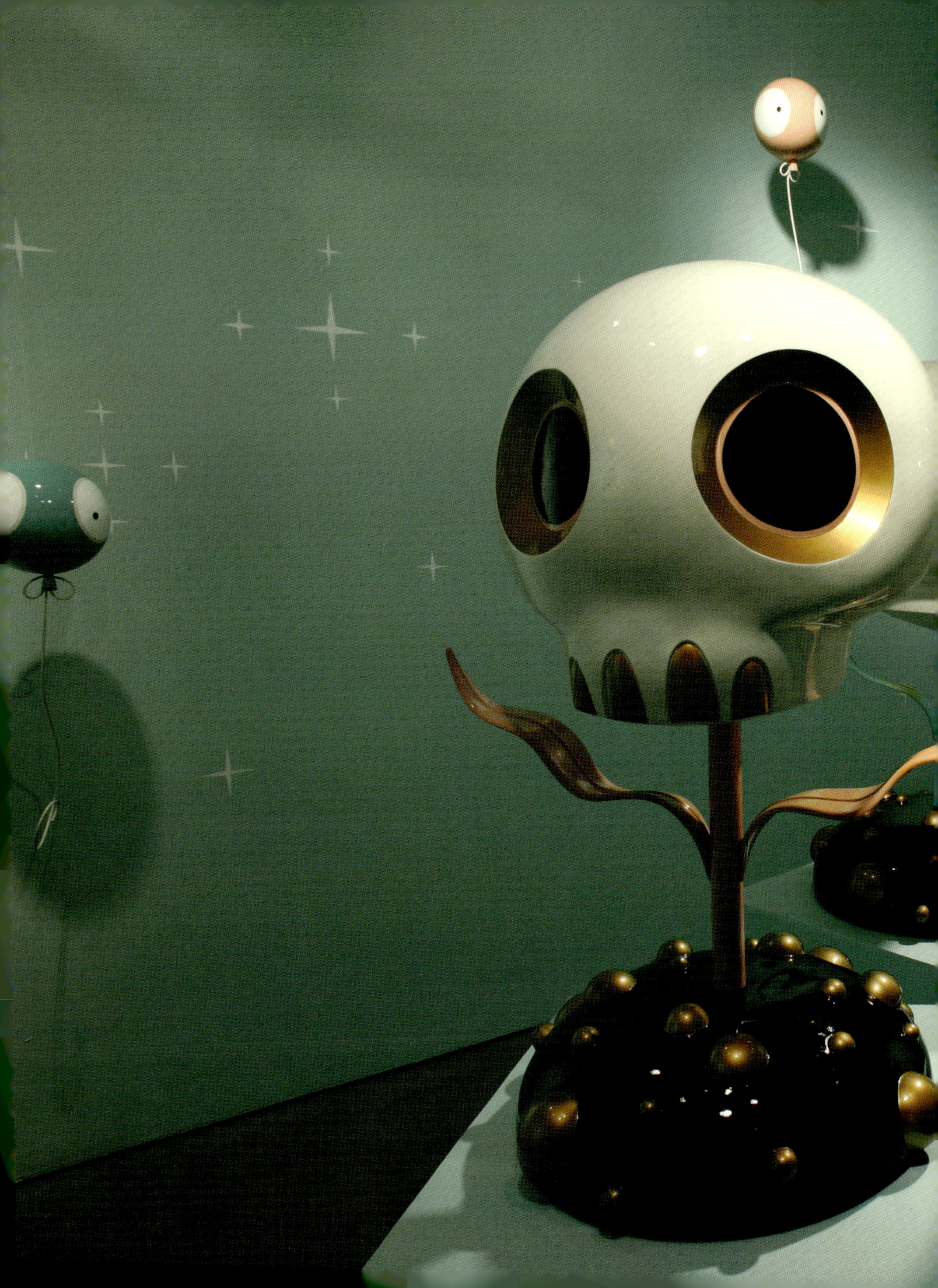

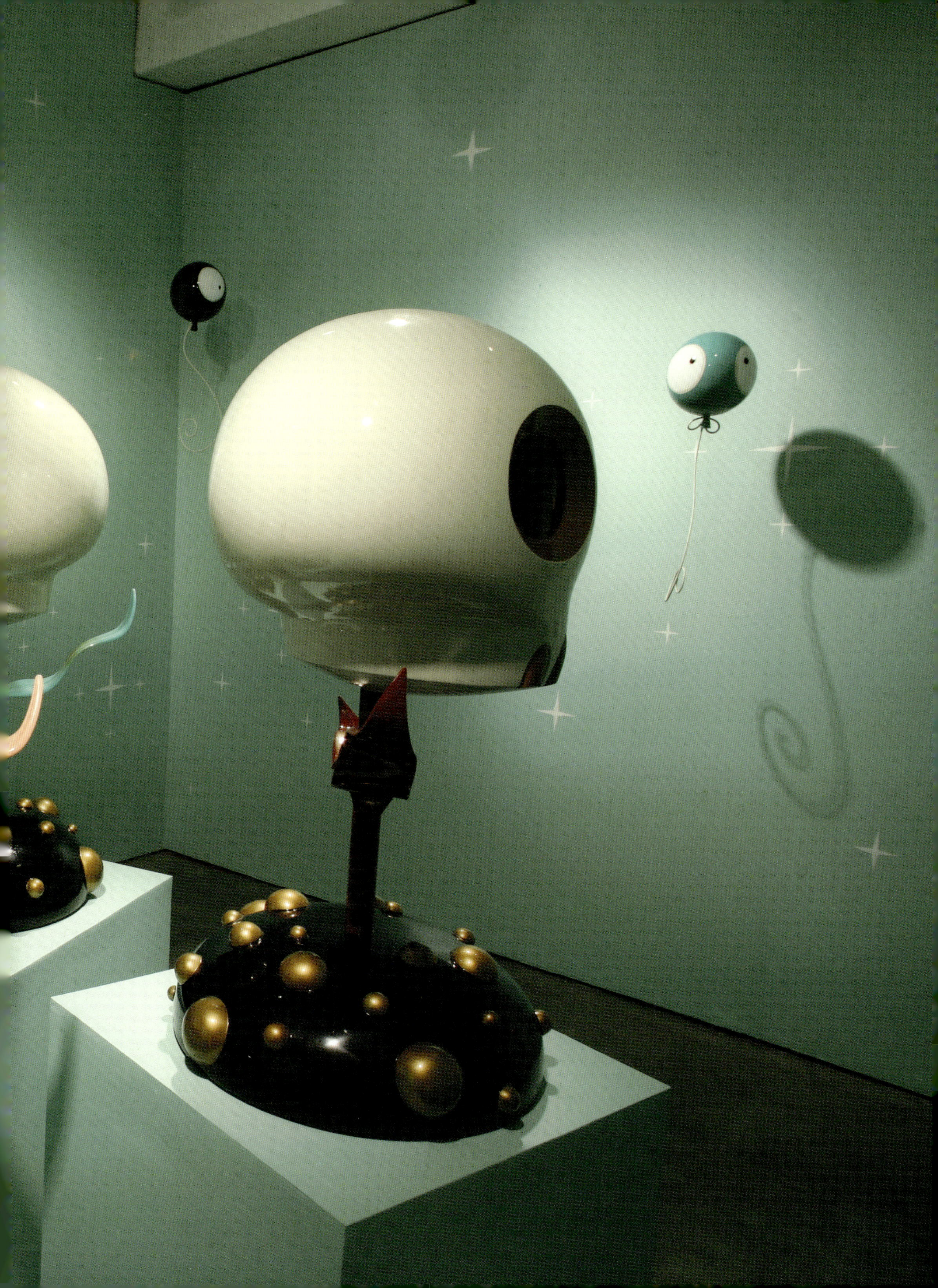

Skull Flower—Pink

polyester resin, polyurethane, aluminum, paint
20" x 37"
2008

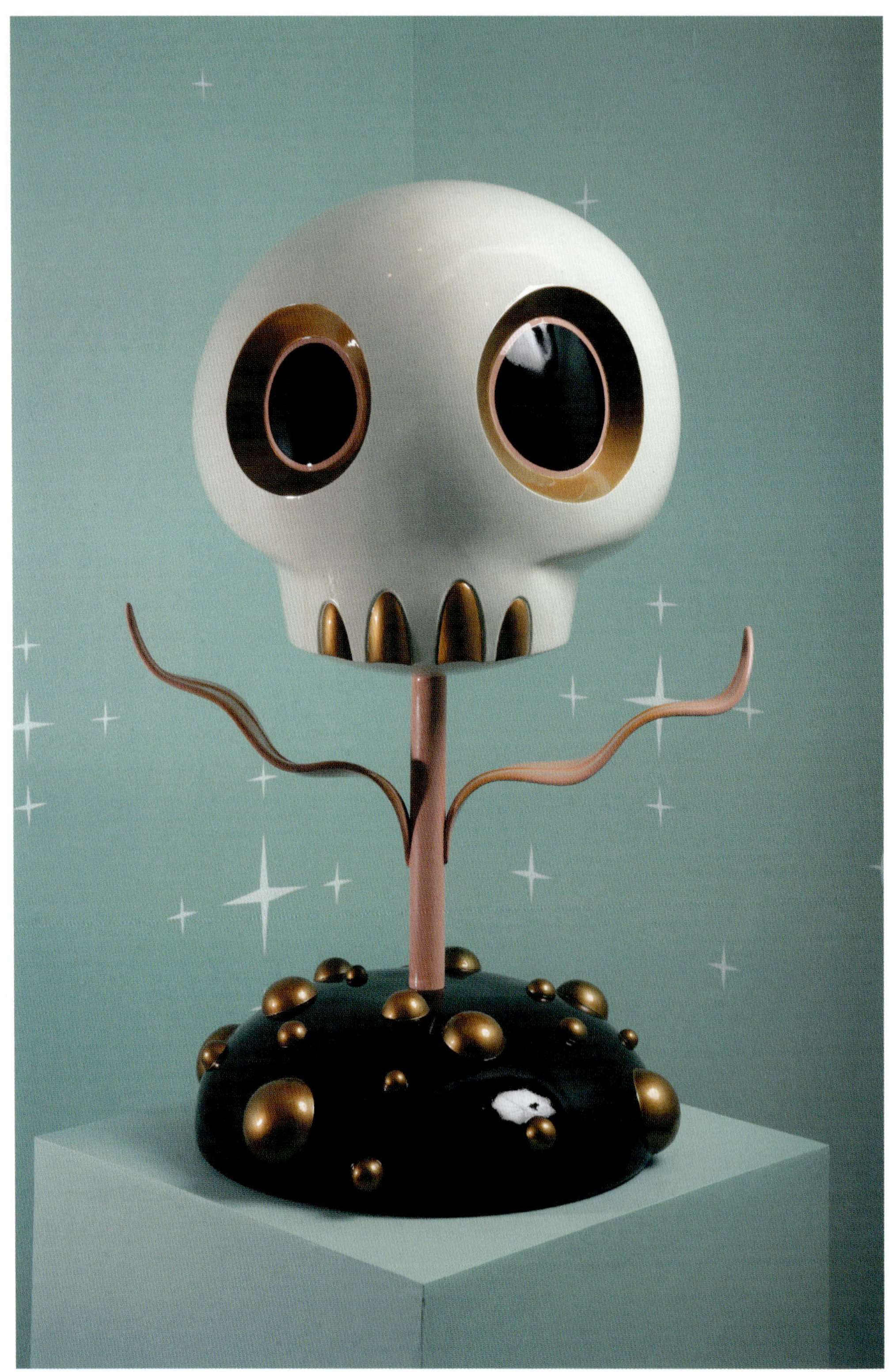

SKULL FLOWER—TURQUOISE

polyester resin, polyurethane, aluminum, paint
20" x 37"
2008

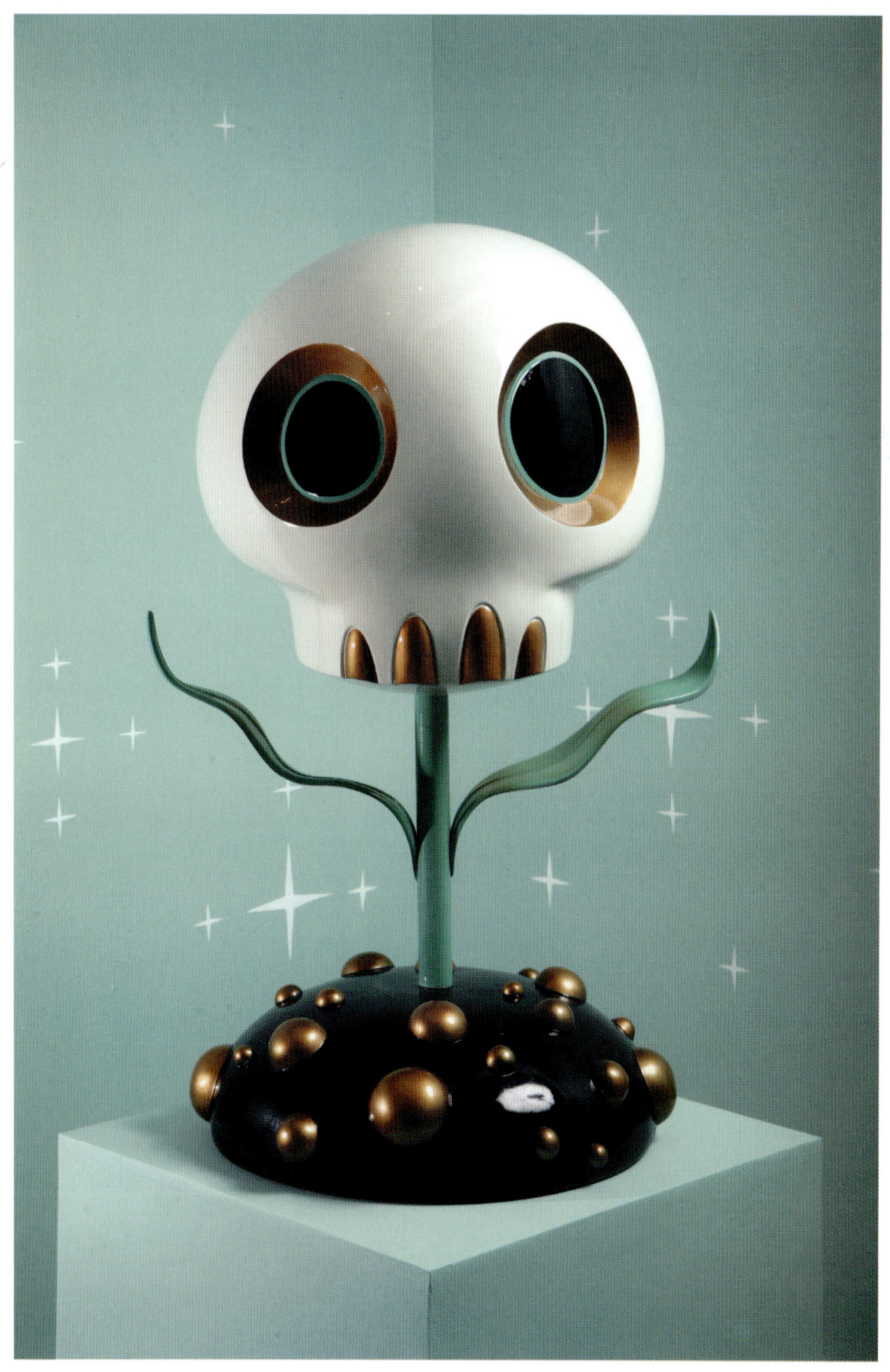

Skull Flower—Red

polyester resin, polyurethane, aluminum, paint
20" x 37"
2008

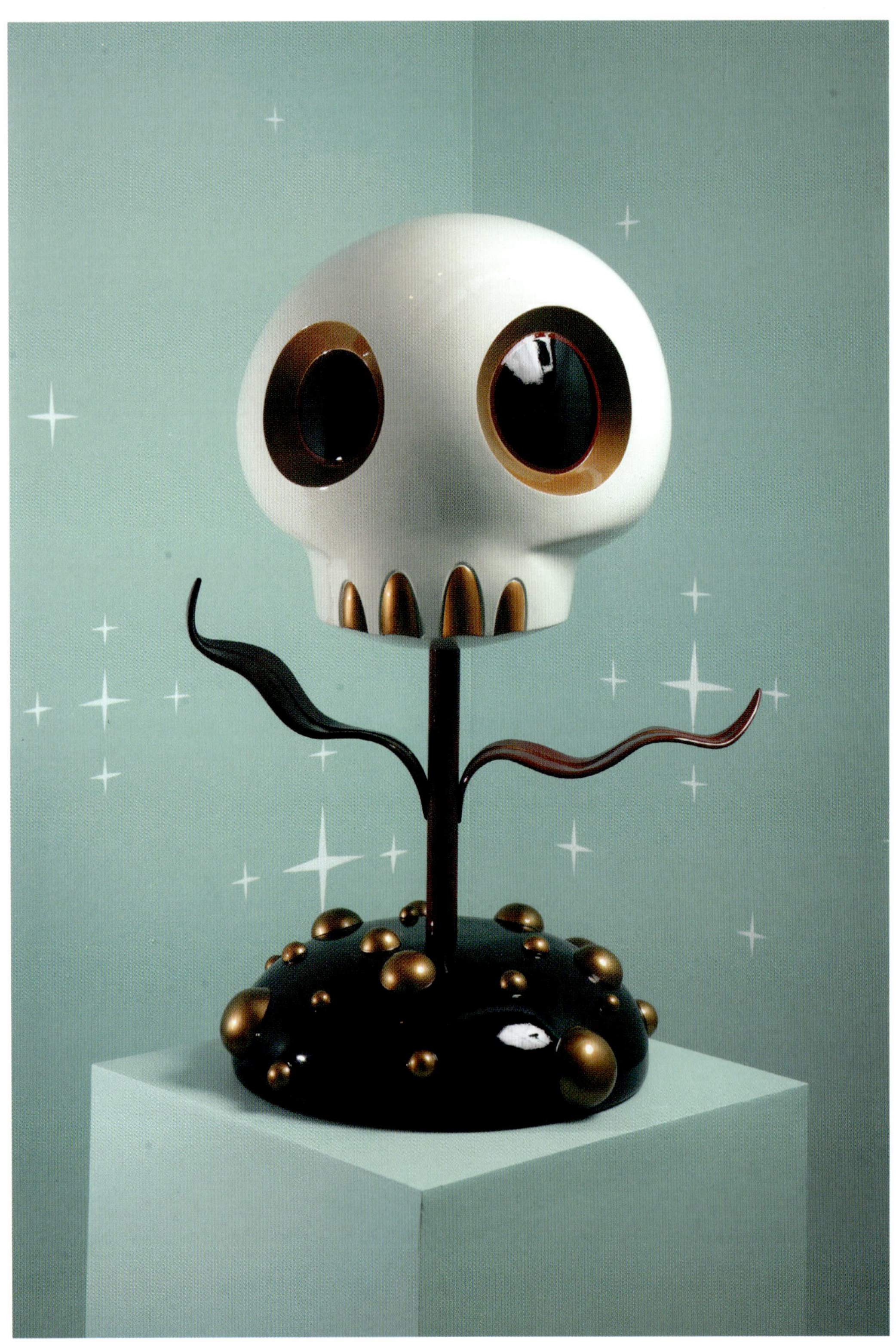

MR. WIGGLES GANG—PINK

polyester resin, polyurethane, aluminum, paint
8" x 24"
2008

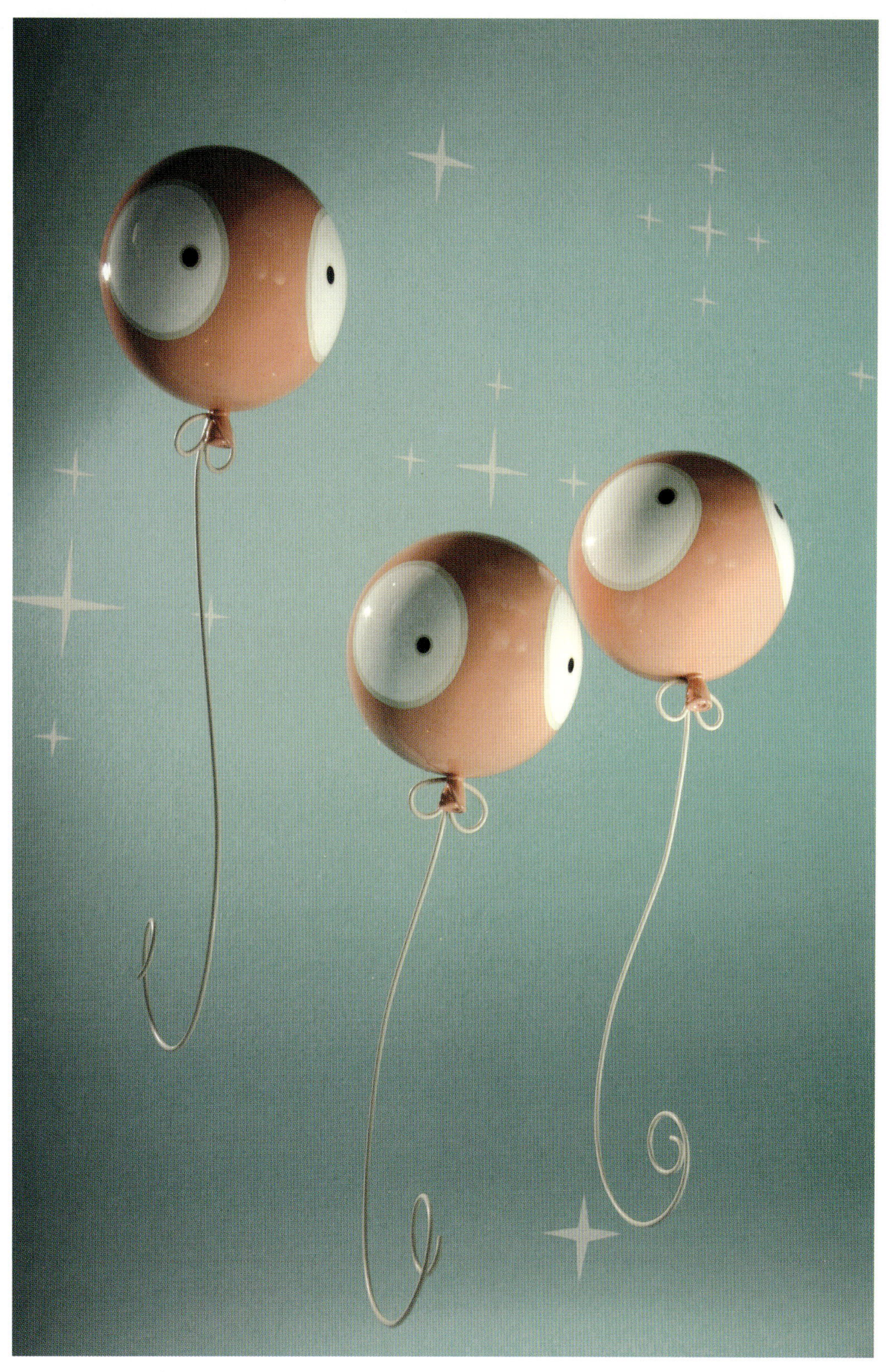

Mr. Wiggles Gang—Black

polyester resin, polyurethane, aluminum, paint
8" x 24"
2008

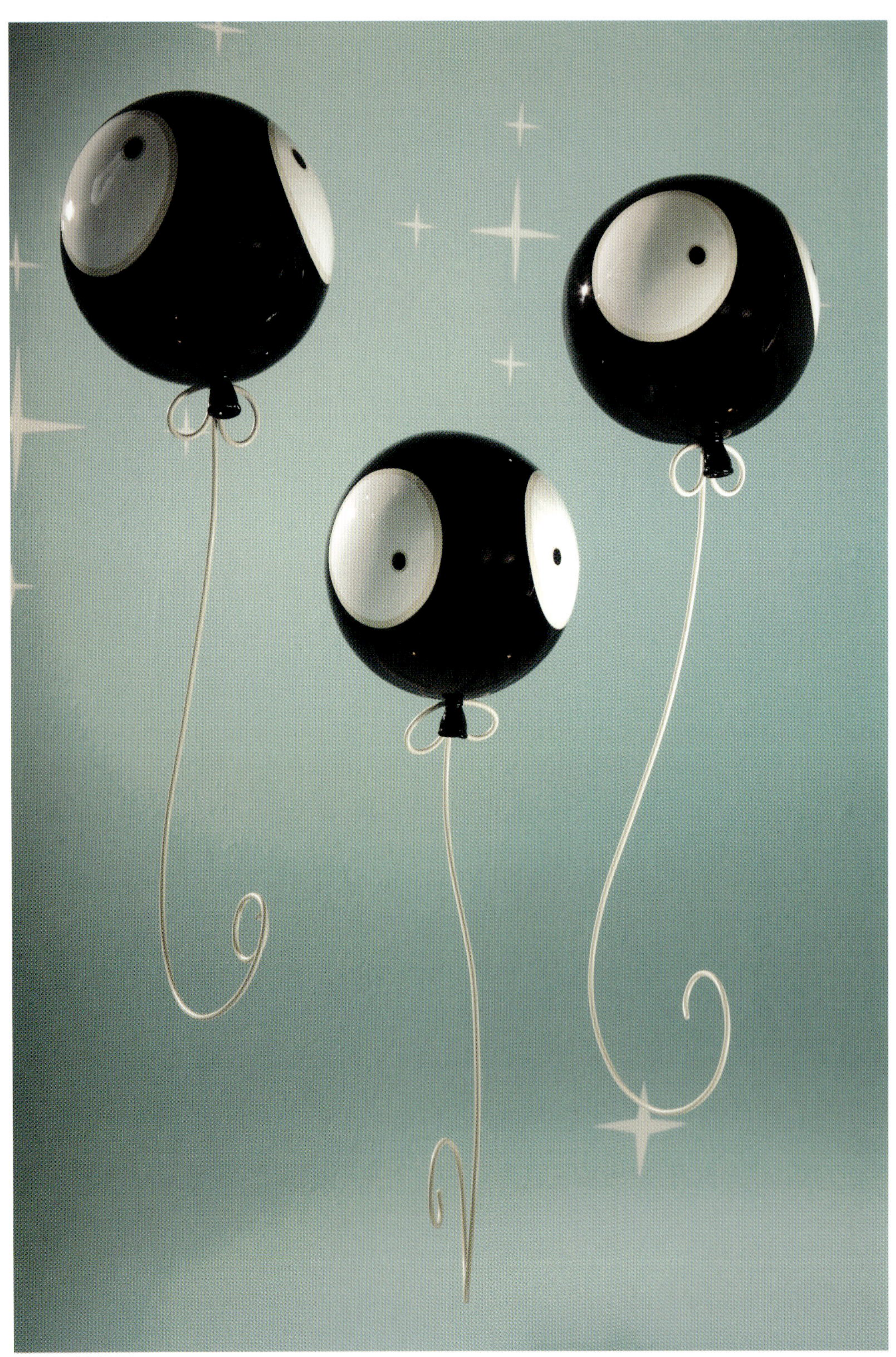

Mr. Wiggles Gang—Turquoise

polyester resin, polyurethane, aluminum, paint
8" x 24"
2008

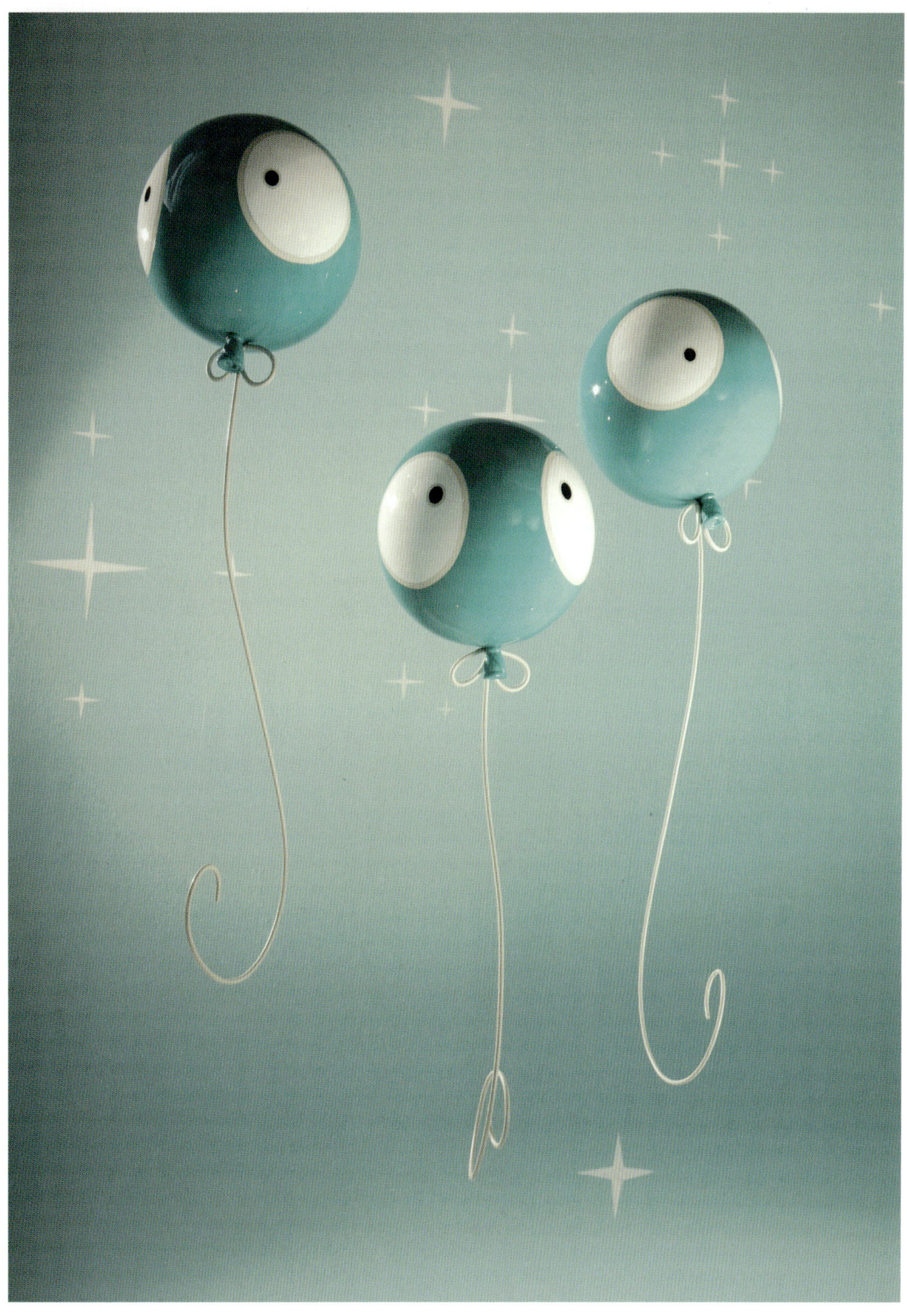

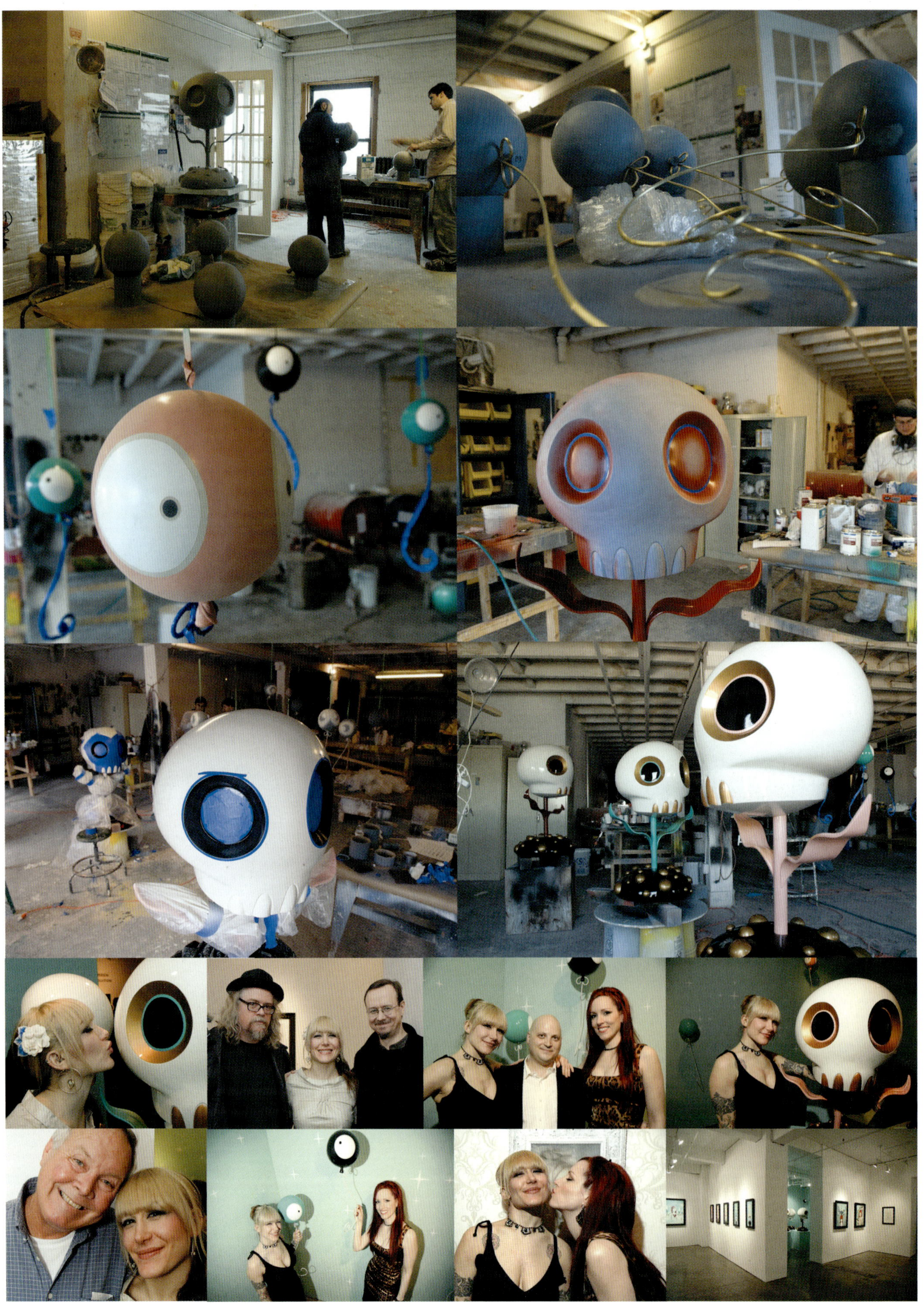

Sculpture-in-progress photos by Svetlana Bahchevanova

Opening reception photos by Adam Wallacavage

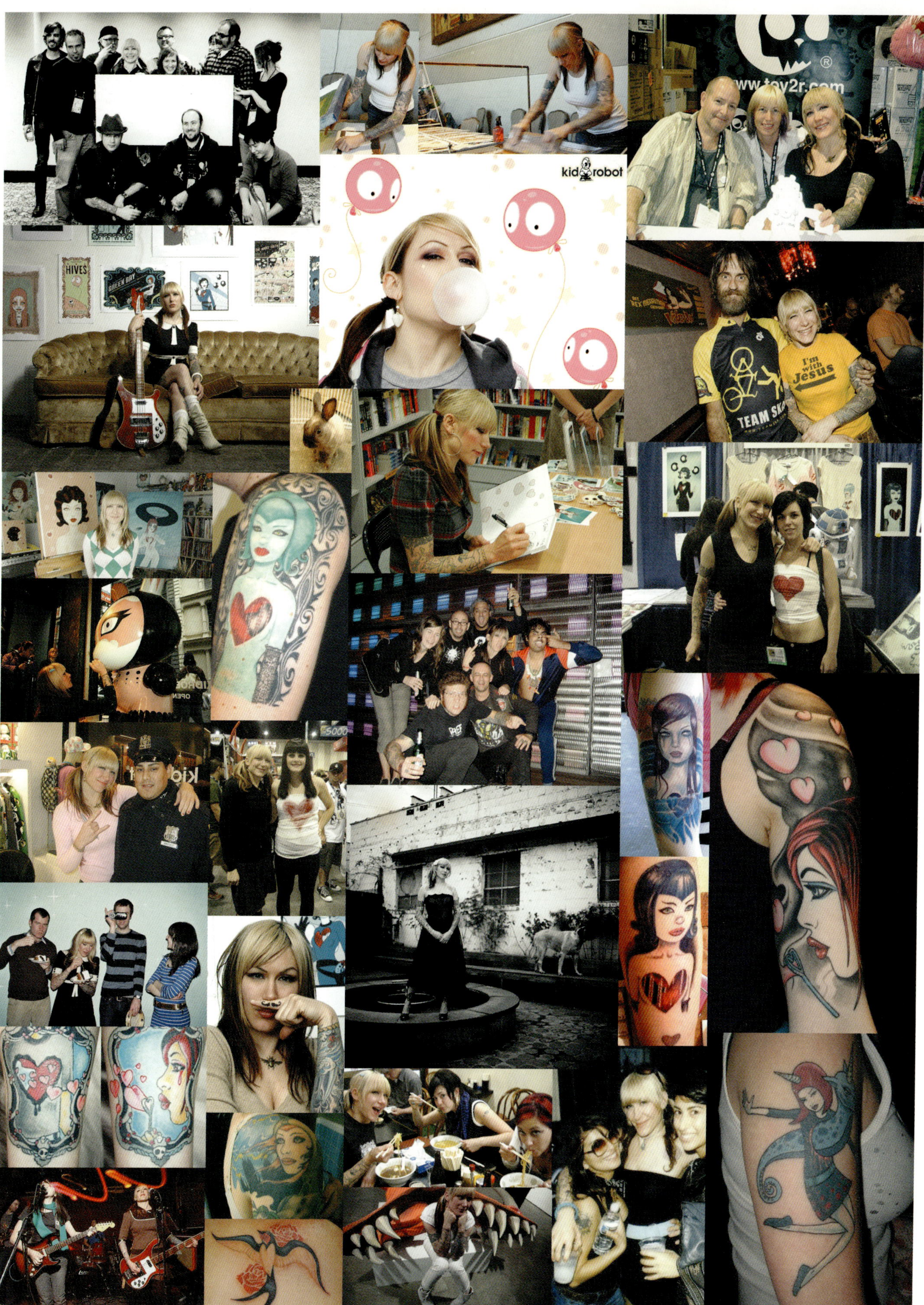

Photos by lots of awesome friends . . .

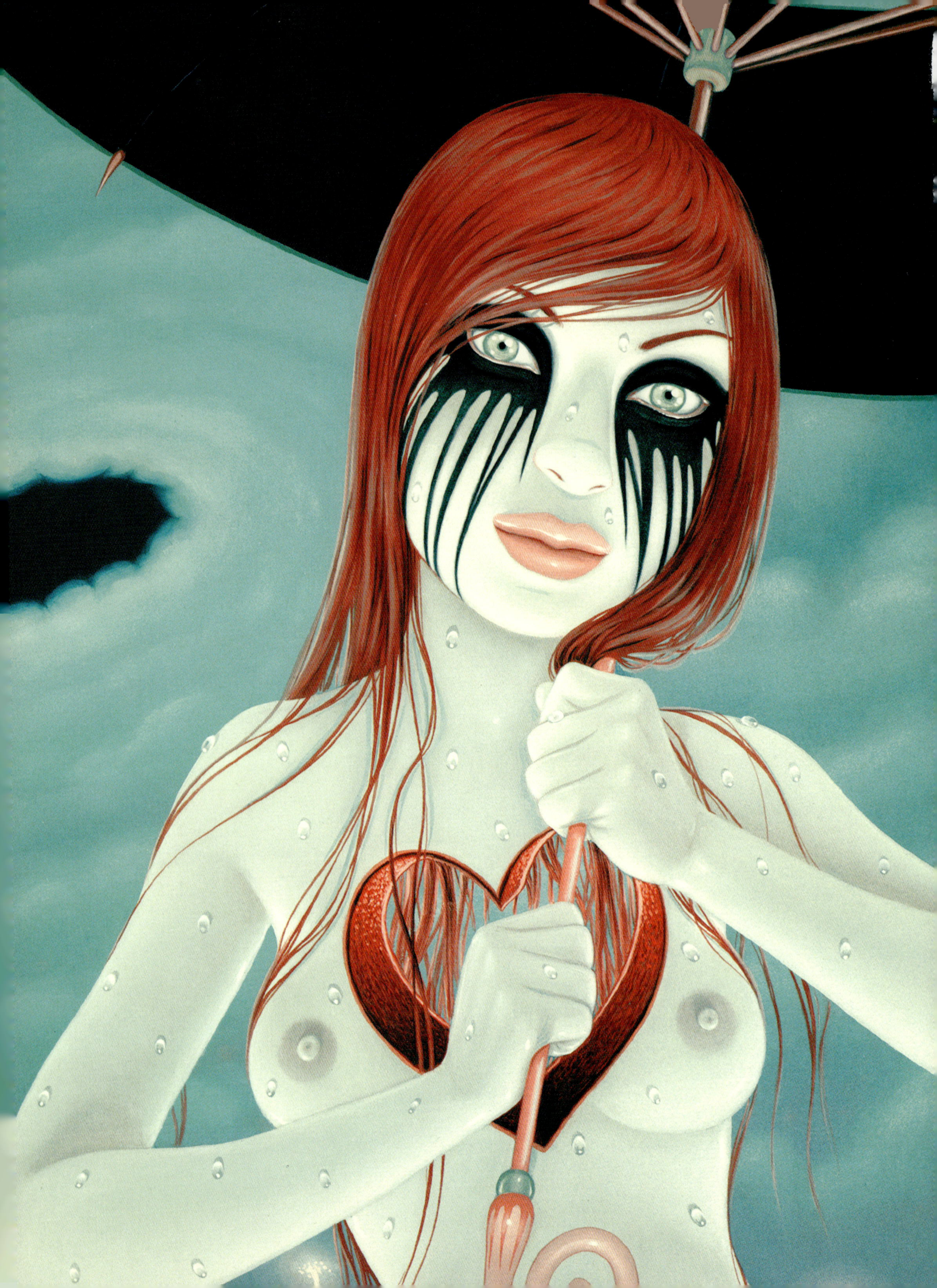